W9-DFW-670

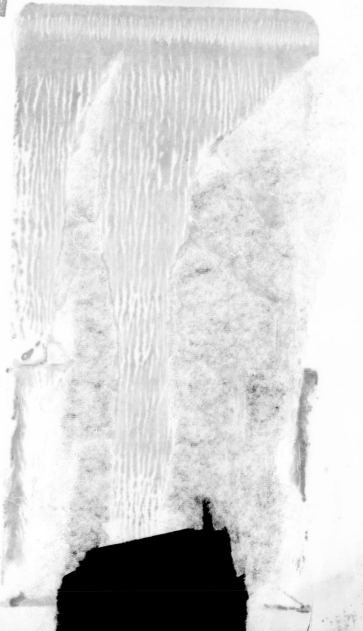

Our National Passion

OUR

ILLUSTRATED

NATIONAL PASSION

200 Years of Sex in America

Edited by

Sally Banes

Sheldon Frank

&

Tem Horwitz

FOLLETT PUBLISHING COMPANY

CHICAGO

PHOTOGRAPHS AND ILLUSTRATIONS ON THE FOLLOWING PAGES ARE COURTESY OF:

Chicago Historical Society—64, 65, 108

Dellenback—181

Douglas Kenyon Gallery—22

Historical Pictures Service, Chicago—5, 6, 11, 15, 16, 19, 20, 26, 29, 30, 34, 38, 39, 40, 60, 62, 71, 72, 73, 76, 94, 104, 107, 113

Magnum Photos, Inc., photograph by Bob Adelman—114, 118

Magnum Photos, Inc., photograph by Burt Glinn—116 (left)

Massachusetts Historical Society—9 (top)

Planned Parenthood Association, Chicago—130, 131, 132

UPI—53, 54, 55, 158, 160, 161, 164, 171, 174, 184, 185, 188

Library of Congress Catalog Card Number: 74-28651
ISBN: 0-695-80550-9

First Printing

Contents

1 Sex and the Puritans   3

2 Sex on the Frontier   15

3 Sex Scandals   41

4 Victoria Waives the Rules
  Sex, Marriage, and Feminism in the Nineteenth Century   59

5 Utopian Sex
  In Search of a New Amorous World   79

6 Prostitution in the U.S.   101

7 Wishbones, Condoms, Pessaries, and the Pill
  A History of Birth Control   121

8 Sex in Two Dimensions
  Erotic Movies   137

9 I Lost it in the Back Seat
  A Personalized History of America's Auto Romance   157

10 Manual Sex
  From Kinsey to Comfort   179

11 Above the Fruited Plain
  Gay Life in San Francisco, 1974   197

12 Slightly Far Out in California   213

Index   225

Preface

The image of a sexual revolution taking place in America is sorely overused (one imagines armed troops in every bedroom), but there's no doubt that right now more people are talking more openly about how to live their sexual lives than at any time in our nation's history. Inspired by the human potential movement, women's liberation, gay liberation, the barrage of sex manuals and how-to books, contemporary men and women are feverishly experimenting with open marriages, semi-open marriages, slightly-ajar marriages, non-marriages, group activities, and anything else you can imagine. Nirvana may lie somewhere between the pleasures and constraints of monogamy and the joys and terrors of variety. How it will turn out is anybody's guess.

Puzzled by the present we look at the past. Believe it or not, we are not the first generation to discover sex; living with the libido has never been easy for anyone. But how different are we from our ancestors? What were sexual relations like in our distant and recent past? Realizing that we couldn't hope to fully answer this question,

we chose a group of subjects that seemed particularly interesting and a group of writer friends with disparate styles and similar sensibilities.

We tried to discover how our ancestors lived their sexual lives and how certain key institutions affected their sexual behavior. The focus of our attention was on sex, so we tried to ask direct questions of the historical material. What were the sexual practices of the Puritans? How did nineteenth-century feminists order their lives? What kinds of experiments were tried by our more adventurous ancestors who settled in communes and utopian communities? How did these experiments work out? How were people's lives altered by the automobile, the bedroom on wheels?

The final essay is an exception to our emphasis on the historical. After surveying the past, it seemed appropriate to face the present. "Slightly Far Out in California" is a personal sketch of one man's difficulties on the new sexual frontier. Living with the possibility of sexual freedom isn't all cakes and ale, and Peter Ellis's idiosyncratic, at times bitter, at times euphoric, account of life amidst sexual plenty reminds us that we all must make our own personal peace with the demands of the libido.

What have we concluded? We have learned that we are not the first generation that has experimented freely with sex, nor are we the first generation that has attempted to look at sex clearly and honestly. Our writers have found significantly more variety in sexual styles than we had expected; not surprisingly, our ancestors were struggling with the same problems and possibilities that baffle, energize, and trouble us.

About the Authors

SALLY BANES is a performancemaker and writer. A graduate of the University of Chicago, she is cofounder of Community Discount Players, a loose amalgam of performers. In addition to writing book reviews for the *Chicago Daily News*, art reviews for the *New Art Examiner*, and acting as the dance editor of the Chicago *Reader,* she is currently working on a book on contemporary dance and, along with Sheldon Frank and Tem Horwitz, is coauthor of the recent guidebook, *Sweet Home Chicago.*

SHELDON FRANK graduated from Harvard College with a degree in American history and literature and attended graduate school at the University of Chicago. He has published stories in *Fiction Midwest* and *Chicago Review* and received a National Endowment for the Arts award to finish his novel *I Can See Clearly Now.* He also writes book reviews for the *Chicago Daily News, Chicago Sun-Times, The New Republic, The National Observer, The Nation,* and *Harper's;* does art criticism for the Chicago *Reader;* is another cofounder of Community Discount Players; and is the founder of Bozo's Youth Entourage, a conceptual performance group.

TEM HORWITZ is a photographer and writer residing in Chicago with his colleagues. After receiving a B.A. from Haverford College and an M.A. from Columbia University, he managed a steel warehouse and a dance center, and cofounded the MoMing Collection, an avant-garde performance troupe. In addition to these activities, he has exhibited his photography at several galleries and teaches Tai Chi Chuan.

NANCY BANKS is a sexy twenty-five-year-old Chicago freelancer who writes a weekly column for the Chicago *Reader.*

DON DRUKER is a filmmaker and film critic for the Chicago *Reader.* He has written for *The Real Paper, The Journal of Popular Film, Take One, December* and other film journals, and has taught film, popular culture, and American history at the University of Chicago.

PETER ELLIS is a novelist residing in California.

JACK HAFFERKAMP is a staff member of *Panorama,* the weekly feature section of the *Chicago Daily News.* A connoisseur of the rock scene, he has written for *Rolling Stone, Creem, Earth, Clear Creek,* and *Oui.*

FLORA JOHNSON is a writer and a feminist.

DAVID MOBERG is a writer and anthropologist living in a placid urban commune. He has done research on utopian and millenarian movements, and is currently writing a book about American workers.

MICHAEL SCHUDSON has written for *Daedalus,* the *Harvard Educational Review, The New Republic,* and *Social Science Quarterly.* He won Harvard's Bowdoin Prize in 1970 and 1973.

CHRIS TANZ is a psycholinguist and author of children's books.

R. WILLIAMS, who worked on the design of *Our National Passion,* is a book designer at the University of Chicago Press, and art director for *Poetry* magazine.

DAN ABRAHAM, whose drawings appear in the last chapter, is an illustrator and law student.

Our National Passion

Sex and the Puritans

What are the origins of the peculiar American squeamishness about sex? Why are we as a people so uptight and prudish about doing, or even talking about, a natural human activity that even our parents may have enjoyed? Well, analyzing national characteristics is a dubious historical enterprise, but it is necessary to clear up one major misconception. In the twenties H. L. Mencken blamed the Puritans for practically all our social and sexual ills. And it has since soaked into our popular consciousness that those self-righteous New Englanders are responsible for our excessive discomfort about intercourse and related human activities. We have been told in article after article, talk show after talk show, that it was those peculiar, God-obsessed colonists who poisoned our sexual spirit, and who twisted a wholesome human activity into something disgusting and dirty. Sorry, but it just isn't so. The Puritans are not to blame. They were indeed an odd, complicated group of people whose ideas and attitudes did so much to shape the American character, but they can't be held responsible for our prudery and squeamishness.

Blame the Victorians; don't blame the Puritans. It is our nineteenth-century ancestors who are responsible for our twisted sexual attitudes. In the mishmash of ideas that passes for popular thought, two quite separate intellectual threads—the Puritan and the Victorian—have been sewn together for too long. Let's try to separate them and get things straight.

Our very notion of civilized behavior is a Victorian creation. It was the nineteenth century that constructed a society where women were seen as vessels of purity who fainted at an indelicate word; and men were portrayed as lust-driven animals out to snatch the goodies from every virgin. It was a world where nice men never talked about sex, and nice women never participated in it. It was a world of hollow decency and profound false consciousness. No doubt about it, the Victorians were off the wall on the subject of sex. No wonder pornography and prostitution were booming industries, and the marriage bed was a scene of nightly horror. If you're looking for the source of American prurience, look at the Victorian world; that's where our sexual chaos began. It was the Victorians who were prudish, squeamish, and self-deceiving about sex; the Puritans are another story.

To begin, it is essential to forget Victorian drawing rooms and lace doilies, and to imagine life in a simpler, largely rural society in seventeenth- and eighteenth-century New England. As Edmund Morgan (whose article, "The Puritans and Sex," written in 1942, is still the best work on the subject) remarks: ". . . the Puritans were a much earthier lot than their modern critics have imagined. It is well to remember that they belonged to the age in which they lived and not to the more squeamish decades of the nineteenth or twentieth centuries." Early eighteenth-century men and women still talked honestly and directly about subjects that in the nineteenth century could be approached only by circumlocution or not at all. They were good, hardy, plain, country folks, not creatures of patent leather and crinoline.

And remember, they were farmers, and farmers have always been more honest and less prudish about the facts of life, whether animal or human. Puritan kids growing up on a New England farm could see cows and sheep engaged in continuing their species. They could daily see the sexual organs of the farm animals, larger than life, but organs nonetheless. They assisted in the births of calves and colts, and they did what farm boys and girls have done since time immemorial. It is difficult to deny the existence of what you see every day, and for most Puritans in Colonial America sex was a fact of daily life.

Yes, they were earthy, robust men and women, but they were also Puritans, adherents to a strict, Protestant orthodoxy. So, as Puritans, what was their attitude toward sex? Not what you might expect. The Puritans believed that as long as the man and woman were married, sex was a gift of God. Sex between husband and wife was an activity to be enjoyed, but not abused. It was neither disgusting nor dirty; it was part of a couple's normal marital life that, when exercised properly, was a joyful, healthy activity. In its proper place, sex could and should be a source of pleasure. Much of our confusion about Puritan sexual mores involves a misunderstanding of what the Puritans believed was proper. The key point is that only sex in marriage was proper. And in marriage, it was not only proper, but also essential.

Of course the Puritans believed that marriage was a spiritual partnership, but they also knew that it was and *should be* more than just a union of two souls. In a famous passage, John Cotton, one of the major New England theologians, discussed the case of a newly-married man who wanted a marriage of pure spirituality, a marriage unsullied by sexual consummation. People mistakenly believe, Cotton wrote, that this desire for a solely contemplative life is an ". . . instance of no little or ordinary Vertue; but . . . I can account it no other than an effort of blind zeal, for they are the dictates of a blind mind they follow therein, and not of that Holy Spirit, which saith *It is not good that man should be alone.*"

The Puritans, quite simply, were not ascetics. The Catholic ideal of celibacy was not their religious ideal. They believed that "the Use of the Marriage Bed" is "founded in mans Nature," and that a marriage without sex was unnatural. It is important to note that male impotence was definite grounds for divorce in

A stolen frolic in a Puritan farmhouse. It was the Victorians who were prudish, squeamish, and self-deceiving about sex; the Puritans are another story.

Sex and the Puritans

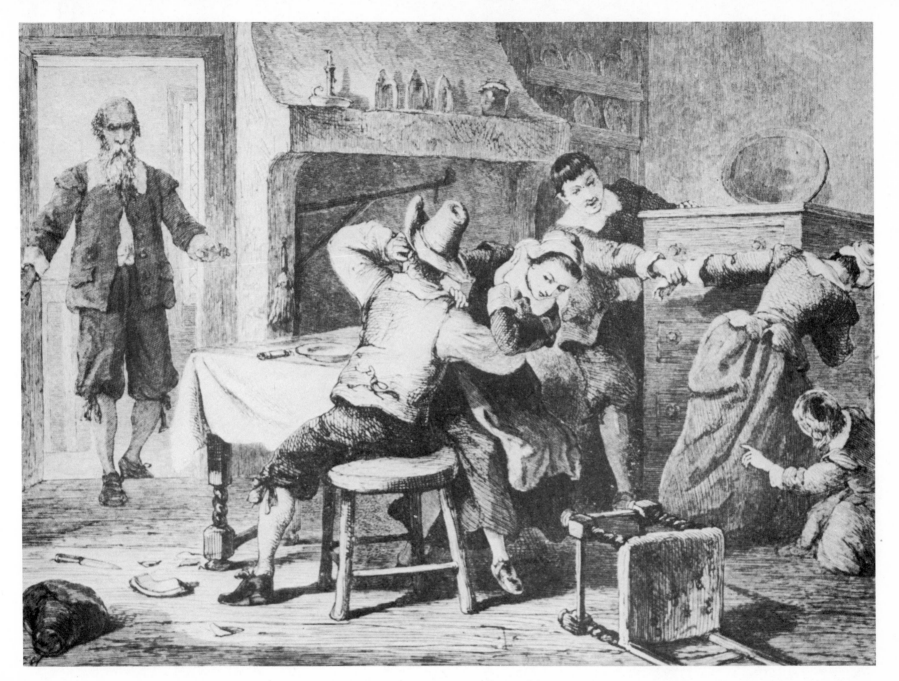

Sex and the Puritans

Anne Bradstreet.
"If ever two were one, then surely
we . . ."

In their interpretation of the Bible, the Puritans understood that God had created two sexes and had given each sex appropriate sexual organs and they were not given to us to atrophy from disuse. God had ordained that man and woman should marry and that they should have sexual intercourse. The only limitation they placed on sex in marriage was that it must not interfere with man's main purpose on earth—to glorify God. Man could glorify God by obeying His commandments to marry and have intercourse, but he could also lose sight of God by loving someone too much. To quote Cotton again:

> . . . sometimes a man hath a good affection to Religion, but the love of his wife carries him away, a man may bee so transported to his wife, that hee dare not bee forward in Religion, lest hee displease his wife, and so the wife, lest shee displease her husband, and this is an inordinate love, when it exceeds measure.

The love of a man for a woman is a beautiful thing, graced by God, but it must never become so strong that it leads us away from God.

In a Puritan family the man was clearly the dominant figure, the patriarch of his "little commonwealth" of wife, children, and servants. And the woman was still viewed, to a certain extent, as the descendant of Eve, the source of sexual and spiritual corruption. But this link to Eve was often softened in Puritan thought. The Pilgrim minister John Robinson wrote that God had created man and woman in equal perfection, and "neither is she, since the creation more degenerated than he from the primitive goodness." Given this muted link to Eve, it is not surprising that the Puritans, unlike the Victorians, realized that women had sexual desires and sexual needs, and that the Puritan wife felt as free as her husband to enjoy sexual pleasure.

In trying to imagine the relation between husband and wife in Colonial New England, the modern image of a stern, pleasure-hating couple must be discarded. "The love which proceeded from Christian charity," writes Edmund Morgan, "conceived in reason and conscious of God's sacred order, was warm and tender and gracious." A Puritan couple loved each other openly and expressively, in a manner few couples since the Victorian nightmare have been able to achieve. A fine example of the feelings between Puritan wife and husband can be seen in Anne Bradstreet's famous poem, "To My Dear and Loving Husband:"

> If ever two were one, then surely we.
> If ever man were lov'd by wife, then thee;
> If ever wife was happy in a man,
> Compare with me ye women if you can.
> I prize thy love more than whole Mines of
>   gold,
> Of all the riches that the East doth hold.
> My love is such that Rivers cannot quench,
> Nor aught but love from thee, give
>   recompence.
> Thy love is such I can no way repay,
> The heavens reward thee manifold, I pray.
> Then while we live, in love let's so
>   persever,
> That when we live no more, we may live
>   ever.

Anne Bradstreet, to our knowledge, was an exceptional woman, but there is no reason to believe that the feelings she expressed were unusual for a Puritan; she merely put into poetry what countless other women also felt about marriage.

As Morgan notes, Puritan men felt equally free to express their feelings of love toward their spouses. Remarking on the relationship of John and Margaret Winthrop, he writes: "John usually closed his letters with phrases such as these: 'I kiss and love thee with the kindest affection, and rest Thy faithful husband; so I kisse thee and wish thee Farewell;' and 'I kisse my sweet wife and remaine allwayes thy faithfull husband'. . . ."

So, for the Puritans sex within marriage was both necessary and good. But sex outside of marriage was an unacceptable sin. The same God that approved conjugal sex condemned pre-, extra-, and nonmarital sex. The Puritans believed that sexual sins were serious sins and deserved serious punishment. In the New England codes, adultery was punishable by death, fornication by a whipping. But what must be noted is that the death penalty was applied only three times (and there were many instances of reported adultery), and the whippings were rarely severe. Yes, sexual sins must be punished, but the Puritans also understood that man is, in fact, a fallen creature and that he and she could be expected to disobey God's laws with frightening regularity. Their wise assessment of human capacities, Morgan remarks, ". . . led the Puritans not only to deal leniently with sexual offenses but also to take every precaution to prevent such offenses, rather than wait for the necessity of punishment. One precaution was to see that children got married as soon as possible." He writes that the Puritans realized that the Catholic vow of celibacy could not be obeyed by fallen man, and would only lead to sexual trouble. "The way to avoid fornication and perversion," Morgan continues, "was for parents to provide suitable husbands and wives for their children." In a similar fashion, "As marriage was the way to prevent fornication, successful marriage was the way to prevent adultery. The Puritans did not wait for adultery to appear; instead, they took every means possible to make husbands and wives live together and respect each other." If a man left his wife, the Puritan authorities dragged him back home and watched his behavior carefully. If two people were suspected of having an illicit affair, they were forbidden to see each other. Using all the tools at their disposal, the Puritans tried to make marriages work. If the situation was hopeless, and only then, was divorce an acceptable solution.

Here again the profound differences between Puritan and Victorian are evident. Where the Victorians wished the women didn't have vaginas and hoped that if they stopped talking about sex it would go away, the Puritans understood how men and women actually did behave. Since the task of salvation was a genuine matter of eternal life or eternal death for them, they could not afford the luxury of self-deception. The Puritans were forced by their religious beliefs to be acute psychologists, alert to the subtle vagaries of the human will. They fully acknowledged that the flesh of both sexes was weak, and they realized that if they enforced their laws as strictly as they enacted them, they would have decimated their small colony.

For the same reasons, the Puritans were not prurient in their attitude toward sexual irregularities. Because they understood the ways of fallen man, few things surprised or disgusted them.

Prurience of the Victorian variety is the product of a society that lies about reality, that wishes to deny how people really behave, that refuses to face facts. The Puritans never flinched from the facts, and did not waste their energy in feigning shock at man's tireless waywardness. Morton Hunt writes of the results of one scholar's research into this area of Puritan sexual attitudes:

> . . . Dr. Emil Oberholtzer, a diligent historian, recently read all the 1,242 confessions of fornication, or reports of such confessions that exist in church records from 1620 to 1839, and concluded that what is most remarkable about them is how unremarkable they seemed to the Puritans; the vast majority were recorded in a perfectly matter-of-fact manner without comment, as though they were nothing but routine business.

Hunt explains that these 1,242 confessions are but a small sample of the illicit sexual activity in New England, the tip of the iceberg of sin. Exactly how many Puritans were straying from the path of righteousness is beyond our calculations. But, Hunt notes, there is ". . . one exceedingly important statistic to be gleaned from these records. Dr. Oberholtzer tabulated by type all disciplinary cases of every sort mentioned in the records of the Massachusetts churches he visited, and discovered that a plurality of them concerned fornication." One must conclude, therefore, that fornication was "the most prevalent and most popular sin in Puritan New England."

As an indication of how remarkably matter-of-fact these Puritans could be about sexual sins, witness the attitude of Samuel Sewall. Judge Sewall was, in many ways, a quintessential

Sex and the Puritans

Puritan whose diaries are a treasured source of information about the Puritan mind. Even the crime of sex with an animal scarcely disturbs the unflappable Sewall; in a diary entry for 1674 he writes:

> April 2. Benjamin Gourd of Roxbury (being about 17 years of age) was executed for committing Bestiality with a Mare, which was first knocked in the head under the Gallows in his sight. N. B. He committed that filthines at noon day in an open yard. He after confessed that he had lived in that sin a year. The causes he alledged were, idlenes, not obeying parents, etc.

Sewall's casual diary entry highlights the complexity of the Puritan sexual attitudes. Yes, they could execute someone for committing bestiality and, yes, even they could label such behavior as "filthines;" but Sewall neither elaborates nor moralizes about this sexual crime. It's just another event to be recorded for posterity.

It is this complexity that we must try to understand. The Puritans never believed in easy answers to any of the problems of human behavior; they were aware, as few of us are, of just how strange a creature man could be. They had left a spiritually corrupt England to create a religious utopia in America. They came here equipped with a detailed moral code based on a sternly Calvinistic interpretation of the Bible. But life in America didn't turn out quite as they expected. It's one thing to punish a wrongdoer in a small English town, it's quite another to attempt to regulate people's behavior on the edge of a wilderness. The basis of Puritan sexual regulations was not a Victorian impulse to force people to deny their sexual desires. Instead, it

Samuel Sewall.
"He committed that filthiness at noon day in an open yard. . . . The causes he alleged were, idleness, not obeying parents, etc."

Sex and the Puritans

was an effort to limit those transgressions that threatened the fabric of their tiny society. At the heart of the Puritan experiment was the family, the "little commonwealth" that served as a paradigm of the larger commonwealth of the Puritan colony. Sexual sins threatened the family, and family stability had to be maintained at all costs. Thus adultery was a far more serious crime than mere fornication, and sex between an engaged couple was rarely punished, except if the betrothed's belly seemed too full.

As time passed and the colonists took increasing advantage of the freedom available in a new land, the Puritans became more and more resigned to their inability to make people conform to God's rule. John Demos has calculated that by 1750 between one-third and one-half of all new brides went to the altar pregnant. As Edmund Morgan writes: "The Puritans became inured to sexual offenses, because there were so many." The Puritans fully appreciated their dilemma of trying to control sexual excess, while knowing at the same time that excess was built into man's corrupt nature. Whatever else they were, the Puritans were not fools; they did the best they could to establish their brave new world, but they never closed their eyes to man's real ways.

The classic account of the complexity of the Puritan response to man's wayward sexual ways appears in William Bradford's history of the Plymouth colony. Bradford was the leader of the Pilgrims who landed at Plymouth in 1620, and his *Of Plymouth Plantation* is indispensable for understanding the early years of this Puritan colony. There were slight theological differences between the Pilgrims at Plymouth and the Puritans at Massachusetts Bay, but as far as sexual mores were concerned, the Pilgrims and Puri-

tans were virtually interchangeable. So when Bradford describes his puzzlement at the goings-on in his colony, we can view his attitudes as those of a representative Puritan.

We are concerned with events that occurred in 1642, only twenty-two years after the Mayflower landed at Plymouth. Bradford had survived extraordinary hardship and unremitting struggle in attempting to build a society based on the rule of God, and he had not yet given up hope that such a utopia was possible. Unlike the eighteenth-century Puritans, Bradford was not "inured" to sexual offenses; he still believed that man's carnal nature could be effectively controlled. But the events of 1642 left even this resolute Puritan shaken, for that year witnessed, in Morgan's words, an "epidemic of sexual misdemeanors" plus a few sexual felonies. Writing in his history, Bradford relates the story of that terrible year:

> Marvilous it may be to see and consider how some kind of wickednes did grow & breake forth here, in a land wher the same was so much witnessed against, and so narrowly looked unto, & severly punished when it was knowne. . . . And yet all this could not suppress the breaking out of sundrie notorious sins, . . . espetially drunkennes and unclainnes; not only incontinencie betweene persons unmarried, for which many both men & women have been punished sharply enough, but some married persons allso. But that which is worse, even sodomie and bugerie, (things fearfull to name,) have broak forth in this land, oftener than once.

Only twenty-two years had passed since the founding of the holy colony and already sin was

Sex and the Puritans

abounding, even the fearful sin of bestiality. Why, Bradford wondered, in a land where even simple sins were so closely observed and so severely punished, were so many Christians doing so many foul deeds? Good Puritan that he was, he searched for explanations. ". . . one reason may be," he wrote, "that the Divell may carrie a greater spite against the churches of Christ and the gospell hear. . . ." and therefore works harder to make people sin in Plymouth so he can "cast a blemishe & staine upon them in the eyes of [the] world. . . ." Another reason he offered was the possibility that, in fact, sin was no more common in Plymouth than elsewhere,

but at Plymouth sin was more frequently discovered. Perhaps the wayward Christians in the new land were just as sinful, no more no less, than wayward Christians everywhere.

It was Bradford's third explanation for this epidemic of sexual license that was most interesting, that demonstrated the remarkable psychological acuteness of the Puritan mind. It was an analysis worthy of Freud:

. . . it may be in this case as it is with waters when their streames are stopped or dammed up, when they gett passage they flow with more violence, and make more noys and disturbance, then when they are

A Puritan governor interrupting the Christmas sport.
Why was there so much sin at Plymouth?

Sex and the Puritans

11

suffered to rune quietly in their owne chanels. So wikednes being here more stopped by strict laws, and the same more nerly looked unto, so as it cannot rune in a comone road of liberty as it would, and is inclined, it searches every wher, and at last breaks out wher it getts vente.

The libido would find its way. Bradford suggested that it was the strictness of the Puritan code that was perhaps responsible for the outbreak of flagrant sexual crimes. In most societies, where people's behavior was not closely watched and frequently punished, sexual energy would take the path of least resistance, and people would engage in run-of-the-mill peccadilloes. But in a holy commonwealth, where every Christian was constantly observed for signs of sin, if people were not given acceptable channels for their sexual impulses, they would turn to any source for sexual satisfaction, even to animals.

Bradford fully understood the dilemma of Puritan moral leadership. On the one hand, severe

Sex and the Puritans

punishment was necessary because God's will must be obeyed; on the other hand, even the most severe of punishments could not contain man's impulse to sin and, in fact, could drive man to greater sin. There was no final solution to this dilemma. Both God and man must be given their due; in practice the Puritan compromise was to provide all the acceptable channels possible and to be lenient to those who violated God's sexual commandments.

But some sins, even for the Puritans, were too horrible to tolerate. Sex with animals was an affront to the total fabric of Puritan society and an offense completely disgusting to God. Bradford wrote of one such offense in that dreadful year of 1642:

Ther was a youth whose name was Thomas Granger; he was servant to an honest man of Duxbery, being aboute 16. or 17. years of age. (His father & mother lived at the same time at Sityate.) He was this year detected of buggery (and indicted for the same) with a mare, a cowe, tow goats, five sheep, 2. calves, and a turkey. *Horrible it is to mention, but the truth of the historie requires it.* [italics mine] He was first discovered by one that accidentally saw his lewd practice towards the mare. (I forbear perticulers.) Being upon it examined and committed, in the end he not only confest the fact with that beast at that time, but sundrie times before, and at severall times with all the rest of the forenamed in his indictmente; and this his free-confession was not only in private to the magistrats, (though at first he strived to deny it,), but to sundrie, both ministers & others, and afterwards, upon his indictmente, to the whole court & jury; and confirmed it at his execution. And

whereas some of the sheep could not so well be knowne by his description of them, others with them were brought before him, and he declared which were they, and which were not. And accordingly he was cast by the jury, and condemned, and after executed about the 8. of September, 1642. A very sade spectakle it was: for first the mare, and then the cowe, and the rest of the lesser catle, were kild before his face, according to the law, Levit: 20. 15. and then he him selfe was executed. The catle were all cast into a great & large pitte that was digged of purpose for them, and no use made of any part of them.

An awful deed had been committed and the sinner had to pay with his life; but Bradford did not write with the voice of wrath or vengeance. He was disgusted by the deed, but he was also saddened. Again we see the remarkable lack of prurience, the Puritan necessity to be honest even in the face of the foulest things. As he explained, he owed it to history to tell the whole story. We are so accustomed to history written by participants that is self-serving, apologetic, which glosses over the sordid, that Bradford's honesty seems extraordinary. But Bradford could not hide behind a screen of false decency; since God sees everything and knows everything, we must be truthful to ourselves and to others.

The accepted image of the Puritans as neurotic repressers of sexual behavior bears no relation to the reality of life in Colonial New England. Make no mistake about it, life in a holy commonwealth put severe limits on personal freedom; there were laws and regulations covering every imaginable area of human activity. The

"Horrible it is to mention, but the truth of the historie requires it."

Puritans most definitely wanted people to behave in specified ways, to live lives that glorified God at every turn. But they weren't repressed and squeamish about sex. Far from it. They appreciated its power more than we. They knew its strength and its mystery. And, within the limits they placed upon it, they also knew its joy.

SHELDON FRANK

A Note on Sources

This essay has relied heavily on the pioneering work of Edmund S. Morgan, in particular his article, "The Puritans and Sex," *New England Quarterly* XV (1942): 591–607, and portions of his book, *The Puritan Family*, New York: Harper Torchbook, 1966. Other useful studies of Puritan behavior are John Demos, *A Little Commonwealth*, London: Oxford University Press, 1970; Emil Oberholtzer, *Delinquent Saints*, New York: Columbia University Press, 1956; and Morton Hunt, *The Natural History of Love*, New York: Alfred A. Knopf, 1959. The poems of Anne Bradstreet and *Of Plymouth Plantation* by William Bradford are available in a number of editions, while *The Diary of Samuel Sewall 1674–1729* has been edited recently by M. Halsey Thomas, New York: Farrar, Straus & Giroux, 1973.

Sex and the Puritans

Sex on the Frontier

Alden Brooks was a portrait painter from Winnetka, Illinois, who left a diary of his *Grand Trip Across the Plains* in 1859. The trip was a "constitutional" of sorts. Brooks had come down with consumption from overexposure in a Wisconsin snowstorm, and it was thought that outdoor living was good medicine for his ailment. So when a neighbor set out for California in a prairie schooner, Brooks paid $50 for his board, and made ready to walk alongside across the continent. The party had its adventures with Indians, a death, and a marriage. They also found time for intellectual pursuits. After driving their fifty head of cattle onto an island in the Platte River, they made camp and set up a debating society to discuss weighty topics. The question set for one evening was: "Resolved that the love of money is greater than love for women."

The answer they reached on this pause in their journey is unrecorded. But the great Westward journey that took a hundred years and spread millions of people across the continent, and of which Brooks's "grand trip" was only a

miniscule fragment, provides an answer of its own, or even several answers, sometimes mutually contradictory.

The frontier, we are likely to forget, was many places. Each part of what was to become the nation had its turn. Where I write, in central Illinois, the frontier passed through about 150 years ago. Where you are as you read was once frontier territory too. But wherever the frontier happened to be, one thing appears to have been constant: the men outnumbered the women.

Sir Walter Raleigh's colony of Roanoke had a population of ninety-one men and seventeen women. Some attempts were made to redress this early imbalance. In the seventeenth century when prisoners and vagrants were shipped off to the colonies by authority of the Privy Council, the shipments also included girls from small villages who had been drafted to ameliorate the life of the settlers. A settler could claim one for the cost of her transportation—about $500 in tobacco.

Given half a chance, nature would quickly have restored the balance of the sexes. No

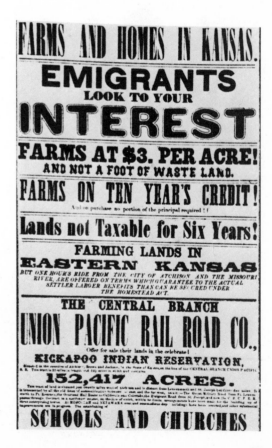

Sex on the Frontier

matter how disturbed the ratio becomes in one generation, that generation's allotment of children will still be properly distributed—half boys, half girls. But as long as heavy immigration continued, the balance stayed tipped in favor of men. Writing in 1876, William Dixon calculated that "England and Germany owe to America more than 800,000 females, a debt in the face of which all other claims for compensation are the merest bagatelles."

Many of the young immigrants were unmarried. But married men often came alone too, leaving wives and children behind. There is a correspondence between one such husband and father, settled in Kansas, and his parish overseer back home in Devon. The parish wrote to him to send for his family. He replied, in July 1850, as follows:

> Sir, what made me leave England was distress. I could not gain a living for myself, wife, and children. There was nothing more to look for but relief from the parish, if I had stayed in England. Sir, if you will send my wife Mary Fervins and children here I am ready to receive them and here I can maintain them if they were here.

The parish must not have been eager to cover the cost of their passage, since there is another letter from George Fervins, dated half a year later:

> I love my wife and children, but if you love to keep them and maintain them you can do so and be damned. . . . You can kiss my arse, I am living in the land of the free.

Internal immigration only aggravated the problem that began at the ports of entry. It is estimated that in 1849, 50,000 people traveled westward; 42,000 of them were men. And when Denver was founded in 1859, with a population of about 1,000, the number of women was five.

These conditions could not but shape relations between the sexes on the frontier and in the settlements behind it. And these facts alone are testimony on the question debated by Brooks's riverside lyceum. For if love for women were greater than the love of money, the frontier would not have leaped across the continent at all. In the vanguard of settlement were men who were willing to leave women behind, and instead pursue otters or gold or Indians or herds of cattle across the prairies.

Indians

Although the men of the frontier left their women behind, they encountered others at each step of the way—Indian women. *Because* they left their own women behind, the encounter was intimate. A French trader working on the upper Missouri, Jean Baptiste Truteau, described the young trappers arriving in the Indian villages. They were "usually seen to be galloping at full speed like horses that have broken loose into the field of Venus."

The spirit of all this galloping was probably more lighthearted than it usually is at the meeting of two cultures. Initially it did not depend on conquest and subjugation. Many of the Indian tribes did not adhere to ideals of virginity for unmarried women. According to another Frenchman, Baron de Lahontan, a young woman among the Huron "is master of her own body, and by her natural right to liberty is free to do what she pleases."

Whether or not white observers fully under-

Arrival of the young women at Jamestown.
A settler could claim one for the cost of her transportation—about $500 in tobacco.

stood the conditions they were describing, they made it clear that tribal practices in many circumstances allowed and even welcomed contact between white men and Indian women. In the journal he kept on his famous expedition, Meriwether Lewis noted that he cautioned his men "to give [certain Indian husbands] no cause of jealousy by having connection with their women without their knowledge. . . . To prevent the mutual exchange of good office altogether I know it is impossible to effect." Apparently the only critical issue was going through the proper channels.

Among some tribes it was a canon of hospitality for men to offer their women as bedfellows for visiting guests. And the women themselves seem to have been warmly inclined toward white men, if we are to believe Amerigo Vespucci. The Italian explorer who gave his name to the continent boasted delicately that its natives "showed themselves very desirous of copulating with us Christians."

Records of the white men's amazement at this practice are scattered across several centuries. *Their* idea of hospitality (which may well have been kinder to women) was slightly different: On a cold night during a campaign General Custer loaned a fellow officer a sleeping companion—the loudest-snoring member of his large pack of dogs.

Ultimately, as they surveyed each other across the Indian women, the white men and the Indian men reciprocated each other's attitudes precisely: wonder tinged with contempt. The Indians were willing to offer their women, but they were amazed that the white men were so full of lust they could accept them. An Aricara chief once asked, "Why is it that your people are so fond of women? One might suppose they had never seen one before."

After the first Europeans had come, all subsequent white men to penetrate the woods knew something about the Indians. But the Indian discovery of white men continued into the nineteenth century. Records of these first encounters show that it was the women who were the most intrepid explorers of the unknown territory of the white men's skin. If they weren't terrified, they were often charmed and amused.

A trader named Pattie described what happened when his party bumped into some Indian women in California:

> At length they made up to one of our companions who was of a singularly light complexion, fair soft skin, and blue eyes. They wanted him to strip himself naked, that they might explore him thoroughly, for they seemed doubtful of him being alike in every part of his body. This, as mildly as possible, he refused to do.

But after they brought him a present of dried fish he relented and "oblige[d] these curious and good-natured women by giving them a full view of his body. . . . This delighted them, and they conversed and laughed among themselves, and then came one by one and stood beside him, so as to compare their bodies with his."

Ross Cox, an Irish trader on the Columbia River, described a similar inspection which ended with an examination of his friend M'Donald's flowing red hair in search of "certain animalculi which shall be nameless." The woman doing the inspection was disappointed not to find a "solitary ferlie" and pronounced the man "too clean."

Indians at a fur trader's hut.
"The Indians were willing to offer their women, but they were amazed that the white men were so full of lust that they could accept them."

An occasional black man traveling across the country was an even greater attraction. Lewis and Clark had a slave named York on their expedition; and Lewis pondered the fact that "instead of inspiring any prejudice, his color seemed to procure him additional advantages from the Indians. . . . Two very handsome young squaws were sent aboard this evening and persecuted us with civilities. The black man York participated largely in these favors."

White men were reciprocally interested in observing Indian women. But unlike white men, Indian women did not have to undress to stand for inspection since they were already naked.

Sex on the Frontier

A fur trader in the council teepee. The white men had more tradable goods than any Indian ever dreamed of, but they were poor in females of their own.

And this seemed to be as amazing to the men as white skin, multicolored hair, and blue and gray eyes were to the women.

If there were no absolute standards of virginity and chastity standing in the way of interbreeding, there might still have been the specter of bastardy. But the Indians loved their children. Orphans reputedly did not suffer from neglect. And it appears that even in tribes which punished adultery, the sins of the parents were not visited upon the children. Half-breed children, in fact, were often specially prized. A New England Puritan wrote about an infant with gray eyes whose "father shewed him to us and said they were English mens eies. [He desired the child to] have an English name, because of the likeness of his eies which his father had in admiration, because of novelty among their nation." The New Englander went on to report that "I tould the father that his sonne was . . . bastard." It is not clear whether this was the extent of his proposals for English names. In any case, it made no impression on the father.

Children of mixed blood were appreciated for qualities other than their novel coloring. A Cree chief in the early 1800s held that the best warriors were sons of an Indian mother and a white father. The Mandan believed that in sexual intercourse the white man transmitted his powers to the woman, and she in turn could transmit them to her husband.

This system of thought led to a strange experience for Truteau among the Cheyenne. He was brought into the middle of a ceremonial ring by a young chief who then stripped him down to his breeches and shoes. The man spoke to his wife and "she did something I never expected— she stretched out her hands toward me and

rubbed me from head to foot, and then she passed them over her whole body. I was so astonished at the action of this man and this woman that I stood stock-still with my arms crossed, and let her do all she wished." He later learned that her actions were supposed to keep her future children from sickness and make them live a long time.

In the regions where the frontier stabilized, where white men "settled" to carry on some years as trappers and traders, but where the real settlers, agricultural families, did not immediately follow, the pattern of relations changed. An 1805 census of the North West Company's trading posts recorded at least 400 Indian wives of traders.

The spirit in which marriages were undertaken ranged broadly. When one of the young clerks in Ross Cox's party, "having become tired of celibacy resolved to take a wife," an interpreter was sent to the local Spokan village, to inquire "whether any unappropriated comely young woman was willing to become the partner of a juvenile chief." A seventeen-year-old girl was found. Gifts of blankets and kettles were presented to her family, and when negotiations were complete her mother delivered her to the fort. Here she was "consigned to the care of one of the men's wives, called 'the scourer,' conversant in such affairs, who had her head and body thoroughly cleansed from all the Indian paint and grease with which they had been saturated," and thus purified, was handed over to her new husband.

Other marriages were even less ceremonious. The famous trader Alexander Henry the Younger kept a daily journal of his adventures in

Sex on the Frontier

northern Minnesota. The entry for New Year's Day 1801 reads: "Liard's daughter took possession of my room, and the devil himself could not have got her out." Liard was a Saultern chief. Ten years later his daughter still occupied Henry's house, along with three children.

Occasionally a marriage was performed with full tribal ritual. Pierre Michel, a hunter and interpreter for the Flatheads, asked for a sixteen-year-old girl who was the niece of the chief. A young Indian from the tribe also wanted her and had received her mother's promise that she could be his. A tribal council was called. The warchief asked the Indian if the girl had herself promised to be his wife. When the answer was negative, the chief spoke in behalf of Michel's suit, praising his bravery and his services to the tribe, and urging the marriage as a way to "forever make him as one of their brothers." His influence prevailed, and brotherly feeling triumphed all around with the defeated Indian rival shaking hands with Michel and assuring the girl that if he could not be her husband he hoped she would treat him as a brother.

Later, at a ceremony where the peace pipe was passed around, the bride was exhorted to be "chaste, obedient, industrious, and silent, and when absent with her husband among other tribes, always to stay at home." A procession led by warriors carrying cedar torches escorted them to Michel's fort. They lived happily together, if not forever after, at least as long as Cox stayed in the country. But he ends his description with a concession:

> I may as well state that he was the only person of our party to whom the Flatheads would give one of their women in marriage.

Several of our men made applications, but were always refused.

Willingness on the part of the women also varied, and gave the tribes different reputations. Flathead women were indifferent to the "superior comforts" of a white man's wife. Spokan women were not, and reputedly "made excellent wives." The painter Rudolph Kurz married an Iowa girl, but in their first winter together she grew homesick and vanished to return to her family, taking all his gear with her.

The white men were also driven by a mixture of motives. Some of their motives were even divine. A shrewd Dutch Protestant of the Colonial period, Dr. Douglas, speculated cheerfully about an advantage the Protestant missionaries had over Catholic ones: they could gain entry into the tribes by marriage while Catholic clergy could not.

Mercenary motives, not surprisingly, were an important spur to marriage. A trader with an Indian wife could feel relatively safe in the territory occupied by her tribe, and he could expect preferential terms of trade. The Indians, on their side, became aware of the white men's trade benefits in having an Indian wife and were able to strike increasingly profitable bargains in return for their women.

In Cox's view (he never married in "the country" but went home to Dublin and married a woman there), the men who entered into these marriages seldom expected them to be permanent. Few men wished to have children with their Indian wives: "a sterile woman [was] therefore invaluable. They [were], however, scarce."

Cox had a friend who was particularly cautious

Sex on the Frontier

in this matter. When he learned that an Indian who had been married for five years without having a child had recently drowned, he promptly proposed to the widow. Nine months later he was a father. Horrified, the man "dissolved the connexion" and resolved never to take such a risk again.

The same man, Mr. J---, as Cox discreetly calls him, was transferred to a new district to replace another trader who was quitting the country and leaving his wife of eight years behind. Mr. J--- regarded her to be a fine woman. On top of that she was, at the age of twenty-five, a veteran of two marriages totaling eleven years, and had never had a child. Mr. J--- therefore, in his own words, "determined to secure such a prize." She accepted his proposal. The letter Mr. J--- sent to Cox, describing the whole sequence of events, reports:

> On the 1st of April we became *one* (the day was ominous), and on that day nine months precisely (it is a melancholy coincidence of dates) she presented me with a New Year's gift in the shape of a man-child!

The fertile Mr. J--- tried to find some way to extricate himself again, but not knowing how to break his intention, delayed, and found his wife pregnant again. His letter ended with an expression of his resigning himself, the governor permitting, to stay with her.

The records kept by frontiersmen are often punctuated by descriptions of social customs surrounding sex that astonished them. One type of ritual especially, elaborated in different forms by various tribes but prevalent across the whole continent, gets singled out for attention in nar-

rative after narrative. A soldier at Fort Cumberland described it simply:

> It is the custom with them, once or twice a year, for the women to dance and all the men to sit by. . . . Each woman takes out her man that she likes, dances with him, and lies with him for a week, and then [they] return to their former husbands and live as they did before.

But the nitty gritty seems to have gone without comment. One must conclude either that the white men encountered nothing that seemed remarkable to them, or that they were reluctant to cast an anthropological eye on activities in which they themselves were intimately involved.

Although they sometimes took part in them, most white men described the Indians' sexual rites as "abominable" and "detestable." They interpreted the practice of offering a woman to a guest as prostitution. In time, their misperceptions were corrected, not by being revised, but by transforming reality until it came to match their ideas of it.

The white men had more tradable goods than any Indian had ever dreamed of. And while they were rich in goods they were poor in females of their own. Even if they had brought a supply of wives and daughters into the woods, it is doubtful that they would have entered into fully reciprocal exchange agreements with the Indians. So gradually transactions became more and more purely commercial.

Every trading post came to have its "squaw town." The companies tolerated them; it was to their advantage to have their men spend their money fast. Later, when the fur trade collapsed

Indian agent Clifford, his Indian wife, and friends in the 1890s.

Lady's Chain—a scene from a frontier mining camp.
"It was a wild, free, disorderly, grotesque society! *Men*—only swarming host of stalwart *men* . . ."

and the mountain men were replaced by soldiers, buffalo hunters, railroad crews, and miners, the situation was aggravated. With fur no longer an item of trade, all the Indians had to sell was women. The white men's enterprises no longer depended on their cooperation or toleration. Instead the white men were everywhere driving the Indians off their traditional lands. Endemic poverty and hunger completed the transformation of Indian-white sexual relations into prostitution.

Like prostitution (and scalping), the worst of the venereal diseases were apparently imported by the white man. By the late days of the frontier they were widespread. Through syphilis white men managed to distribute the sterility which they had found "invaluable" in Indian women.

Sex on the Frontier

The scarcity of women on the mining frontier was even more drastic than among traders and trappers. Although it was frontier territory the mining region was also urban. Here were instant cities with sudden concentrations of population, banks, hotels, saloons, newspapers, houses thrown up in continuous rows—all the paraphernalia of real towns except for women and children and families. When news got around of a woman in the vicinity there would be a woman rush. Mark Twain was there and wrote about it:

> It was a wild, free, disorderly, grotesque society! *Men*—only swarming host of stalwart *men*—nothing juvenile, nothing feminine, visible anywhere!
>
> In those days miners would flock in crowds to catch a glimpse of that rare and blessed spectacle, a woman! Old inhabitants tell how, in a certain camp, the news went abroad early in the morning that a woman had come! They had seen a calico dress hanging out of a wagon down at the camping-ground—sign of emigrants from over the great plains. Everybody went down there, and a shout went up when an actual, bona fide dress was discovered fluttering in the wind! The male emigrant was visible. The miners said: "Fetch her out!"
>
> He said: "It is my wife, gentlemen—she is sick—we have been robbed of money, provisions, everything, by the Indians—we want to rest."
>
> "Fetch her out! We've got to see her!"
>
> "But, gentlemen, the poor thing, she—"
>
> "FETCH HER OUT!"
>
> He "fetched her out," and they swung their hats and sent up three rousing cheers and a tiger; and they crowded around and gazed at her, and touched her dress and listened to her voice with the look of men who listened to a *memory* rather than a present reality—and they collected twenty-five hundred dollars in gold and gave it to the man, and swung their hats again and gave three more cheers, and went home satisfied.

It is one of the few marvels of the West that he exaggerated little. For it seems that one of the main genres of mining tales was about the strenuous lengths a man would go to in order to catch a glimpse of a woman.

The fascination with all things touching on the domestic side of life was so great that an enterprising miner in Shasta, California, was able to sell tickets to his own wedding. At five dollars per head he collected enough to pay for the lavish affair and a household of furnishings besides.

If a woman offered services of any kind, the market was insatiable. Mrs. Phelps was the first woman to arrive in Nevada City, also in California. She crossed the plains with her husband and a cook stove. The latter made her fortune. Upon her arrival in town she began producing dried apple pies which sold briskly at one dollar apiece. For miles around the miners would set the stakes in their nightly gambling sessions at payment for Mrs. Phelps's pies. Soon she had to buy a second stove, but even then demand exceeded supply. On Sundays "her place (was) literally thronged with miners waiting for her pies to come out of the oven, and as soon out, devoured."

But other things could be even more profitably

The frontier towns had all the paraphernalia of real towns—except for women, children, and families.

peddled than pies. A legendary personage was Julia Bulette, reputedly the *second* unattached female in Virginia City. Where she came from and how she found her way to Nevada nobody seems to know for sure. Although France and England are both mentioned as possible places of origin, the consensus seems to be that she was a Creole from New Orleans.

New Orleans before the war was regarded as a city of self-indulgence and vice:

> Ladies [in that city] think nothing of expending a large proportion of the profits of a year's trade on a few dresses. . . . Land in America is too cheap to create adequate social distinctions. Your wife's back is the only place to display your wealth.

Julia Bulette brought these opulent standards to Virginia City. It was an inflationary situation. Her goods were scarce and money was daily dug out of the ground. Soon her fee rose to $1,000 per evening. Like Mrs. Phelps she was pressed to expand her operations and began importing girls from San Francisco.

Her house was the first of the grand rococo structures that eventually sprouted in Virginia City. It was known as "Julia's Palace." Inside, festive French meals were served and washed down with imported French wines.

Travelers in the mining towns were struck by the dismal absence of anything green to soften the harsh landscape. But inside Julia's Palace the atmosphere was brightened by fresh cut flowers, hauled in from California by the Wells Fargo stagecoach each day.

The respectable women in any mining town received lavish and sentimental praise for their uplifting and cheering influence. But an equally

Sex on the Frontier

salutary influence on the manners of the frontier was credited to the high-class prostitutes. In Julia Bulette's Palace no disorderly conduct was permitted. Chivalry prevailed, as did good table manners.

Outside there was a tidy row of white clapboard cottages with red lights over the doors after dark.

Julia was generous in performing other neglected feminine functions. Tales circulate about how she nursed the miners when influenza epidemics struck the camp, and turned the Palace into a hospital when several hundred men fell ill from drinking bad water.

The miners focused all their love and nostalgia for women on her. And the firemen honored her with a supreme accolade, membership in the Virginia City Fire Engine Company No. 1. In a town where mining explosions were not uncommon, and where the town itself burned down more than once, this was no trivial honor. Julia Bulette treated it as a responsibility, donating money for new equipment and priming firemen with coffee if there was a long blaze.

At the height of her fame, her French maid found her one morning in her bed, strangled, her jewels missing. The whole lode was plunged into mourning. On the day she was buried, the miners stayed above ground. Risking disaster, all of the town's fire companies put on their uniforms and joined the funeral procession. The Brigade Nevada Militia Band, recruited for the occasion, marched home afterwards playing "The Girl I Left Behind Me."

One year later a man tried to peddle some of the stolen loot. He was arrested, tried for murder, convicted, and sentenced to die. A special gallows was designed and constructed for the ceremonious occasion. Committees were appointed to handle the routing of traffic. On the day of John Millain's hanging the miners again took the day off. Again the firemen left the town unprotected so that they could attend the proceedings. Even the saloons were closed. The prisoner, escorted by a company of National Guard, arrived stylishly in an open carriage from the town's best livery. Before he died, he "thanked the good ladies of Virginia in a ringing voice for their favors of fried chicken, cupcakes, and homemade preserves." Some of them apparently had felt sympathy for the man who had sped Julia Bulette on her way.

In its heyday, and Julia Bullette's, Virginia City "boasted of a red-light district superior to any other from Denver to the coast, both in size and in the variety and amiability of its inmates." After an excursion through the mines, noted visitors to the town would be taken for a tour of its double row of white cottages that lined D Street for two blocks.

The cities of the East also had thriving industries in prostitution. A contemporary report of the New York Magdalen Society provided the following statistics for New York in 1830: 20,000 women were engaged in prostitution; "more than one-half of the male population, married and unmarried, were customers thrice weekly." But it was only in the frontier towns of the West that some prostitutes emerged, however briefly, as civic leaders. An Eastern lady traveling in California one hundred years ago noted with scorn that while in other cities prostitutes emulated the fashions of upper-class women, in San Francisco the picture was reversed.

Although few of them could match Virginia City, almost all the mining towns had their

Virgin Street or Maiden Lane. The old camp ballad tells the story:

First came the miners who worked in the mine,
Then came the ladies who lived on the line.

Only a handful managed to live in luxury. "The line" usually consisted of a row of shanties each with just a bed, a stove, and a dresser. The story of how these women made their way to the mining towns would be an interesting one if it were known, for the white prostitutes were probably the only women who responded on their own to the lure of the frontier and the fortunes that could be made there. Excluded from the activity of mining, they found a way to share the land's wealth; gold diggers among the gold diggers. But except for the few who won fame or notoriety, their stories are lost. The chroniclers of the time (and many of the mining towns had lively newspapers) wrote about them only to report an occasional shooting or knifing. Otherwise the lives and personalities of the prostitutes, always referred to with a euphemistic leer as "ladies of joy," "women of easy virtue," "daughters of Venus," and "the fair but frail," did not surface in the pages of the journals.

There were those who did *not* come under their own steam. In the period when shiploads of Chinese laborers, having heard the call to "go East, young man," arrived at the docks of San Francisco, the cargos sometimes included young women as well. The men were often indentured workers who could eventually pay off their debts to the legendary Six Companies of China and be free. The women were more often slaves. They were bought or kidnapped in China and sold on arrival in the U.S. Some were sold to whites, others to Chinese, to serve as prostitutes or household servants. The Chinese men, on arrival, had to pay a "landing fee" to the Sixth Company, the one on the American side of the ocean. This was to cover the cost of shipping their bones back to China after they died, to assure burial in their native soil. The fact that women did not have to pay landing fees was a measure of their inferior status: when they died their bones could remain where they were.

Some of these women were channeled inland to the mining camps. A decade after the official end of slavery in the United States they continued to be the property of the men who bought them. One such girl, arriving in San Francisco in 1871 at the age of eighteen, turned up in Warren, Idaho, in the possession of the local Tong leader. He was the head of a group of about a hundred Chinese men working in the claims. He was also an inveterate gambler. The story goes that one night in an unlucky streak of betting he gradually lost every ounce of his gold. His opponent, a young white card shark, suggested continuing the game by staking the girl. He did. He lost. Like another sack of gold dust she passed into the hands of the winner. The story continues that a few months later, on his next visit to Warren, the young man, Johnny Bemis by name, had another streak of luck at faro. This time he shouldn't have been so lucky because his disgruntled opponent put a bullet in his chest. Johnny Bemis lost a lot of blood, and his friends gave up hope for his survival. It was the girl, Polly, who took charge and in faltering English ordered him strapped to a horse and hauled him back to their cabin. She nursed him

In 1865, due to the scarcity of women on the frontier, the president of Washington's territorial university collected about 400 young ladies who emigrated as teachers, housekeepers, and husband-hunters.

Sex on the Frontier

ON DECK

Sex on the Frontier

Some women came and found husbands; others found another way to share the land's wealth—gold diggers among the gold diggers.

for a few months, in the course of which he fell in love with her. On the next trip to Warren they were married. This true romance is authenticated by the Idaho Historical Society which, however, does not guarantee its representativeness.

The California state government tried to bar the entry of these women, and a long court battle ensued. State officials were upheld through the state courts. But the U.S. Circuit Court overruled them, prohibiting the closing of ports. A legal battle over frontier morality? In the mountain mining communities there was little regulation of prostitution. Those camps which did pass ordinances against it never enforced them, but only drew revenue from the fines they were entitled to collect. And in fact, California officialdom didn't really consider the importation of Chinese women a "question of the minor morals" but rather of being inundated by "Asiatic scum." "We are little more than 30 millions of White people," a senator is quoted as saying in the 1870s. "They are upwards of 360 millions of Yellow people. So, to spare us 50 millions would be nothing to them, while the gift would be death to us."

The Civil War just over, and the red man

Sex on the Frontier

disappearing, the stage was being set for the nation's third racial conflict. To keep the shores pure of new arrivals by sea, equally new arrivals from the continent quickly organized themselves as "Native Sons and Daughters of the Golden West":

The miners came in '48,
The whores in '51,
The two soon got together
And produced the Native Son.

Meanwhile, there was plenty of traffic in girls from South America and Mexico. Santa Fe had a lively trade in captured Indians, both male and female; but the price of a man was never more than half the price of a young and pretty girl.

Marriage to Indian women declined with the formation of "urban" outposts in the mountain country and the attendant concentration of white men and subsequently, white women. It came to be looked upon with increasing scorn.

On the early frontier rape was uncommon. It would have been a dangerous undertaking for a lone trapper. And in the close communities of Colonial America justice was evenhanded enough to make the rape of an Indian punishable by law. But the mining communities of the West had less to fear from the Indians, and Indian women suffered by consequence. A California Indian agent received a report in 1855 complaining about the miners in Klamath County: "They have singled out all the squaws, compelling them to sleep with some man every night. This causes great excitement. The Bucks complain daily of it."

The immediate cause of the Piute War of 1860 was that a group of white men at Williams Station, Nevada, captured two Piute girls, put them in a cellar, and raped them. The Indians retaliated by killing every man at the station. Virginia City drew up a volunteer army of 105 men to punish the Indians. The volunteers were caught in a trap and wiped out. Virginia City was panicked. A second army was mustered. This time, 750 strong, they defeated the Piute. Books of Nevada lore often say that this force was rallied for the protection of Julia Bulette.

In our time, when the women's liberation movement was revived in the late sixties, feminists dramatized their grievances by calculating the market value of the services a woman performs for her family. On the mining frontier there was no need for this speculative exercise. Women's services were actually placed on the market, and all of them could command glamorous prices—professional pies, as we have seen, professional board in general, professional sex, professional laundry. (Laundry was such a problem for these womenless men that some forty-niners in California were shipping their dirty clothes off to China to be washed.)

The high value of women brought about by their scarcity made itself felt in many ways—small and large. In the West a woman could get away with straddling a horse, instead of having to ride sidesaddle. In the West a woman could get away with murder, if we can trust William Dixon, a jaundiced critic of the times. He records a justice of the Supreme Court of California complaining:

A judge will never get twelve men to find a female guilty of wilful murder in San Francisco, nor in any other town west of the Rocky Mountains. An excuse is always found by the jury; a petticoat being too much for bar and bench.

In the West a woman could get a divorce. This was what distressed Dixon most.

The domestic relation is everywhere disturbed. Marriage is a career; marriage, divorce, remarriage, times without end, and changes without shame.

According to him it was the women who made the most applications for divorce. They could always find a new husband if they wanted one. Old Westerners would gladly admit they used to marry "anything that came off the stage coach."

Divorce laws and proceedings were more liberal in the West than the East, a legacy no doubt brought about by the frontier woman shortage. It seems likely that other improvements in women's conditions should also be attributed, at least in part, to the same cause. The wild territory of Wyoming was the first place in the world to give women the right to vote. The issue of suffrage was closely tied to the issue of marriage and divorce, at least for the rear guard who opposed it. C. K. Nuckolls, a legislator who fought for repeal, argued that "women were made to obey. . . . They generally promise to obey, at any rate, and I think you had better abolish this female suffrage act or get up a new marriage ceremony to fit it."

Wyoming did not abolish the female suffrage act, although the price of its refusal almost turned out to be forfeiture of statehood when the territory applied for it twenty years later. It was a long time before the East was ready to have women voting. In fact the first twelve states to ratify female suffrage were all far west of the Mississippi.

Saints

Next door to present-day Nevada, in the region that was to become Utah, there was no shortage of women and there were no "single men's wives" as someone once called the Virginia City prostitutes.

On the contrary, there was even a slight surplus of women, a condition unknown anywhere else on the frontier. And all wives were the wives of married men. Emphatically so; some were married to men who were already much married.

Joseph Smith, the founder of Mormonism, was a big, handsome man, proud to display his physique in wrestling, his intellect in the study of Egyptian papyri, and his authority by wearing a lavish gold and lace trimmed uniform.

When God spoke to him about marriage in Nauvoo, Illinois, these are some of the things He said:

If any man espouse a virgin, and desire to espouse another, and the first give her consent; and if he espouse the second, and they are virgins, and have vowed to no other man, then he is justified; he cannot commit adultery, for they are given unto him. . . . But if one . . . of the virgins . . . , after she is espoused, shall be with another man, she has committed adultery, and shall be destroyed.

God also had a personal message for Joseph's wife Emma, which Joseph kindly delivered:

And I command my handmaid, Emma Smith, to abide and cleave unto my servant Joseph, and to none else. . . . And again, verily I say, let thine handmaid forgive my servant Joseph his trespasses, and then shall

she be forgiven her trespasses wherein she has trespassed aginst me.

There was some consternation when Joseph Smith divulged his revelation to a few leaders. And in Nauvoo, polygamy was little practiced except by Smith himself, who had twenty-eight wives. Even so, it caused a furor among the surrounding "Gentiles" (as non-Mormons were called), who also resented the Mormons's prosperity and the political power they derived from voting as a bloc. Resentment soon exploded into violence in the form of fires, thefts, and personal assaults.

Brigham Young and his family on their way to church, entitled "Scenes in an American Harem," from an 1857 *Harper's Weekly.*

Sex on the Frontier

Seeing the threat, Joseph Smith dispatched a delegation to go West and investigate locations in California and Oregon as possible sites for emigration. But as one last effort to forestall the exodus, he announced his candidacy for the presidency of the United States. If he won, "the dominion of the Kingdom of God" would be established; if he lost, the Mormons could still flee.

His plans were shattered in 1844 when the *Nauvoo Expositor* published charges against him which Smith considered libelous. Somehow the paper was burned down and Smith arrested.

Under pledge of protection, he and his brother were placed in a jail in nearby Carthage. But when a mob stormed the jail they met little resistance and murdered both men.

Two years later under the leadership of Brigham Young, Mormon advance companies set out for the West. Instead of going on to California or Oregon they chose to stop in the empty desert of Utah where they would be able to live without interference. To the extent that they were sexual refugees, they were the first and only group to brave the rigors of the frontier for such a cause. By 1852, established in their re-

Sex on the Frontier

mote mountain outpost, the Mormons felt secure enough to proclaim plural marriage to the world as doctrine.

Mormon doctrine evolved the position that no woman could make it to heaven without being married. As for a man, the more wives he had, the higher would be his position in the Eternal Kingdom. And though in Salt Lake City, unlike New Orleans, a wife's back was not the place for a man to display his wealth, he did pull rank by the number of backs.

Credit could be earned by marrying widows as well as virgins, and this had the good effect that older women were seldom left to solitude and neglect. Young ones were snapped up very quickly. The cosmopolitan world traveler Richard Burton, stopping in Salt Lake City in 1860, observed that girls seldom remained single past the age of sixteen. In England, by contrast, if Burton is correct, the average age of marriage was thirty. He remarked that in Utah any girls "would be the pity of the community if they were doomed to a waste of youth so unnatural."

(Englishmen had been surprised by this same age disparity for over a century, early marriage having been a constant of the American agricultural frontier from Virginia through the Northwest. Travelers on the Columbia told of coming across married women in the woods playing with their dolls.)

As in heaven it was required that a woman be married, so on earth it was considered her right. A man could be compelled to marry on her initiative. And young men were urged to take a wife as soon as they could support one.

While the marriage of a man to many women was the highest of virtues, adultery remained the lowest of sins. Burton stressed this fact to squelch the defamatory notion, widely held "back in the States," that the Mormons of Utah "all pig together." As evidence he testified that a man who murders his wife's lover is invariably acquitted. Brigham Young, according to Burton, would counsel adulterers, "because unable to hang or behead them, . . . to seek certain death in a righteous cause as an expiatory sacrifice, which may save their souls alive."

In subsequent years travelers who took the northern route across the prairies counted the Mormons among the many marvels of the West. Every journal offers some account of a visit in a Mormon household and, according to the writer's predilections, a verdict on how the women appeared—ugly or pretty, morose or cheerful, wholesome or depraved.

Utah was the more astonishing by its perfect contrast with the surrounding settlements—not only in the abundance of women and the multiplicity of wives but also on every point. Mark Twain told a story about a miner "huge . . . bearded, belted, spurred, and bristling with deadly weapons" just down from a long campaign in the mountains. Coming upon a woman carrying her three-year-old daughter he stopped still and barred her way:

> His face lit up with pleasure and astonishment: "Well, if it ain't a child!" Snatching a little leather pouch from his pocket, he offered it to the woman. "There's a hundred and fifty dollars in dust there, and I'll give it to you to let me kiss the child!"

Twain swore "that anecdote was *true.*"

But in Utah children were prodigious. A farmer could have eight "stalwart sons" to help him thresh his wheat, and inside the house, as with one Mr. Robbins, "two . . . Mrs. Robbinses nursing babies of the same age" and several intermediate Robbinses "chirping about." Brigham Young, capitalizing on the advantages of a long life, superior wealth, and exalted status, managed to produce fifty-six children.

Having chosen their new home for its isolation, the Mormons were caught by surprise when the first gold-seekers began streaming in no more than three years after them. Some were tempted to join in the hunt that was going on all around them. But Brigham Young prohibited prospecting in Utah. Instead of digging gold, "the business of a Saint is to stay at home and make his fields green."

While Nevada was constructing its famous tunnel to carry cooling water into the scalding mines, Utah was building irrigation ditches. Thousands of acres of land were activated into farming. In Nevada mining towns a green plant was a landmark; in Salt Lake City every house was set in a garden. What Nevada lacked in children and green plants it made up in liquor. An estimate of whisky consumption in Virginia City was one quart per man per day. In Mormon communities liquor was prohibited.

And finally, the Mormon towns had no prostitutes, at least not until the U.S. Army arrived in its campaign to wipe out polygamy.

Most visitors were impressed with the achievements of the Mormons, and even if they opposed polygamy, they measured it on balance with the general orderliness and well-being of the community. But for the outside world, polygamy was the dominant fact. People in the States were greedy for intimate details of Mormon life, and a flood of books came out to satisfy their curiosity, most of them "thinly disguised pornography." At Mormon expense, Americans got to read imaginary tales of fantastic orgies, and feel self-righteous at the same time. The Republican platform of 1856 called polygamy and slavery "the twin relics of barbarism," and the Democrat Stephen Douglas concurred in part, denouncing Mormonism as "the loathsome ulcer of the body politic."

Polygamy had a powerful and effective team of defenders in Orson Pratt and Belinda Pratt, one of his eight wives. Pratt studied Scripture and noted that all the old patriarchs had had numerous wives. Even more telling was the fact that they were "never reproved by the Holy Ghost, nor by angels, nor by the Almighty." When Congress passed its first anti-polygamy act in 1862 he raised this compelling objection:

> Baptism is a religious sacrament; marriage is a sacrament. Congress will not pretend to legislate for baptism. It will not ordain whether [a man] shall be sprinkled or immersed, or how much he shall be sprinkled or immersed . . . What right has it to say how we shall be married, or how much we shall be married?

Pratt's debates with anti-Mormon spokesmen received national press, and the consensus was that he always won, although he was still wrong.

Belinda Pratt did not give public sermons, but a letter she wrote to her sister in New Hampshire was widely published.

"What," she asked her sister, "appears to be the great object of the marriage relations?" And she answered, "the multiplying of our species. . . . To accomplish this object, natural law would dictate that a husband should remain apart from his wife at certain seasons."

Belinda Pratt reasoned that when the embryo was being formed, the mother's "heart should be pure, her thoughts and affections chaste, her mind calm," and that her body should not be subjected to "any thing calculated to disturb, irritate, weary, or exhaust any of its functions. . . . [A kind husband] should refrain from all those untimely associations which are forbidden in the great constitutional laws of female nature, which laws we see carried out in almost the entire animal economy, human animals excepted." So the presence of additional wives served to protect the chastity of a pregnant woman. As for single women, they would not be forced to marry drunkards or idlers as the only alternative to prostitution or celibacy, if they also had the option of marrying reliable, industrious, proven family men.

Belinda Pratt reproached her sister for asking, "Why not a plurality of husbands as well as a plurality of wives?" It was clear that "such an order of things would work death and not life or, in plain language, it would multiply disease instead of children."

Some women discovered more quotidian virtues in polygamy. They found it sociable. A visitor to Salt Lake City recalled being asked by a young woman what he thought of her friend who had briefly stepped out of the room. He replied that she was a charming girl. "Indeed she is," the young woman exclaimed, "I do wish B--- (her husband) would marry her. I should like to have her with me all the time."

The same man observed that Utah farmers' wives did not have the overworked air of women in other rural districts who single-handedly had to bear all the children and do all the household work for a family.

When one Gentile woman asked her Mormon friend how she could bear the knowledge that her husband was with another woman, the latter replied, "Certainly it is not pleasant to think of, but we have this advantage over you, we know where our husbands are—you don't."

All these arguments were to no avail. In one skirmish of a continuing battle with the federal judiciary over jurisdiction in Utah, Brigham Young was indicted by a grand jury for "lewd and lascivious cohabitation." This particular case came to nothing. But members of the federal bench were bent on overruling Utah law. This was particularly galling to the Saints in the case of one Justice Drummond when it was discovered that he had abandoned his family in the East, and that the woman he had brought to Utah as his wife and whom he liked to have sit beside him on the bench was a whore.

Before the Civil War the government used the issue of polygamy partly as a diversion from continuous strife over slavery. After the war, it attacked in earnest. In 1882 a bill was passed making polygamous living a felony punishable by fine and by loss of the right to vote; 12,000 people were disenfranchised. Church leaders were forced into hiding. For six years Mormons suffered nighttime raids by U.S. deputies on "polyg hunts." Finally in 1890 they gave up.

Although they got no thanks for it, the Mormons had tried to construct a social system that embodied the prevailing wisdom of the nation as a whole in the second half of the nineteenth century. All men and women were to live in the comfort of a family. Within its circle men could indulge in sex, and women could be spared it.

Sex and the Frontier

This excursion began with a question that agitated the minds of a group of pioneers midway in their journey across the continent: Is the love of money greater than the love for women? Here is the opinion of an old Pawnee chief who watched the white man's strange antics from the outside, still with a sympathetic interest, before the white man and red man were irreconcilably at war:

> There is nothing more beautiful nor admirable, my brother, than the manners, the customs, and especially the industry of the white men in all they do. . . . [But] I find three great faults in their way of living and in their customs, that we, although completely savage, do not have. Their ambition to amass that white iron, called

silver, their hardheartedness in the matter of food, which they sell even to the people of their own village and their own family, and their weakness towards women.

For him the money/woman debate would have seemed entirely beside the point, and in itself symptomatic of his conclusion, that white men loved *both* too much.

Nineteenth-century sermonizers believed that energy for the pursuit of either one boiled down to basically the same thing: sperm. Then as now the great problem was conservation of energy. Men were warned not to squander sperm in sex ("Sturdy manhood . . . loses its energy and bends under the too frequent expenditure of this important secretion") so that they would have enough left to cut down forests, throw up rail-

Sex on the Frontier

roads, and dig mines. Conquest of self was the condition and the model for the conquest of nature.

The very language of the nineteenth century reveals how intimately the two preoccupations—money and sex—were interconnected. Sexual terms were used to talk about economic concerns, economic terms to talk about matters of sex. To *come* in the nineteenth century was to *spend.*

At an earlier period in American life when most people were farmers, work and sex were not seen to be in competition. The work unit *was* the sexual unit. Husbands and wives labored together; their children worked with them. If there was enough land to expand into, then the more children the better.

By the nineteenth century, the heyday of the Wild West, more and more people in the East lived in cities and worked in factories. The unity of work and sex was shattered. Husbands and wives were separated at the most elementary level: they no longer spent their days around the same place occupied in a common enterprise. As for the children, the more the hungrier. The idea that sex drained men's energy and that women diverted men from serious work grew up in this context, and supported the enforced separation of the sexes.

The frontier was an exaggeraton of this separation. It became an historic symbol of men leaving women behind, not just for the day—to return after putting in their hours at the factory or office—but for long enough to accomplish the manly work of nation-building.

CHRIS TANZ

Sex on the Frontier

A Note on Sources

In writing this essay three books have proved invaluable: Dee Brown, *The Gentle Tamers* (New York: Bantam Books, 1974); Walter O'Meara, *Daughters of the Country* (New York: Harcourt, Brace & World, 1968); and J. F. McDermott, ed., *Travelers on the Western Frontier* (Urbana, Illinois: University of Illinois Press, 1970). The quotes from the introductory section came from McDermott and O'Meara, and also from William Hepworth Dixon, *White Conquest* (London: Chatto & Windus, 1876) and John Clark, ed., *The Frontier Challenge* (Lawrence: University of Kansas Press, 1971). For the *Indian* section McDermott, Brown, O'Meara, and Leslie Fiedler, *The Return of the Vanishing American* (New York: Stein & Day, 1968); Ross Cox, *The Columbia River* (Norman: University of Oklahoma Press, 1957); and Arthur Calhoun, *A Social History of the American Family* (Cleveland: Arthur Clark Co., 1919) were the sources of the various quotations. Calhoun, Dixon, Brown, and O'Meara, and Mark Twain, *Roughing It* (New York: Holt, Rinehart & Winston, 1965); Charles Ferguson, *Experiences of a Forty-Niner* (Cleveland: Williams, 1888); Lucius Beebe, *Legends of the Comstock Lode* (Oakland: Grahame Hardy, 1950); Oscar Lewis, *Silver Kings* (New York: Alfred Knopf, 1947); Sidney Ditzion, *Marriage, Morals, and Sex in America* (New York: Bookman, 1953); and James Horan, *Desperate Women* (New York: Putnam's, 1952) provided the material for the *Miners*.

For the *Saints*, Calhoun and Richard Burton, *The City of the Saints* (New York: Harper, 1862); John Codman, *The Mormon Country* (New York: U.S. Publishing Co., 1874); WPA Writers Project, *Utah* (New York: Hastings, 1941); and Robert Riegel, *American Women* (Rutherford, New Jersey: Fairleigh Dickinson University Press, 1970) were used.

Finally, for the concluding section, the Pawnee quote is from the McDermott book and the quotation connecting ejaculation with enervation comes from the *Boston Medical and Surgical Journal* of 1835, as quoted by B. Barker-Benfield in "The Spermatic Economy" (Gordon, ed., *The American Family in Social-Historical Perspective,* New York: St. Martin's Press, 1973).

Sex on the Frontier

Sex Scandals

In small societies and small circles, we gossip to maintain position. We must give and get information. Persons rise with the quality of the information they pass on, and their status is enhanced by the eagerness with which others share gossip with them. Gossiping is not only acceptable, it is required. A British anthropologist, Max Gluckman, has observed that outsiders in a community are more "efficient" than insiders in performing simple errands. When Gluckman first moved to a new neighborhood, he could buy a newspaper at the corner store and be back home in a minute. But once he was part of the community it would take him twenty minutes to buy a packet of tobacco because he gossiped with the storekeeper. "I find that when I am gossiping about my friends as well as my enemies," he writes, "I am deeply conscious of performing a social duty."

That is one side of gossip in a small society, but the same anthropologist knows another side as well: "When I hear they gossip viciously about me, I am rightfully filled with righteous indignation." On the one hand, gossip seems vital; on the other hand, gossiping seems malicious. When we draw near gossip we feel seduced—but involved; when we draw back from it we feel virtuous—but left out.

So our feelings about gossip are complicated. Even in the warmth of a face-to-face community we are wary of "talking behind someone's back," of gaining pleasure or gaining status by trading on our knowledge about someone else. With "scandal" we are even more conflicted. With scandal the matter is more serious; the moral senses cut nearer the bone. Gossip can be "idle," it can be chatter, it can be offhand, it can be dismissed. Scandal shames, disgraces, horrifies, shocks.

If we know the persons involved in the scandal we will be shocked and outraged or perhaps even feel some sorrow. But when we hear of public figures involved in scandalous activities, we do not know what to feel. We don't know if we should laugh as at a spectacle or be straight-faced as at a trial. We don't know what we *should* feel in the presence of a scandal.

People want to talk about personal things. We

41

"This confession is not made
without a blush."

want to touch one another, to feel in others the frailty and confusion we feel in ourselves but we do not know these objects of scandal, we only know about them. We read about them or watch them on television. Magazines and newspapers and movies fill our eyes with a popular culture of political leaders, screen stars, and sports heroes. This culture is what we share and what gives us the illusion of human connection.

But some part of us recognizes the illusion for what it is. This makes us ambivalent about our own curiosity and uneasy about our own moral sentiments. While we can rely on the well-established role of "citizen" to feel righteous in following political scandals like Watergate, we search more vainly to justify our reading about the sex lives of celebrities. By what right can we make it our business to read about and talk about the private lives of public figures?

In the early days of the American Republic, newspapers confined their attention exclusively to the worlds of politics and commerce. The human interest story and the focus on ordinary everyday life came much later. So scandals, which made their way into print or originated in print, could only be those involving the domestic lives of prominent political men. One of the most significant involved Alexander Hamilton. Hamilton carried on an affair with Maria Reynolds for more than a year, even entertaining her in his own house on weekends when his wife and children were in the country. Maria Reynolds was the wife of one James Reynolds, by all accounts a cheap swindler who earned his living by buying up or forging veterans' claims to government monies. It appears that Reynolds had abandoned his wife for another woman for half a year, and during that time she struck up

Sex Scandals

the liaison with Hamilton. Reynolds returned to his wife, discovered the affair, and decided that forgery did not compare to blackmail for employment. But he could not shed his past quickly enough and one of his forgeries landed him in jail in 1792. When Hamilton refused to intercede on his behalf, Reynolds spilled the beans to enemies of Hamilton in the Congress—Frederick Muhlenberg, Abraham Venable, and James Monroe. As it happens, these gentlemen were most interested in Reynolds's allegations that Hamilton had embezzled Treasury funds. When they faced Hamilton with the charges of embezzlement and adultery, he denied the former, admitted the latter, and counted on the decency of his enemies to be discreet.

They were discreet, or largely so. But the matter was leaked in time to journalist James Thomson Callender who, in 1979, announced it to the world. Hamilton figured truth would be the best policy and so he published an answer to Callender:

The charge against me is a connection with one James Reynolds for purposes of improper speculation. My real crime is an amorous connection with his wife. . . . This confession is not made without a blush.

This did not free Hamilton from popular suspicion in the Treasury matter but served as final proof of the adultery. John Adams wrote privately that Hamilton's ambitions sprang from "a superabundance of secretions" and Jefferson observed that Hamilton's confessions actually increased the belief that he was an embezzler. All of this appears to have sealed Hamilton's political fate several years before Aaron Burr determined his mortal destiny.

Thomas Jefferson met Callender in 1797 when Callender was publishing the series of tracts that included the story of Hamilton's affair. Jefferson began to subsidize Callender with small sums of money and apparently found Callender "a man of genius." But by 1800 Jefferson had become disillusioned with Callender, wary of his bitterness and his venom. When Jefferson became president in 1801, he nonetheless officially pardoned Callender, who had been imprisoned for sedition. However, by then Callender was as disillusioned with Jefferson as Jefferson with him, and he joined the staff of a Federalist paper and dug into Jefferson's private life. On September 1, 1802 he printed the news of Sally Hemings.

Sally Hemings was a slave on Jefferson's plantation at Monticello and for years after the death of Jefferson's wife, she was his mistress. The liaison began in 1788 while Jefferson was in France. Sally Hemings, then fourteen or fifteen, arrived in Paris as servant to Jefferson's daughter Maria. When she returned to Monticello two years later, she came with Jefferson's child in her womb and with his promise that all of her children would be freed when they reached twenty-one. She was to have five children by Jefferson, four of whom lived to adulthood and were freed. All of them, according to other slaves, visitors, and neighbors looked remarkably like Thomas Jefferson. At Monticello, Sally Hemings took care of Jefferson's chamber and wardrobe and looked after her children, but Jefferson never confessed that the relationship was nearer and dearer. One of Sally Hemings' sons wrote later, with some bitterness, "We were the only children of his by a slave woman. He was affectionate toward his white grandchildren, of whom he had fourteen, twelve of whom lived to manhood and womanhood."

Republican editors quickly raged against Callender's revelations. They denied the story, but other Federalist papers gleefully picked it up. John Quincy Adams was inspired to verse and printed a ballad in a Boston paper, part of which goes:

Of all the damsels on the green,
  On mountain, or in valley,
A lass so luscious ne'er was seen,
  As Monticellian Sally.

You call her slave—and pray were slaves
  Made only for the galley?
Try for yourselves, ye witless knaves—
  Take each to bed your Sally.

The rest is only worse. Thus Jefferson's enemies turned to ridicule a relationship that, from the little evidence we have, was as loving as it was conflicted.

One scandal bred another. Callender uncovered an early Jefferson misadventure—his attempted seduction of the wife of a neighbor. John Walker was one of Jefferson's best friends, and Jefferson served as a "brideman" at his wedding in 1764. In 1768, when Walker was away for a few months, Jefferson was alleged to have seduced, or tried to seduce, Betsy Walker. But it was twenty years before she confessed this to her husband and another decade before, in 1805, Walker wrote down his version and demanded satisfaction from Jefferson. Walker's account is farcical, even declaring that Jefferson had slipped into Betsy Walker's gown sleeve "a paper tending to convince her of the innocence of promiscuous love." Jefferson denied that the affair went on a year, as Walker claimed, and said it was a single attempt at seduction without premeditation and occasioned by an accidental visit. In order to avert a duel with the offended Walker, Jefferson admitted his guilt in writing: ". . . when young and single I offered love to a handsome lady. I acknolege its incorrectness."

Journalists continued to be the leading scandalizers in the nineteenth century. But with the entry of an enlarged middle class into the political world and the commercial revolution in the press that made cheap newspapers available to large numbers, the arena for scandal widened. A "social world" intruded in the space between public and private, making that very distinction harder to keep in focus. Newspapers began to take as their legitimate preserve not only business and politics but the everyday life of the ordinary citizen as seen in the courts, the streets, the ballrooms, and the theaters. For the first time the behavior of anonymous citizens could become celebrated public scandals.

On April 9, 1836, Helen Jewett, a prostitute in New York, was murdered with an axe. A few years before, this would probably not have found its way into the newspapers at all, but now the penny papers promoted it—and themselves with it, James Gordon Bennett tripling the circulation of the *Herald* in a week's time. The alleged murderer, Richard Robinson (later acquitted), was a hardworking clerk of respectable background. Both his presumed respectability and the apparent gentility and refinement of the prostitute helped fan the interest in the case.

In 1844 the *Herald* covered the trial of the abortionist Mme. Costello. The young woman who had had the abortion, Zulma Marache, was forced into it by her fiance, Napoleon Lareux, who insisted that for his own reasons he could

Sex Scandals

not marry her until it would be too late to make the infant's birth respectable. The *Herald,* while continuing to publish the advertisements of known abortionists, lamented that the Costello case illustrated the "present state of licentiousness in this city."

Actual abortions were mirrored in the fiction of the time. Countless tales described the "three-fold murder" of an abortion—murder of a woman's chastity, her body, and her unborn child. The union of sex and death reappeared in a scandal standing somewhere between reality and fiction, a scandal manufactured to add fuel to the flames of anti-Catholic nativism. This was the publication in 1836 of *Awful Disclosures of the Hotel Dieu Nunnery of Montreal* by Maria Monk. In this book, which sold some 300,000 copies before the Civil War, Maria Monk described her Protestant upbringing, her conversion to Catholicism, and her entrance into a nunnery where she was instructed to "obey the priests in all things" including the command to live with them in "criminal intercourse." The progeny of such intercourse were summarily baptized and strangled. Nuns, she wrote, were executed if they refused to obey the lustful will of priests, and she claimed to have witnessed the strangling of two babies. She left the nunnery when she found herself with child and did not want to see it murdered.

So ended the first volume (more would follow) and so began a year in which the tales of Maria Monk were the center of attention in a growing anti-Catholic movement, which had begun in earnest with the burning of the Ursuline Convent in Charlestown, Massachusetts, in 1834.

As it happens Maria Monk's tale seems to have been wholly fabricated. Early on the book

A Nun Stabbing a Priest.

Death Pit—Trap-Door—Cell.

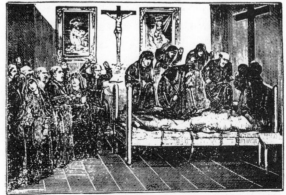

The Smothering of the Nun.

Jumping on the Maria Monk bandwagon, in 1836 these pictures were published in *Decisive Confirmation of the Awful Disclosures of Maria Monk,* by S. B. Smith ("late a Popish priest").

was given credence by much of the religious press in America, but later her mother, a Protestant woman in Montreal, denied Maria's story. Maria had escaped, not from a nunnery, but from the Catholic Magdalen asylum in Montreal. She had been aided by one of Montreal's leading anti-Catholic clergymen, and he persuaded two other anti-Catholic New York clergymen to write her book. They claimed that she dictated it to them. So scandal became a weapon in warfare between ethnic groups as a once homogeneous society found itself becoming pluralistic.

Fact and fiction merged again in a bestselling novel by George Lippard, who modeled his book on an actual incident of a man who killed his sister's seducer and was acquitted for the murder. The novel itself reflected back on reality by moving public opinion to pass anti-seduction legislation in New York in 1849. No doubt Lippard's novel, or others like it, fired the imagination of the Pennsylvania farm girl mentioned in H. L. Mencken's memoirs, who in the 1890s, after making love with her longtime beau, felt she was ruined and could never regain her honor. The novels she had read told her that the very touch of sex was pollution and a single sexual experience would make her capable of any crime. She left home in the dead of night and made her way to Baltimore to find a bordello in which to spend the rest of her dishonored life.

The focus of scandal on the prominent had a magnetism that the events of the anonymous could not touch. The prominent status of the priesthood, as well as its mystery and foreignness, were part of the appeal of the Maria Monk disclosures. Even in reporting on Zulma Ma-

rache, editor Bennett suggested that the greater scandal lay in the worlds of the wealthy. One of his editorials, "The Morality of the 'Upper Classes'" commented briefly on abortionist Mme. Costello but only then to argue that corruption is not confined to the lower orders. Mme. Restell, who began the abortion business in New York, had more than 12,000 applications for her "professional" services, according to Bennett, "from persons connected with the first families all over the country, and amongst the police depositories some of the most revolting stories are to be obtained in relation to persons of the highest rank in fashionable, respectable, and religious society in the city of New York."

Probably the most celebrated of all American sex scandals involved a figure not only prominent but putatively proper—the Rev. Henry Ward Beecher, probably the most famous of all American clergymen of the nineteenth century. When the scandal first reared its head in 1870, Beecher was in his third decade as pastor of America's largest congregation, the Plymouth Church of Brooklyn. He was earning $20,000 in salary and at least another $15,000 in lecturing. He was one of the country's great orators and one of its leading liberals. He had been an outspoken opponent of slavery, advocated women's suffrage, later would support evolutionary theory, and always interpreted religion liberally: "What is Orthodoxy? I will tell you. Orthodoxy is *my* doxy, and Heterodoxy is *your* doxy, that is if your doxy is not like *my* doxy."

Beecher was unusually attractive to women and was attracted by them. Henry C. Bowen, the wealthy founder of Plymouth Church who brought Beecher to Brooklyn, had reason to regret this. His wife confessed to him on her deathbed in 1862 that she had visited Beecher at his study at the church, for the most intimate of purposes (and that, indeed, she had once seen another woman enter, similarly sporting her own key to the study). Bowen ultimately was expelled from Plymouth Church in 1876 for slandering Beecher—accusing him of adultery but not mentioning the name of the woman involved.

But this scandal played second fiddle to Beecher's alleged adulterous relationship with Elizabeth Tilton, wife of Theodore Tilton who, with Bowen and Beecher, formed the "Trinity of Plymouth Church." Tilton was editor of the *Independent,* a liberal religious paper owned by Bowen, endorsed by Beecher, and boasting a circulation of 60,000, the most profitable religious journal in the world. Elizabeth Tilton, sentimental and immodestly religious, came under the spell of Beecher and in the 1860s would write letter after letter to her traveling, lecturing husband of her (spiritual) love for Beecher: "Oh, how my soul yearns over you two dear men!" In 1870 she confessed to Tilton that for a year and a half, prompted by a "pure affection and a high religious love," she had been carrying on an affair with her pastor.

What followed was a snarl of cover-ups and revelations, accusations and denials that culminated in 1874 in a six-month civil trial that scandalized the nation—and ended in a hung jury voting nine to three for Beecher's acquittal. The scandal was first made public by Victoria Woodhull, who announced it in her weekly newspaper.

Woodhull had been nominated for president by the Equal Rights Party in 1872, but her career quickly foundered as her financial and moral

supporters changed their minds. Angrily she vowed to expose secrets in the lives of the famous. She attacked some of the suffragist leaders she felt had abandoned her and finally broke with her friends and supporters, Tilton and Beecher. She revealed all she knew of their private lives. True to her belief in free love, she insisted that Beecher's appeal for women "instead of being a bad thing as the world thinks, or thinks it thinks, or professes to think that it thinks, is one of the grandest and noblest of the endowments of this truly great and representative man." What was evil, she felt, was the false conviction that "lovers own their lovers, husbands their wives, and that they have the right to spy over and to interfere." To her, Elizabeth Tilton's love for Beecher was true marriage and her marriage to Tilton, prositution. She urged Beecher to come forth and express what she claimed was his true abhorrence of marriage, his devotion to the theory and practice of free love.

For some time Beecher and Tilton agreed to maintain silence. Their mutual confidant, Frank Moulton, feared that revelations of the scandal "would tend to undermine the very foundations of social order." Bowen, Beecher, and Tilton signed a covenant renewing their old relations of "love, respect, and alliance." But the scandal refused to die and Tilton finally, in October, 1873, was read out of Plymouth Church for slandering Beecher and for having associated with Woodhull. Still the scandal would not fade. Before his church, Beecher denied and denied—no, he had not returned Elizabeth Tilton's affection except in perfectly proper ways; no, he was not a free lover in theory or in practice. The scandal had had already too much attention—

Elizabeth Tilton.
"Oh how my soul yearns over you two men!"

"Not a great war nor a revolution could have more filled the newspapers than this question of domestic trouble, magnified a thousand-fold and, like a sore spot on the human body, drawing to itself every morbid humor in the blood." Beecher's statements received more attention from the press than the impeachment of Andrew Johnson. Tilton could not but respond, and he filed a complaint charging Beecher with alienating Elizabeth Tilton's affections and demanding $100,000 for the loss of "the comfort, society, aid, and assistance of his said wife."

The press and the nation were for Beecher.

But the evidence kept coming. Elizabeth Tilton's love letters were published; stories of earlier Beecher seductions came out; and prominent figures with inside knowledge of the scandal, like suffragist Elizabeth Cady Stanton, pointed fingers.

Meanwhile, Elizabeth Tilton kept changing her story—first accusing Beecher, then retracting her charges, then retracting the retraction. She did not testify at the trial and it was only some years later, in 1878, that she made her last public statement, admitting to an affair with Beecher just as she had told her husband in the

Sex Scandals

first place. Beecher responded that Mrs. Tilton was an unbalanced clairvoyant and, as his popularity was in general on the rise, her confession seems to have had little effect. Victoria Woodhull moved to a life of respectability in England. Tilton was never forgiven for having sullied the reputation of Beecher, and he left America in 1883 to spend the rest of his days in Paris. He scarcely noted Beecher's death in 1887. Thousands came to see Beecher lying in state, the vast majority of them women. As for Elizabeth Tilton, she retired from the public eye, living out her life in the home of one of her daughters. It was remarked at the time that the trial had brought about the abolition of privacy, but she, at least, was able to regain it.

A decade after the Beecher trial, Grover Cleveland ran for president. Beecher, appalled at the corruption of the Republican candidate James G. Blaine, split with his party and campaigned for Cleveland. This proved embarrassing for the preacher because ten days after Cleveland's nomination, the *Buffalo Evening Telegraph* printed a story of Cleveland's amorous escapades, declaring of Cleveland in an editorial, "The libertine is a foe of the home, and is therefore, in a certain sense, a traitor to the Republic." While the *Telegraph* was a disreputable rag, more established Republican sheets picked up the story. Support for Cleveland began to melt away. Beecher kept on, though it brought his own scandal back to haunt him. "I will not be prudent," he declared, ironically admitting what others had long been convinced of. But if Beecher was steadfast, others demanded that Cleveland withdraw from the race; staunch supporters wavered; some newspapers withdrew their support. One historian estimates that if the scandal

had emerged at the convention or had been delayed until the few weeks just before the election, Cleveland would have lost.

What was Cleveland's transgression? Ten years before, he had had a liaison with Maria Halpin, a widow, head of the cloak department at Flint and Kent dry goods store in Buffalo. She lived just down the street from Cleveland. September 14, 1874, she gave birth to a son whom she named Oscar Folsom Cleveland in honor of the man she thought to be the father—or wanted as the father. Cleveland did not know if he was the father; Maria was also sharing her bed with several other men, all of them married. Cleveland, as the only bachelor, was most likely to be charged with paternity, and he took responsibility for the child. Cleveland supported Maria and her child and when Maria began drinking he placed the child in an orphanage.

After the original unchastity, Cleveland's behavior seems to have been beyond reproach, or so his defenders said. One of his friends asked him what to tell people about the scandal and Cleveland replied in the words that became a campaign slogan, "Tell the truth."

The moral issue was enormously important in the campaign. Even into the last days of the campaign the issue of Cleveland's personal morals would not be silenced. However, there was a second moral issue, and that concerned the allegations that James G. Blaine had used public office for private gain. Republicans and Independents circulated a petition reading, "The paramount issue of the Presidential election of this year is moral rather than political," and it was Blaine's morality they were talking about. In a piece of pro-Cleveland literature entitled "A Dialog Between an Independent and a Clergy-

Did the Rev. Henry Ward Beecher *(left in chair)* alienate $100,000 worth of Elizabeth Tilton's affections and deprive her husband, Theodore *(above),* of her "comfort, society, aid, and assistance?"

A cartoon of Grover Cleveland, Maria
Halpin, and little Oscar Folsom Cleveland
in *Judge*, a Republican weekly.

Sex Scandals

man," the Independent forces the Puritanical clergyman to agree that "an unchaste man, assuming that he can be honest, is not so dangerous to society as is a dishonest man, even though he be chaste."

The scandalous act rarely involves anything exotic. Not sexual deviations but ordinary sex—with an inappropriate partner—is the usual stuff of scandal; and this seems unchanged from the days of Alexander Hamilton to our own. Of course, standards of sexual morality change. But this essay is not a chronicle of American sexual mores, nor should it be. Of all the elements of a sex scandal, the scandalous act itself may be the least important. What emerges as centrally significant is the relationship between the scandalous, the scandalizer, and the scandalized. A history of scandal has less to do with the physical details of two-person relationships than with the community in which they exist; less to do with the facts of sexual intimacy than with the social meanings of privacy; less to do with the pathologies of passion than with the epidemiology of arousal. A history of scandals must necessarily attend less to the doings of the scandalous than to the findings of the scandalizers and the lookings of the scandalized.

The role of the scandalizer is one that some take to as avidly as did Callender in the case of Hamilton and Jefferson. This role is pretty straightforward: enemies exploit each other's follies or sins to the delight, outrage, or horror of public morals. Victoria Woodhull's scandalizing presents a more complicated case. Woodhull sought not only to embarrass people she believed had betrayed her, but intended also to promote through scandal her political and social ideal of free love.

Others are most uncomfortable in the role of scandalizer and seek to get out of it no matter how accidentally they fell into it. Edward Livingston, who designed a liberal criminal code for Louisiana in the 1830s, feared that if he spelled out the nature of sexual crimes, he would be writing a sexual handbook to encourage the very acts he sought to forbid. He finally left sexual crimes out of his code altogether. In a New York prostitution case a generation ago, the presiding judge barred the press because, he said, it was not the function of the judiciary to satisfy the public appetite for "lurid and salacious details."

Just as the word "gossip" can signify the gossiper as well as his topic, so in scandal the scandalizer can become the scandal. In some measure this happened to James Callender and to Victoria Woodhull. It also happened, to some extent, to RKO Films and Ingrid Bergman in a more recent case.

Ingrid Bergman left her husband and child in 1949 to live with her new lover, Roberto Rossellini. She was pregnant with Rossellini's child while they worked together on *Stromboli,* and the film's promoter, RKO, used this to advertise the film. RKO was the chief scandalmonger, scheduling the film's opening to coincide with the expected date of birth of the child and spicing the publicity for the film with allusions to the scandalous private life of the heroine. But Bergman herself was as much the scandalizer as she was the scandalous person, making no effort to hide a private life she believed in.

Women's clubs, church groups, city censorship boards, and at least one state senate condemned Bergman, the film, or both. Many filmhouse operators refused to show the movie. The climax of criticism came when Sen. Edwin

Johnson of Colorado brought the scandal to the floor of the U.S. Senate. He attacked Bergman and Rossellini as "free-love cultists" and "moral outlaws" but he also reserved some choice words for RKO's role in the affair. He charged RKO with playing up "the moral turpitude of the leading lady to pack their theaters," and added a film review of his own:

> . . . even in this modern age of surprise it is upsetting to have our most popular but pregnant Hollywood movie queen, her condition the result of an illicit affair, play the part of a cheap, chiseling female, to add spice to a silly story which lacks appeal of its own.

Johnson introduced a bill to license actors, actresses, writers, directors, and producers in Hollywood so that no one would be licensed "who admits committing acts constituting the essential elements of a crime involving moral turpitude."

Johnson withdrew his bill two months later, and it was never debated in Congress. It was debated in Hollywood, however. The motion picture industry took Johnson very seriously and feared his attacks would keep people from going to movies featuring erring stars. Johnson's words gave force to the association of theater owners which had repeatedly pressed producers to fire or suspend stars for improper off-screen behavior.

No one wanted to regulate private morals, but many hoped that some semblance of moral order, public and private, could be retained, and this is what Bergman, Rossellini, and RKO seemed to threaten. The concern was that notoriety sold movie tickets and that RKO was becoming to the movies what Hearst had been

to journalism—a sensationalist, a scandalmonger. What was also at issue was that Bergman was a public figure, much observed and much admired, and she was flaunting behavior that many considered improper. Senator Johnson observed that, like baseball heroes, movie stars have chosen a public life and must live accordingly: "If a movie queen insists upon a private life, let her divorce herself from the movies."

The attention we pay to the world of popular public figures—politicians, professional athletes, and entertainers—makes people much less fussy than Senator Johnson most uneasy. Even some of the writers and reporters who have helped create that world have backed away from their Frankensteins. As Theodore White, who more or less invented a reporting style for presidential campaigns that pays as much attention to the private as the public lives of the campaigners, told Timothy Crouse in *The Boys On the Bus:*

> McGovern was like a fish in a goldfish bowl. There were three different network crews at different times. The still photographers kept coming in in groups of five. And there were at least six writers sitting in the corner—I don't even know their names. We're all sitting there watching him work on his acceptance speech, poor bastard. He tries to go into the bedroom with Fred Dutton to go over the list of Vice-Presidents, which would later turn out to be the fuck-up of the century of course, and all of us are observing him, taking notes like mad, getting all the little details, which I think I invented as a method of reporting and which I now sincerely regret. If you write about this, say that I sincerely regret it. Who gives a fuck if the guy had milk and Total for breakfast?

Sex Scandals

Roberto Rossellini and Ingrid Bergman. "If a movie queen insists upon a private life, let her divorce herself from the movies."

Virginia Rappe (*above*) and Roscoe "Fatty" Arbuckle (*second from left, opposite*) with court bailiffs and attorneys. It was never clear just what happened in their half hour together.

If the position of the scandalizer is problematic, so is the role of the scandalized—and, for that matter, the role of those of us who frequently follow scandals without feeling scandalized. All of this might be dismissed as a kind of collective voyeurism. The unifying sexual element in scandals might then be seen not to lie in the acts of the scandalous but in the sexual arousal of the scandalized.

Gossip in a small community is a regulatory agency, a familial trade commission for the supervision of rights and duties. Scandal in a mass society also regulates—as the purveying of the Watergate scandal has helped regulate political morals. More important, perhaps, than the legislation it led to, is the self-regulation it promoted—publicity of community moral standards inhibits the transgression of those standards by private persons who fear publicity. And it educates many others for whom the standards were not well-defined. Much behavior that has moral implications goes on beyond the law or in the law's interstices, and so the moral standards need to be recalled, repeated, almost ritually reenacted.

In the ritual of scandal, some people are genuinely shocked and offended. The scandalous act is something they do not recognize. It shakes their sense of reality, it attacks boundaries of their world. It threatens to make them redefine their society and so to reconsider themselves. They are genuinely scandalized because they are actually innocent. One does not have to be terribly prudish or unduly moralistic to be scandalized. Hundreds of thousands of provincial people are shocked by cosmopolitan behavior; hundreds of thousands of unpretentious, ordinary people are shocked by the sexual trap-

pings of wealth and power. And as we are all in some respect innocent, we all have the capacity in some respects and in some moments to be scandalized.

We also may want to protect innocence, even if it is not our own. Frequently in the scandals in American public life, the call for censure of the scandalous appeals to the innocence of an outside party, not the scandalized but the scandalizable, the impressionable—the young. Boston and Philadelphia papers that picked up Callender's accounts of Sally Hemings manufactured scenes of Jefferson's daughters "weeping to see a *negress* installed in the place of their mother." Edward Livingston decided to leave sexual crimes out of his criminal code because he hoped the law would become part of the education of youth and feared "the shock which such a chapter must give to their pudicity." *The New York Tribune* fretted over the Beecher scandal to the same effect: "Ten thousand immoral and obscene novels could not have done the harm which this case has done in teaching the science of wrong to thousands of quick-witted and curious boys and girls."

This appeal to the innocence of children is readily invoked in scandals involving film stars. This was true not only in the Bergman scandal but in the affair of Roscoe "Fatty" Arbuckle, one of the leading men of Hollywood's silent films. In 1921 Arbuckle became the center of a scandal involving a drunken orgy in his San Francisco hotel suite. Arbuckle persuaded or pulled a young actress from the main room to an adjoining bedroom and locked the door. It was never clear just what happened in their half hour together, but when Arbuckle emerged the woman lay on the bed moaning and two days

later died of peritonitis caused by the rupture "of an important organ." Arbuckle was tried for manslaughter and after two hung juries was finally acquitted. The scandal focused on the fact that a movie star has responsibilities as a public figure—especially in his influence on the young. Arbuckle was the subject of women's club resolutions and Sunday sermons across the nation, one minister in Pittsburgh proclaiming, "The moving picture is poisoning the mind of the youth of America and they are slipping away from the Sunday School, the Christian Endeavor, and the Church."

In both the Arbuckle and Bergman scandals, and in other scandals as well, women have been especially prominent among the scandalized. This may be because of the special responsibility women have traditionally felt toward children. Or perhaps women on the whole have been more innocent than men and so have been more likely to be scandalized. But it is just as reasonable to suppose that women have been *less* innocent than men and have followed sex scandals because the affairs of home and family have been so central to cultural definitions of "woman's place."

This last explanation would account for the prevalence of women among those who follow scandals but it would not explain their prominence among those actually scandalized.

For this we have to go further. We are familiar with social "types" who feign knowledge; young sophisticates rising in the social world learn that they must not be surprised or shocked. They come in time not only to affect knowledge but actually to deaden their own innocence. Just as these people feign knowledge to gain status, others feign no-knowledge to the

same end. While the sophisticate develops the capacity to not be scandalized, traditionally women perfected displays of innocence, for they had to live up to a social role which demanded it. "Woman is appointed for the refinement of the race," declared Henry Ward Beecher, expressing a sentiment that pervades our culture. "Man is said to have been made little lower than the angels; woman needs no such comparison; she was made full as high." The "virtue" of a man may be an ambiguous term, but the "virtue" of a woman in our language and culture is her sexual innocence. She reinforces it for herself and convinces others of it by a visible capacity to be scandalized.

If some participate in the ritual of scandal because they are innocent, others because they want to protect innocence, and still others because they are forced to feign innocence; yet another group avidly follows scandals without any pretense of being scandalized. Here the charge of voyeurism comes back more strongly. For these people, for many of us, the public scandals of the day do not violate our dreams of innocence, for we have no such dreams. What, then, can they be for us but vicarious fulfillments of our dreams of violation?

But this still goes too far. The world is not neatly divided between those who are innocent, still cosseted by old-time religion and small-town morals, and those who are worldly, liberated by the city, by travel, by knowledge, by experience. And we do not have to hurl psychiatric epithets to explain that in our culture, as in others, the symbols and structures of sexual life are enormously powerful. It is no wonder that sex scandals are an absorbing rite for so many when we acknowledge, with anthropologist

Sex Scandals

Mary Douglas, that "no other social pressures are potentially so explosive as those which constrain sexual relations. We can come to sympathize with St. Paul's extraordinary demand that in the new Christian society there should be neither male nor female." If the innocents in our society and in each of us read of scandal with eyes opened wide, the sophisticates in our cities and in our breasts read with eyebrows raised archly. But if the latter are less earnest in their attention to scandal, they are nonetheless attentive. The innocents—provincial, prudish, wary of sex, and acknowledging guilt, find their own fascination with scandal alarming; the sophisticates, denying guilt, find *their* fascination baffling. When the innocents observe the ritual of scandal, they know they participate in an event bristling with moral significance. When the sophisticates "observe" the ritual as onlookers from a safe remove, they think they engage in a casual pastime. But in whatever terms they bracket the experience or set it apart from deeper feelings, they are left with a lingering puzzlement and suspicion that sex scandals connect to their own roots, too.

MICHAEL SCHUDSON

A Note on Sources

Fawn M. Brodie, *Thomas Jefferson: An Intimate History* (New York: W. W. Norton, 1974) is the best account of the scandals involving Hamilton and Jefferson and a sensitive portrait of Jefferson's personal life. Robert Shaplen, *Free Love and Heavenly Sinners* (New York: Alfred A. Knopf, 1954) is a good book-length account of the Beecher scandal. Constance Rourke, *Trumpets of Jubilee* (New York: Harcourt Brace Jovanovich and World Harbinger Book, 1963) covers the same ground with more wit and more sense of history, and much more briefly.

Max Gluckman, "Gossip and Scandal" in *Current Anthropology* (vol. 4, 1963) deals almost exclusively with simple societies, but provides some useful insights. Mary Douglas, *Purity and Danger* (Baltimore: Penguin Books, 1966) does not deal with gossip or scandal directly at all, but it is one of the most imaginative works in anthropology of recent years and a provocative place for amateur and professional alike to start thinking about sex, rituals, and social roles.

Victoria Waives the Rules

Sex, Marriage, and Feminism
in the Nineteenth Century

4

It is impossible to talk about sex or about men and women or about feminism in the nineteenth century without talking about *marriage*. The early leaders of the Women's Rights Movement were less interested in sex than in getting the vote, and less interested in suffrage than in improving women's legal status, increasing opportunities for education and employment, gaining guardianship of children and control of property. For most of these women—white, middle-class, Victorian—sexual behavior was not a central issue, as it is among radical feminists of our day.

Victorian women simply didn't talk about sex.

As bodies, women have always felt vulnerable. They get pregnant. They get raped. In societies which forbid them to become educated and work, women depend on men for food and shelter. In nineteenth-century America, when feminism first became an active social force, women were weak and unhealthy from bad medical care, constricting clothing, and lack of exercise. For most people, pregnancy was a dangerous but unavoidable side effect of sexuali-

ty. And Victorian women were, not surprisingly, fond of denying that they had bodies. They would not so much as mention an article of clothing in front of a man: "shirt" was a dirty word. A French visitor to the United States reported in the early nineteenth century that women referred to their bodies as though "from the waist down is ankles." They were reluctant, as well, to allow doctors to examine them. Bodilessness was necessary to be a "good" woman; by denigrating their bodily functions, women sought to transform themselves into special incorporeal creatures—ladies. "Bad" women were those who allowed themselves to be treated as bodies.

Marriage was based on the "you break it, you buy it" principle of sexuality. A man paid, with marriage, for the privilege of defiling a good woman. A bad woman was one you didn't have to marry. Sex for women was part of the domestic bargain, a necessary but unpleasant duty in exchange for which she became the ruler of the Home, the most sacred unit of nineteenth-century society.

Victoria Waives the Rules

Yet once married, a woman had the civil status of a slave. She could not sign contracts, sue or be sued; all her property and earnings, including those she acquired after marriage, belonged to her husband, even the unmentionable shirt on her back. If she had children, her husband owned them just as he owned their mother. If a woman left her husband, not even her own family could legally give her sanctuary.

"Both [slaves and wives] were expected to behave with deference and obedience towards owner or husband; both did not exist officially under the law; both had few rights and little education; both found it difficult to run away; both worked for their masters without pay; both had to breed on command and to nurse the results. . . . The authority of a husband was as absolute and unquestionable as that of a plantation owner," Andrew Sinclair pointed out in *The Better Half*.

The women's rights movement grew out of the antislavery movement, not so much because of this theoretical analogy, but because women active in abolitionist work found that, as ladies overstepping the boundaries of the Home, they aroused hostility—even among their coworkers—when they spoke and organized publicly.

When Sarah and Angelina Grimké, who grew up in South Carolina, freed their slaves and began a lecture tour in New England, the powerful Council of Congregational Ministers in Massachusetts denounced them:

> We invite your attention to the dangers which at present seem to threaten the female character with widespread and permanent injury. . . . If the vine, whose strength and beauty is to lean upon the trellis-work and half conceal its clusters,

thinks to assume the independence and the over-shadowing nature of the elm, it will not only cease to bear fruit, but fall in shame and dishonor into the dust.

Both sisters responded by emphasizing women's rights in their speeches, and the entire abolitionist movement split over the issue of whether women should be allowed to lecture and to vote or hold office in the antislavery societies.

It was mostly clergymen who felt that women should not take part in public affairs, since God intended them to stay at home. Leaders like William Lloyd Garrison and Theodore Weld were sympathetic to women's rights but feared that feminist activism would sap the energy of the antislavery movement.

In 1838 Angelina Grimké married Theodore Weld. Both privately confessed their anxiety and guilt at feeling passion for each other, rather than for God and abolition. "I laid awake thinking why it was that my heart longed and panted and reached after you as it does," Grimké wrote to Weld. "Why my Savior and my God is not enough to *satisfy* me. Am I sinning, am I ungrateful, *am I an* IDOLATOR? I trust I am not, and yet—but I cannot tell how I feel. I am a mystery to myself. . . . I want to know why those of our own sex *cannot* fill the void in human hearts. This is a mystery I have yet to learn and I want to know why I find myself involuntarily applying to you the language which hitherto I had applied to my blessed master, for instance 'I am my beloved's and my beloved is mine,' etc."

Grimké worried that marriage would cause her to "retire from public view and sink down into *sweet obscurity*," but Weld urged her to

Theodore Weld.
"Am I sinning, am I ungrateful, *am I an* IDOLATOR?" asked Angelina.

Victoria Waives the Rules

continue her commitment to reform. Their marriage would be viewed by the world as a great experiment, he said, since "we have uncommon notoriety, YOU *especially*. . . . all eyes are upon you and almost all mouths filled with cavil. Nine tenths of the community verily believe that you are utterly spoiled for domestic life. . . . Beloved, on account of your *doctrine* and *practice* touching the sphere of woman. I will only add that you are the FIRST woman everywhere known to be on this ground, to whom in the Providence of God the *practical* test of married life will be applied (if we are spared)."

In fact, their marriage was a strange ménage à trois. Sarah, older than Angelina by twelve years, lived with them until her death in 1873. Shortly after the marriage, the Grimké sisters withdrew from public speaking, devoting themselves to writing for abolition, running a school, and eventually taking care of Angelina's three children. The first respectable American women to consistently propagandize in public for women's rights, the first to lecture and write major essays on the subject, they soon came to concentrate almost exclusively on antislavery activity. The passion between husband and wife was complicated by Angelina's illnesses and gynecological disorders; the relationship between the sisters was irritated by Angelina's occasional feeling that it was "unnatural that a wife and mother should ever thus be willing to share the affections of her dearest ones with any human being." But as Gerda Lerner, biographer of the Grimkés, commented, the "strange trio continued in Victorian harmony, tantalizing the biographer and historian with a host of unanswered questions."

Two other disgruntled abolitionists took up

where the Grimké sisters left off. In 1840, Elizabeth Cady Stanton and Lucretia Mott met at the World Antislavery Convention in London where they, along with six other American women delegates, were denied seats because of their sex. Horrified by the injustice, Stanton and Mott spent the convention on a balcony behind a curtain discussing women's rights, and decided to call for a convention to discuss it further with other women.

But both were so preoccupied with other responsibilities that it was eight years before this meeting took place. Stanton, the daughter of a judge who had taught her some law and the wife of a lawyer, knew enough about the legal status of women to want to change it. But living a life in Boston that was intellectually stimulating and emotionally secure, occupied with taking care of three children and a household by herself (since her husband was often away), working for the antislavery movement, "life had glided by with comparative ease." In 1846 when the Stantons moved to Seneca Falls, New York, Elizabeth Cady Stanton was struggling with isolation, sick children (and more of them) and increasing loneliness—Henry Stanton continued to travel and friends were far away.

Later she recalled that it was then that she "fully understood the practical difficulties most women had to contend with in the isolated household, and the impossibility of woman's best development if in contact, the chief part of her life, with servants and children. . . . The general discontent I felt with woman's portion as wife, mother, housekeeper, physician, and spiritual guide . . . and the wearied, anxious look of the majority of women impressed me with a strong feeling that some active measures

Angelina Grimké.

Sarah Grimké.

". . . the strange trio continued in Victorian harmony, tantalizing the biographer and historian with a host of unanswered questions."

Susan B. Anthony.
(Courtesy Chicago
Historical Society.)

should be taken to remedy the wrongs of society in general, and of women in particular. My experience at the World's Antislavery Convention, all I had read of the legal status of women, and the oppression I saw everywhere, together swept across my soul, intensified now by many personal experiences. . . . In this tempest-tossed condition of mind I received an invitation to spend the day with Lucretia Mott . . . and we decided, then and there, to call a 'Woman's Rights Convention.'"

Three hundred men and women came to the meeting and approved a Declaration of Sentiments modeled after the Declaration of Independence. They also passed twelve resolutions, one of which demanded suffrage. But this was the only resolution that was hotly debated and not accepted unanimously. Much more important than the vote to most people were the resolutions calling for the recognition of women as men's equals, the education of women, a single standard of "virtue, delicacy, and refinement of behavior" for both men and women, the right of women to speak and write publicly, the "overthrow of the monopoly of the pulpit, and . . . securing to women an equal participation with men in the various trades, professions, and commerce."

Stanton's husband refused to attend the Seneca Falls Convention—an active abolitionist, he saw the demand for the vote as a dangerous issue—and although she derived great pleasure from her seven children and her relationships with women like Lucretia Mott and Susan B. Anthony, marriage became less and less a source of emotional satisfaction. Her own situation led her to wonder about marriage in general, but the more Stanton approached this ques-

tion, the more the woman's movement—rapidly becoming widespread at a grass-roots level—focused on suffrage.

During the Civil War, the feminists turned their energies back toward abolition and war work. By 1869 enough disagreements were brewing among the women's rights leaders that a formal schism took place between Stanton and

Anthony on the one hand, and Lucy Stone, her husband Henry Blackwell, and their friend and sister-in-law Antoinette Brown Blackwell, on the other. Stanton and Anthony founded the National Woman Suffrage Association (NWSA), which advocated marriage and divorce reform; began to organize women workers; and published a journal, *The Revolution,* which at-

The first International Convention of Women, Washington, D.C., 1888. Susan B. Anthony, *first row, fourth from left;* Elizabeth Cady Stanton, *first row, sixth from left.* (Courtesy Chicago Historical Society.)

THE FASHIONABLE.

THE PROFESSIONAL.

THE RURAL.

THE NATURAL.

A cartoon from *Harper's Weekly*, 1857.
Marriage was based on the "you break it,
you buy it" principle of sexuality.

66   *Victoria Waives the Rules*

tacked religious, moral, and legal codes. "The solemn and profound question of marriage . . . is of more vital consequence to woman's welfare, reaches down to a deeper depth in woman's heart, and more thoroughly constitutes the core of the woman's movement, than any such superficial and fragmentary question as woman's suffrage," wrote one member of the NWSA. Stone and the other conservative feminists preferred to concentrate solely on winning the vote. They organized the American Woman Suffrage Association (AWSA) which, unlike the NWSA, allowed men to join; they avoided volatile issues like marriage, religion, and labor in order to gain as much and as broad support for suffrage as possible. For the AWSA the vote became an end; for the NWSA it was a means for greater social change.

Susan B. Anthony never married, choosing to devote her life to the cause. She severely criticized her friends Stanton, Stone, and Blackwell for being diverted by marriage and "baby-making." Yet throughout her fifty-year friendship with Stanton, she unstintingly shared domestic responsibilities, sometimes moving into the Stanton household so that the two could collaborate on speeches and essays. Stanton explained their collaborative method: "I am the better writer, she the better critic. She supplied the facts and statistics, I the philosophy and rhetoric; and together we have made arguments that have stood unshaken by the storms of thirty long years." The two were so close, worked so intensely together, and argued so heatedly, that they often jokingly referred to their friendship as a marriage. Stanton's writings show that she got emotional support from Anthony that she never had in her relationships with men, wheth-

er her father—who wished she'd been born a boy—or her husband, despite a marriage that continued for forty-six years.

Stanton clearly thought a great deal about sexuality, but confined her discussions of it to entries in her diary or letters to Anthony. "Man in his lust has regulated long enough this whole question of sexual intercourse. Now let the mother of mankind, whose prerogative it is to set bounds to his indulgence rouse up and give this whole matter a thorough, fearless examination," she wrote to her friend. Commenting on Walt Whitman's poetry in her diary: "He speaks as if the female must be forced to the creative act, apparently ignorant of the great natural fact that a healthy woman has as much passion as a man, that she needs nothing stronger than the law of attraction to draw her to the male." Strong words, even in private, from an inhabitant of a society that since the 1830s had grown increasingly sexually repressive.

Stanton and Anthony, believing that women's rights would never be won as long as sexism (as it later came to be called) pervaded social institutions or religious and moral values, were critical of "reformers" who looked for superficial advances. The attacks they made on every controversial front were audacious and persistent; both agitated vociferously for marriage and divorce reform. But the one taboo of their times they could not breach was publicly debating the heart of the marriage question—sex. This stumbling block meant that discussion of marriage and divorce inevitably came to a dead end. While Anthony—who apparently chose celibacy as *her* alternative—and Stanton—who, for all her private scrutiny and personal doubts, continued to ground *her* sexuality

Victoria Woodhull (*left*) and
Tennie C. Claflin.
"If I want sexual intercourse with one
hundred men I shall have it . . ."

in marriage—searched for other theories and hinted most delicately of options, post-Civil War America would simply not have its cornerstone—contractual sex within bourgeois marriage—besmirched. The Comstock Law, passed in 1873, made widespread discussion of sex through the mail impossible, and reflected an ironclad public resistance to even approaching the issue. Stanton and Anthony, like many of their colleagues who had emerged from the abolition, temperance, and social purity movements, simply were not radical enough to insist on personal change so close to home. It was one thing to work for this kind of change in the lives of others—men, slaveowners, prostitutes—and

quite another to make radical changes in the way they lived their own lives.

At the peak of this impasse, and at the height of public hostility toward alternatives to the Home, the women's movement met up with Victoria Woodhull. It was a watershed in the history of American feminism.

For the first time, sexual behavior emerged clearly and defiantly as a feminist concern. But the repercussions of the explosion ultimately erased the issue from the woman's rights movement for almost a century.

Victoria Woodhull was really an anomaly. She liked sex and she didn't mind admitting it. And, the daughter of a fortune-teller and a poverty-

Victoria Waives the Rules

MESMERISM IN WALL STREET.

First Lady Broker, (entrancing subject.)
"There, I've got him to the point now.
Take him at his word, quick."
Commodore V-nd-rb-lt, (murmurs.) "Sell
me one thousand shares Central."
Second Lady Broker. "Booked!"

Victoria and Tennie's bewitching effect
on Vanderbilt is satirized in this 1870
cartoon.

stricken hustler, she had lived a life so utterly untrammeled by normal Victorian inhibitions that she was able to argue unabashedly for Free Love—and Spiritualism and Communism and Women's Rights and her own presidential candidacy—with an ingenuous fanaticism.

When she was fifteen, Victoria Claflin's parents married her off to Canning Woodhull, an alcoholic whom she would take care of, financially and physically, for the rest of his life even though they were divorced in 1866 when Victoria was twenty-eight. A clairvoyant since childhood, she had been visited by the spirit of Demosthenes who promised her wealth, fame, and the presidency. She and her entire family—husband, children, parents, sisters, and brothers—traveled through the Midwest telling fortunes, performing magnetic cures, and avoiding arrest for fraud and running a house of assignation. In the course of these travels, Woodhull met Colonel Blood, a Spiritualist and advocate of Free Love, the man who gave a conceptual framework to her intuitions and furnished energy and support for her schemes for the next ten years. The whole family moved to New York where Victoria and her sister Tennessee opened a brokerage firm, aided by Tennessee's lover Cornelius Vanderbilt. The press and public were shocked and enthralled by the "lady brokers." With the encouragement of Stephen Pearl An-

Victoria Waives the Rules

This 1872 caricature of Victoria Woodhull by Thomas Nast was captioned: "Get thee behind me, (Mrs.) Satan:" WIFE (with heavy burden), "I'd rather travel the hardest path of matrimony than follow your footsteps." Victoria's sign reads "Be Saved by Free Love."

Victoria Waives the Rules

drews, leader of the utopian Pantarchists, Woodhull decided to run for president, and the sisters started a weekly journal to advance the campaign.

Woodhull & Claflin's Weekly treated every subject relevant to Victoria's campaign, from free love to prostitution to women's rights to labor organizing. The motto on the masthead read: "Progress! Free Thought! Untrammeled Lives! Breaking the Ground for Future Generations!"

With the help of Blood, Andrews, and Congressman Benjamin Butler, Woodhull went to Washington in 1871 to present a memorial to the Judiciary Committee, demanding the vote for women under the fourteenth amendment. Members of the NWSA, furious that Woodhull might beat them to the punch, postponed the opening of their convention, which was also taking place in Washington, so that they could attend the presentation and see "Mrs. Satan." The presentation was enthusiastically received, although, finally, the petition was refused. The suffragists were bewitched by Woodhull, much to their own amazement, and invited her to repeat the memorial presentation at their convention.

To those who balked at welcoming "The Woodhull" into their ranks, Elizabeth Cady Stanton argued, "When the men who make laws for us in Washington can stand forth and declare themselves pure and unspotted from all the sins mentioned in the Decalogue, then we will demand that every woman who makes a Constitutional argument on our platform shall be as chaste as Diana."

Woodhull began to travel and lecture on women's rights. At the next NWSA convention,

An 1895 satire on matrimonial agencies.

WOMAN ASSERTS HER RIGHTS.
An 1870 cartoon from *Punchinello*.

she swore that "if the very next Congress refuses women all the legitimate results of citizenship . . . we shall proceed to call another convention expressly to frame a new constitution and to erect a new government. . . . We mean treason; we mean secession, and on a thousand times grander scale than was that of the South. We are plotting a revolution; we will overthrow this bogus Republic and plant a government of righteousness in its stead."

The conservative suffragists disapproved of the NWSA's alliance with this free lover, who attacked the Victorian moral code weekly in her paper and daily in her life, who claimed that the

Victoria Waives the Rules

1776—RETOUCHING AN OLD
MASTERPIECE—1915.
A 1915 cartoon from the
comic weekly *Life*.

Victoria Waives the Rules

Henry Ward Beecher.

institution of the family was nothing more than "a community of hot little hells."

At a Spiritualist convention, Woodhull announced, "If I want sexual intercourse with one hundred men I shall have it . . . . and this sexual intercourse business may as well be discussed now, and discussed until you are so familiar with your sexual organs that a reference to them will no longer make the blush mount to your face any more than a reference to any other part of your body."

In New York's Steinway Hall, Woodhull told a shocked crowd that "promiscuity in sexuality is simply the anarchical stage of development wherein the passions rule supreme. When spirituality comes in and rescues the real man or woman from the domain of the purely material, promiscuity is simply impossible."

Elizabeth Cady Stanton continued to support her: "The men and women who are dabbling with the suffrage movement for women should be . . . emphatically warned that what they mean logically if not consciously in all they say is next social equality and next Freedom or in a word Free Love and, if they wish to get out of the boat, they should for safety get out now, for delays are dangerous."

In her zeal to unveil hypocrisy (probably inspired, too, by her enmity toward Harriet Beecher Stowe and Catharine Beecher), Woodhull fully revealed the Beecher-Tilton story in 1873, three years after the event took place. Woodhull had written a letter to two New York papers in 1871 hinting at the scandal. "My judges react against 'free love' openly, practice it secretly. For example, I know a clergyman of eminence in Brooklyn who lives in concubinage with the wife of another clergyman of equal em-

inence." The former was Henry Ward Beecher, the most popular clergyman in the country, titular head of the AWSA, friend of the conservative feminists. The latter was Theodore Tilton, allied with NWSA, friendly with Stanton and Anthony, and so loyal to his former teacher, Beecher, that he had decided to take no action when his wife, Elizabeth Tilton, confessed that she had slept with him.

Shortly after the publication of this letter, Woodhull had met Tilton and they had become lovers. "He slept every night for three months in my arms," she reminisced. She had then met Beecher, whom she rated eight in Amativeness, a high rating on her phrenological scale. He would not, however, embrace her views on free love publicly.

Woodhull finally decided to reveal the story in detail, she said, because Beecher was "in heart, in conviction, and in life, an ultra socialist reformer; while in seeming and pretension he is the upholder of the old social slavery, and, therefore does what he can to crush out and oppose me and those who act and believe with me in forwarding the great social revolution." She denounced Beecher "as a poltroon, a coward, and a sneak; not, as I tell you, for anything that he has done, and for which the world would condemn him, but for failing to do what it seems to me so clear he ought to do . . . to hasten a social regeneration which he believes in."

The story was printed in *Woodhull & Claflin's Weekly*; almost immediately the sisters were arrested and imprisoned for sending obscenity through the mail. They were released and then arrested for libel.

The uproar surrounding the case and the scandal took years to subside, even though the

Victoria Waives the Rules

libel charge was thrown out and the verdict in the obscenity case was not guilty. Tilton decided, now that everything was public, to sue Beecher. Beecher was investigated by the church and exonerated. Beecher called Tilton a blackmailer, a forger, insane, immoral. The civil suit was deadlocked; Tilton dropped charges and left the country a broken man.

The women's movement wanted nothing more to do with Woodhull, who had struck as close to home as she could get by aiming at this particular cast of characters, drawn from both suffragist groups. Woodhull's interest in religion grew, she repudiated Spiritualism, then Free Love, and finally divorced Colonel Blood. She and Tennessee went to Europe and both eventually married rich respectable men.

The NWSA, staggering under the blow of the scandal, retreated from any issues that smacked of controversy and revised their strategies to resemble those of the AWSA. By 1890 the two suffragist groups had merged. The Woodhull-Beecher-Tilton explosion had ended—with a bang—the feminist inquiry into restructuring the domestic system.

The women's movement had chosen a conservative strategy to appeal to a wide group of supporters, but had sacrificed the growth of radical speculation on sex-related issues. It decided to close the door Victoria Woodhull had opened. After the nineteenth amendment was passed, in 1920, the movement lost its momentum. The vote had become a goal, rather than a tactic; work on deeper issues had no sustaining power. Women outside of the suffrage movement, like Margaret Sanger and Emma Goldman, demanded sexual rights for women, but their voices were isolated, separate from feminist theory and organized activity. It was not until 1968 (two years after *Human Sexual Response,* by Masters and Johnson), when Anne Koedt wrote "The Myth of the Vaginal Orgasm," that personal sexual behavior as a political problem once again emerged in feminist analysis.

FLORA JOHNSON

Victoria Waives the Rules

A Note on Sources

For information on early feminism, and especially on the Grimkés, Stanton, and Anthony, I have found invaluable Alice S. Rossi, *The Feminist Papers* (New York: Columbia University Press, 1973; Bantam Books, 1974). This superb anthology of primary documents also includes detailed and perceptive commentary by Rossi. Among the many studies of nineteenth-century feminism, Andrew Sinclair, *The Better Half: The Emancipation of the American Woman* (New York: Harper and Row, 1956; reprinted, 1965) provides a valuable analysis of the movement in its Victorian context; Eleanor Flexner, *Century of Struggle: The Woman's Rights Movement in the United States* (Cambridge, Massachusetts: Harvard University Press, 1959; New York: Atheneum, 1968) is a basic work; and the six volumes of *The History of Woman Suffrage* by Susan B. Anthony, Elizabeth Cady Stanton, Matilda Joslin Gage, and Ida Husted Harper, were reprinted by Arno and The New York Times in 1969.

Judith Hole and Ellen Levine, *Rebirth of Feminism* (New York: Quadrangle Books, 1971) and Shulamith Firestone, *The Dialectic of Sex: The Case for Feminist Revolution* (New York: Morrow, 1970) both offer brief histories of the early American feminist movement. Gerda Lerner, *The Grimké Sisters from South Carolina* (Boston: Houghton Mifflin, 1967; New York: Schocken Books, 1967) is a valuable study of the strange Victorian trio, with a complete bibliography of writings by and about the Grimkés; the letters quoted here are from Gilbert Hobbs Barnes and Dwight L. Dumond, *Letters of Theodore Dwight Weld, Angelina Grimké Weld, and Sarah Grimké 1822-1844* (New York: D. Appleton-Century, 1934). Portions of Theodore Stanton and Harriot Stanton Blatch, eds., *Elizabeth Cady Stanton: As Revealed in Her Letters, Diary, and Reminiscences* (New York: Harper and Brothers, 1922) have been reprinted in recent years by various publishers.

For the material on Victoria Woodhull, I am indebted to Johanna Johnston, *Mrs. Satan: The Incredible Saga of Victoria C. Woodhull* (New York: G. P. Putnam's Sons, 1967) and Emanie Sachs, *The Terrible Siren* (New York: Harper and Brothers, 1928). A good source for Woodhull's writings is her newspaper; some selections from it appear, with background and commentary, in Arlene Kisner, *Woodhull & Claflin's Weekly: The Lives and Writings of Notorious Victoria Woodhull and Her Sister, Tennessee Claflin* (Washington, New Jersey: Times Change Press, 1972). "The Myth of the Vaginal Orgasm" is reprinted, with other radical feminist writings of the 1960s and 1970s, in Anne Koedt, Ellen Levine, and Anita Rapone, eds., *Radical Feminism* (New York: Quadrangle Books, 1972).

A parade of 9,000 suffragists in Washington, D.C., 1913.

Utopian Sex

In Search of a New Amorous World

5

> *. . . The evil principle of Free Love has spread with marvellous rapidity, until it has manifested itself in almost every class of society. It has not only drawn men and women into organized associations, but has lowered the moral tone of society to an extent which is truly alarming. . . .*
>
> Dr. John B. Ellis,
> *Free Love and Its Votaries;*
> *or, American Socialism Unmasked* (1870)

For hundreds of years the New World has been the nursery of utopias—and their graveyard. People have flocked to American shores with every variety of hope for a better way of life. Some of those dreams have perished through their own inconsistencies. Others were ground up in the great American gristmill and harmlessly digested.

During the nineteenth century there were several separate waves of self-conscious efforts to construct small communities which would escape the viciousness, venality, and chaos of the surrounding society. Inspired by reason or divinity, European immigrants and settled

Americans founded more than 500 settlements based on some form of economic cooperation or communalism. Frequently they were formed as a reaction against the injustices and irrationalities of capitalist industrialism. In Europe such sentiments led to political agitation and revolt. In America, for a long time, the discontented felt they could fashion directly with raw earth and ready spirits a new, better—even perfect—world which would save them and inspire others to follow in their footsteps.

Nearly every time they tried, they were suspected of carrying on outrageous sex lives. Economic communism was weird enough to most moral guardians, but that also implied sexual communism which seemed even more subversive. According to the beliefs of the time, private property and the monogamous, lifelong patriarchal family were parallel sacred pillars of the social order. Unbridled fornication was as abhorrent as violent insurrection.

Although changes in the family and in the relationship between the sexes were important in most of the communities, the sexual behavior

An 1875 map showing location of U.S. communes.

of the utopians was rarely close to the orgiastic fantasies of their opponents. They were concerned above all with community. They wanted warm, closely-knit social lives without tyranny or exploitation. Family life was shaped to help sustain the community, which was usually either religiously motivated or an experiment in secular socialism.

Within each camp there was a wide range of resolutions of how sexual relations should be ordered; and various groups attempted celibacy, monogamy, polygyny, "free love" coupling,

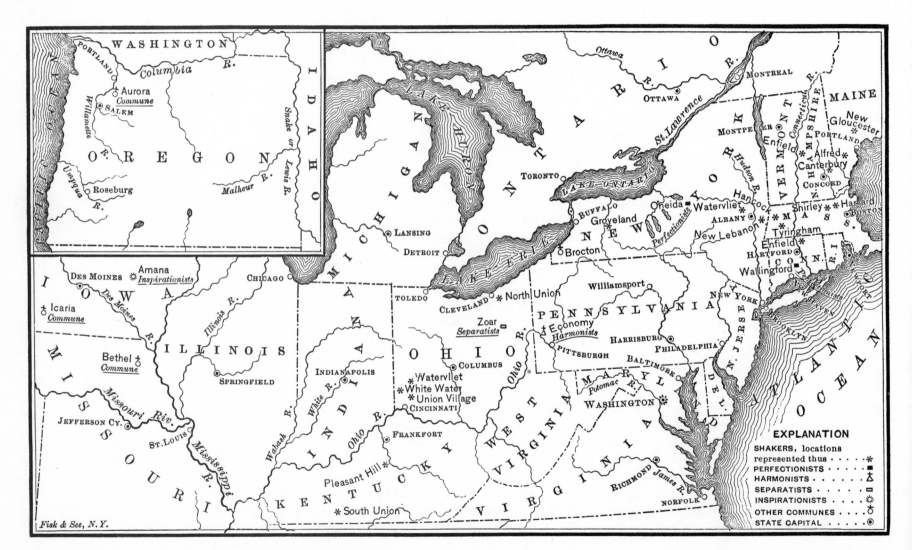

EXPLANATION

SHAKERS, locations represented thus . . . . . ✳
PERFECTIONISTS . . . . ■
HARMONISTS . . . . . △
SEPARATISTS . . . . . ▭
INSPIRATIONISTS . . . . ✸
OTHER COMMUNES . . . . ⚲
STATE CAPITAL . . . . . ◉

Fisk & See, N.Y.

and sexual communism. But their sexual ideologies and practices were virtually always extensions of their religious or philosophical views (though in some cases specific sexual proclivities did seem to give rise to philosophy).

Nearly all the communitarians believed that human beings were basically good, not evil and depraved as the preachers usually stressed. With the right kind of community and proper education, whether profoundly religious or rational in an Enlightenment fashion, most utopians believed people could live together decently and happily, without church and state to guard their virtue.

What place does sex have in decent and happy lives? For the Shakers, an offshoot of the Quakers and officially called The Millenial Church, or United Society of Believers, sex was the cause of humanity's fall from grace and celibacy the return. Shaker leaders advised that possession of organs which could be used for sex did not mean one was obliged to use them. Although procreation itself was not evil, lust was vividly revealed as the "root and foundation of human depravity" in a vision which came to the Englishwoman Ann Lee during the time she spent in prison because of her religious practices. After seeing Adam and Eve copulating in the Garden of Eden, Mother Ann called on her followers among the Shaking Quakers to lead a life of celibacy. A new era had dawned, and further visions revealed to her that Christ had come again, this time in the female form of Ann Lee, and that she should travel to America and establish a new church.

The Shaker settlement in New York in 1776 was not communal at first, but economic expediency soon drew the faithful into a pact of mutual aid which eventually became part of a theology. Their community reincarnated both Eden before the fall and the primitive Christian church with common property, celibacy, nonresistance, separate government. At first families lived together, but without sexual relations. Mother Ann had married and suffered the death of four children, intensifying her already deep fear and hatred of sex (by which she was also apparently strongly, guiltily tempted at times). She continued for a long time to live with her husband who complained of her unwillingness to sleep with him, while she elaborated a theology which uncannily fit her own passions.

In setting up their communities which were successful in recruiting thousands of believers, the Shakers took great pains to separate men and women in all their tasks and associations. A long, detailed confession of all past sins was a prerequisite of admission to the community, although it was clear that few people would join just for the good times.

Life in the Shaker communities was somber and quiet. The slightest suggestion of genitals was avoided. Men arose before the women to empty the chamber pots from their dormitory, since seeing male excrement might suggest carnality to the women. In all their work and religious activity, which together occupied the entire day, men and women were in separate groups, although the two groups would have religious services in the same room while still keeping apart. During only one "Union Hour" a week did small groups of men and women, sitting across from each other, meet for a few minutes of deliberately idle, trivial, amusing talk. But if eyes lingered too long on someone of the opposite sex, or anything gave evidence of "sparking" between men and women, members were disciplined. There is a famous story of an older woman who caught two young girls watching flies copulate and as punishment ordered them to disrobe and beat each other.

To some tastes that may appear to be sexual behavior in itself. Many have hinted that the ecstatic dances of the Shakers, especially in the early years before specific pattern dances were developed, were erotic manifestations— quivering, shouting, gesturing, stamping out the devil, and celebrating the intoxicating gifts brought back from heaven by Mother Ann. Also in the first years of the church, believers enthusiastically mortified their evil flesh. "They often danced with vehemence through the greatest part of the night," a visitor wrote in 1812, "and then instead of reposing their wearied bodies upon a bed, they would, by way of further penance, lie down upon the floor on chains, ropes, or sticks, in every humiliating posture they could devise!"

Even suspicious observers could find no evidence of secret affairs, and the absence of children, as well as the departure of the vast majority of children brought into the communities, supports the view that celibacy was maintained. Although heaven may still seem far away, the Shakers lasted as a thriving community through recruitment and conversion for well over a century; they still exist, though barely.

Another attempt at celibacy was made by the German peasant followers of George Rapp, who settled in 1804 in Pennsylvania, then moved to Indiana and finally returned to Pennsylvania until Harmony Society was dissolved in 1898. They also believed in an androgynous, communist Jesus. God and Adam at first had dual sexuality, but Adam was discontented and God separated out a female part, leading to desire and the fall.

Harmony was designed as a refuge from the sinful world and a means of support for poor peasants who could economically achieve together what they could not singly. At first families lived together, marriages took place, and children were born as usual. But after a few years, under the combined influence of a religious revival sweeping through the area and economic pressures on the fledgling community, Rapp promulgated a plan of celibacy. A few years earlier communal ownership had been adopted as an economic expedient; but celibacy was not quite so successful. From the beginning many members continued to have sexual relations, and children were born despite Rapp's theological criticisms. In 1831, Bernhard Muller, who called himself Count Maxmillian de Leon, joined the community and soon advocated an end to celibacy. The community voted on the issue, and the pseudo-count received 250 votes to Rapp's 500. The dissidents left with money to start a new community, which soon failed under the corrupt leadership of the count.

Although there were reports of the Rappites permitting a month of uninhibited swiving whenever new little Rappites were needed or of cohabiting for a year then separating for six, probably the truth was that the pressures toward celibacy were sufficient to slow population growth and retard sexual dalliance in a more random fashion. Visitors felt the Rappites deliberately cultivated ugliness of dress and appearance to discourage erotic fantasy, also a policy in other celibate communities such as the Shakers. Although less severe than the Shakers, the

Utopian Sex

Harmonists frequently separated the sexes, especially unmarried men and women living in dormitories, yet families did live together. Since they expected the millenium soon (originally scheduled for 1829), true believers were not terribly worried about propagating. "Again a day is past," the night watchman called out to the chastely sleeping followers of George Rapp, "and a step made nearer to our end; our time runs away, and the joys of heaven are our reward."

In other communities, celibacy was much less solidly anchored theologically. German immigrants following the Quietist, separatist leader Joseph Baumeler to eastern Ohio in 1819 adopted communism and celibacy in their colony at Zoar largely to survive, especially since they had much work and many hands which were too

A group of Shakers.

". . . they would, by way of further penance, lie down upon the floor on chains, ropes, or sticks, in every humiliating posture they could devise!"

Harmonists in Economy.
Why was celibacy so popular?

young or too old to be productive. By 1830 they were well established and modified their stand, admitting marriage but lauding celibacy as more godly. Cynics suggest the transformation of doctrine was made by Baumeler so he could marry a pretty young woman who had been working in his house for several years.

In the Swedish colony at Bishop Hill, Illinois, the followers of Eric Janson, "the Swedish Messiah," were twice urged to celibacy, but both times there was too much resistance. Janson felt that celibacy was necessary for economic reasons but, like many other utopian community leaders, he also feared private family attachments would compete with communal solidarity and love. Janson himself was tempted by the

Utopian Sex

flesh, falling into one affair (then condemning the wiles of the woman after he was found out) and announcing four days after his wife's death a divine command to marry another woman with whom he had been sexually linked for several years.

Why was celibacy so popular? Apart from the economic motives and the sexual problems and proclivities of the leaders, celibacy was more God-like and spiritual. By rejecting the pleasures of the flesh, the celibate communists prepared to enter the spiritual kingdom of God.

Not all the emigrant-derived religious communities were celibate (and even the celibate Zoarites were not ascetic in all regards). Two of the largest and most successful groups, the Amana colony (Society of the True Inspirationists) and the Hutterites, formed communities incorporating monogamous families, but transformed them in directions which served community needs and ideology.

The Amana colonizers, who settled in Iowa in 1845, idealized celibacy as spiritually superior, but nearly everyone married despite rigid obstacles. The minimum age for marriage was twenty-four for men and twenty for women, and of course only unions within the society were allowed. Application had to be made to spiritual leaders who lectured the couple on the gravity of their decision and then, if they persisted with the attachment, a year's physical separation was enforced. During the following year only brief and infrequent meetings were allowed until a date was set for the wedding. And after all this, the weddings were gloomy and funereal. One of the texts given great elaboration in the otherwise simple ceremony was the New Testament injunction, "It is good for a man not to touch a woman." That was taken seriously, since the bride and groom were separated for several weeks after marriage, before being allowed to sleep in two small twin beds in the home of one of their parents. When they married, the young couple was demoted to the lowest, children's spiritual level; and to discourage sex and procreation, each time they had a child they were demoted again.

Kids at Amana were strictly admonished not to play with children of the opposite sex. Although taught in the same classroom, they were kept apart otherwise, even taking afternoon strolls in the woods in opposite directions. Young men were warned to avoid the "very highly dangerous magnet and magical fire" which lurked within the female body.

Despite a similar monogamous community, the Germanic Hutterites who came to the northern Great Plains in the late nineteenth century had significantly more enthusiasm about sex, or at least about producing children. They deemphasized the family as a social unit, but gave it great support as a reproductive engine. They made little effort to recruit, yet expanded, and are still expanding, through the fecund marriages that produce an average of ten children. Although not strictly separated, there was little room for romancing between young boys and girls, and marriage partners were strictly limited. But the marriage ceremony itself, though simple, was a time of great joy and celebration. Sex was required in marriage just as strictly as it was prohibited before marriage. Birth control was forbidden, and adultery meant violation not only of the marriage of two bodies but of the simultaneous marriage of soul and body with an omnipotent God. Marriage was for life in both

Grace at Amana.
"It is good for a man not to touch a woman."

theory and practice; only one divorce and four desertions have occurred in a century.

Most of these celibate and monogamous religious communities lived apart from the rest of society and were generally considered simply odd, foreign, or suspicious curiosities. But when average Americans got wind of the polygyny among the Mormons in the Church of Latter-Day Saints, all hell broke loose against what many thought to be the Antichrist's organization on earth. The Mormons' defense and practice of polygyny was a stormy, controversial issue in the late 1800s, a perfect diversion for politicians from all the real questions of the day and the orator's occasion for an impassioned defense of the family.

When the Mormons first started, they had separate property holdings and monogamous families, but Mormon leader Joseph Smith, who was familiar with life in other utopian socialist communities, had a vision of a cooperative society of Mormons. He tried, briefly, to establish this United Order of Enoch several places before settling in Nauvoo, Illinois, in 1840. The order was to be a sanctified theocratic state uncontaminated by the hostile Babylon around it. Like so many other communities at the time, the Mormon settlements were accused of free love and licentious sexual behavior. Unlike others, there seems to have been a very secret kernel of truth to the charges.

Joseph Smith was rumored to have had affairs with various women, to the distress of his wife, and to have been captivated by a biblical passage about Abraham fathering a child by his wife's handmaiden, Hagar. He secretly instituted polygyny among the leaders of the church, while publicly denouncing the practice. While in Nauvoo, however, the lid was lifted, first by a man who penetrated the inner core far enough to learn that members of the hierarchy did have several wives, and then started having affairs of his own. He was attacked by the leaders and forced to leave, but he retaliated by publishing accounts of polygyny among the Mormons. Smith defended his own reputation and denied the charges, but they were made again by a group of dissidents within Nauvoo, along with accusations of embezzlement, dictatorial rule, and obstructing freedom of the press. While Smith was held in jail awaiting trial, a mob attacked and killed him.

During the turbulent Nauvoo period Smith claimed to have received a vision from God settling any lingering doubts he might have had about polygyny. The divine message also ordered Mrs. Smith to accept the arrangement or be condemned. Since Smith's dalliances dated back much earlier, this seems to have been another of the many occasions in which God spoke to earthly messengers with clear statements justifying their own sexual predilections.

Only after Brigham Young took over leadership of the Mormons and led them to Utah was the 1843 revelation made public. Despite reservations by many officials of the church, polygyny and rapid procreation were urged on the faithful, with wives under strict orders to obey their husbands in all matters. Such expansion of domestic labor was valuable in the relatively unsettled frontier territory. Yet many Mormons, especially women, objected to the stud farm model of marriage, and a stronger theological base was needed. Indeed, as Raymond Muncy argues in his *Sex and Marriage in Utopian Communities,* the defense of polygyny led that prac-

Utopian Sex

tice to become the "vital center" of the church. In brief, the Mormons came to believe in a theory of "celestial marriage," in which the faithful were urged to provide homes for souls so they could pass through the earthly life and move on to the celestial realm. Monogamy restricted the rate at which "tabernacles" could be provided for the spiritual souls, and besides, the status of a man in the celestial afterlife was proportionate to his familial kingdom on earth.

Brigham Young took his own teachings seriously enough that he had nine children born to his harem in one week in 1854. Yet despite the admonitions to marry, and marry as much as possible, there were Mormon bachelors, and probably only one-fifth of the Mormon men had two or more wives. Naturally, the richer fared better with women as well as money, and occasionally women would even seek to become the next wife of a well-to-do man for security and comparative freedom from the work a single wife would have. On the whole, however, women seem to have been unhappy with the system, despite the glowing reports given by some female propagandists. Jealousies and resentments within the household were not unknown. Although active courtship was generally discouraged, since it would upset existing wives more than a straightforward business contract of acquiring another wife, romancing did occur. Young and other leaders railed against clothes which were erotically suggestive, yet life among the Mormons was not eternally dull. In fact, long lavish parties were fairly common.

The sexual variety provided for the rich and powerful male Mormons was emphatically denied to the women, however, who were told to refrain from sex from the conception of a child until weaning. They were easily divorced for adultery. Since birth control was forbidden, most wives could expect to spend much of their lives without sex, which was considered healthful for them, although polygyny and an active sex life were defended for men as a guarantor of longevity and physical vigor. Women who defended polygyny did so out of concern for their celestial well-being, rarely finding much good to say about their earthly marriages. In some of the poorer polygynous households, multiple wives meant multiple misery from overcrowding, although in the more substantial families the patriarch tried to provide a separate room, or even a separate house, for each of his wives.

For nearly thirty years, from 1860 to 1890, the United States government passed laws against polygyny and prosecuted Mormon officials as well as ordinary members, denying them various legal rights if convicted of polygyny. The church resisted, and in many areas observers reported the practice was strengthened and expanded as a form of resistance. Eventually, however, Mormon leaders gave in, largely due to the pressure Congress applied by denying statehood to the Utah territory.

To many Mormons the issue was far more a matter of religion than sensual indulgence. Raymond Muncy summed up the emotional implications of polygyny for the Mormons:

Polygyny among the Mormons began and ended in secrecy. Licentiousness may well have given rise to the practice, but its theological justification, which was accepted by its practitioners in Utah, removed it from the pale of purely sensual lust. The objective observers who visited Utah were generally impressed with the sacredness with which the Mormons endowed the institution. William Chandless, a perceptive British observer, reported, "they are not a specially sensual people." Richard Burton was impressed that there were rules and regulations "which disprove the popular statement that such marriages are made to gratify licentiousness, and which render polygamy a positive necessity." He further observed that "All sensuality in the married state is strictly forbidden beyond the requisite for ensuring progeny."

Not all religious communities were so antisensual, however. One of the most daring and radical experiments in communal sex and living in the nineteenth century was also a strongly religious community, influenced by the secular socialist movement. The Oneida, New York, and Wallingford, Connecticut, communities of Perfectionists following John Humphrey Noyes, practiced a "complex marriage" of each with all for more than thirty years. They developed sophisticated theories of birth control, eugenics, sexual pleasure. liberation of women, and the nature of intimate relationships.

Noyes was an intense, thoughtful Vermont banker's son who was smitten with religious fervor in the early nineteenth-century religious revivals, and switched from a law career at Dartmouth to a study of theology at Andover and then Yale. There he became acquainted with Perfectionism, a doctrine which emphasized the ability of human beings to lead morally perfect Christian lives. In the course of his studies Noyes became convinced that the second coming of Christ had already occurred in A.D. 70. Perfectionism was possible: with a thorough

John Humphrey Noyes, founder of the Perfectionists. "Amativeness is to life what sunshine is to vegetation."

Utopian Sex

spiritual cleansing humankind could lead lives as if they were in heaven.

After much prayer and fasting, Noyes had a vision of his own personal baptism and purification, leading him to believe he was perfect. He was extremely agitated by the experience, and began preaching not only among the New Haven religious intelligentsia but also in the slums of New York City, engaging in antislavery propaganda during the same period. He fell in love with one of his first converts, but she soon spurned his attentions, perhaps uneasy with his new mania that had close friends and relatives doubting his sanity, and left him to marry a schoolteacher. Noyes was hurt, pursued her, and declared that whatever happened they were spiritually united forever.

Taking the same text as the Shakers, that in heaven "they shall not marry, neither shall they be given in marriage," Noyes arrived at a much different interpretation. Marriage was narrow possessiveness, unsuited to the saintly life. In a letter published in 1837 in the magazine, *The Battle Axe,* Noyes wrote,

> When the will of God is done on earth as it is in heaven, there will be no marriage. The marriage-supper of the Lamb is a feast at which every dish is free to every guest. Exclusiveness, jealousy, quarrelling have no place there, for the same reason as that which forbids the guests at a Thanksgiving-dinner to claim each his separate dish, and quarrel with the rest for his rights. In a holy community there is no more reason why sexual intercourse should be restrained by law, than why eating and drinking should be; and there is as little occasion for shame in one case as in the other. God has placed a wall of partition between the male and the female during the apostasy for good reasons, which will be broken down in the resurrection for equally good reasons; but woe to him who abolished the law of apostasy before he stands in the holiness of the resurrection. The guests of the marriage-supper may have each his favorite dish, each a dish of his own procuring, and without the jealousy of exclusiveness. I call a certain woman my wife; she is yours; she is Christ's; and in Him she is the bride of all Saints. She is dear in the hands of a stranger, and according to my promise to her I rejoice. My claim upon her cuts directly across the marriage covenant of this world, and God knows the end.

Bold words, indeed, for the time, but Noyes delayed action, instead marrying Harriet Holton and returning to Putney, Vermont, where he joined with a small band of Perfectionists to study and talk. Noyes became greatly disturbed at his wife's four stillbirths and began thinking about how such pain could be avoided, leading him to investigate various contraceptive practices. Coitus interruptus was ruled out since it involved spilling one's seed on the ground (or bed or elsewhere), the Biblical sin of onanism. Various mechanical devices, especially condoms, were associated with the low, sporting life and smacked of lasciviousness. Noyes developed the idea of "male continence" which later became the standard practice of the Oneida community. Men were to learn self-control so they could make love, and according to Noyes, even have orgasm, without ejaculating.

The Perfectionists believed male continence

Perfectionists at Oneida. Most reports agree that both women and men enjoyed sex greatly at Oneida, and there was a constant air of courtship.

had further advantages than simply preventing unwanted conceptions: it conserved the vital strength of men which would otherwise be drained away, and even more important, it elevated the social side of sexual intercourse to its proper place. Noyes believed that sex involved both amative and propagative aspects, the former being the most holy, bringing people together and emphasizing the beauty of "sexual

music" which he thought could be developed as an art, while the propagative side was refined as a science. Love was filling and enveloping, with the amative side predominately female. In the sex act there were three phases, the presence of the penis in the vagina, the motion of the penis leading to female orgasm, and the crisis of male ejaculation. Everything up to the crisis was subject to voluntary control, and thus close to

Utopian Sex

the Perfectionist ideal. When Noyes began practicing male continence, he discovered his wife greatly enjoyed sex, more than ever before.

In the meantime Noyes had developed a following of thirty-five people at Putney who agreed in 1843 to pool their property and live communally. Noyes continued his lectures on the dual sexual nature of God and the place of love in the world: "Amativeness is to life what sunshine is to vegetation." The monogamous family was a question for the community from the beginning. Noyes rejected celibacy, since that would mean a biological end to the community, and decided anarchic love relationships would be socially destructive. Men and women were spiritually united in the community, but it was only after a walk in the woods one May evening that Noyes moved toward physical commingling as well.

He and Mary Cragin, described as beautiful and sexy, had started kissing and fondling each other. She urged him to make love to her, but despite temptations, he resisted and returned to Putney to discuss the matter with his wife and Mary's husband, George. Since they soon arrived at a perfect understanding, they agreed to form a quartet marriage, which was expanded later in the year to include Noyes's two sisters and their husbands (although Noyes reportedly refrained from sex with his sisters; incest, as well as homosexuality, were apparently not permitted among the Perfectionists). "Our love is of God;" Mary Cragin wrote, "it is destitute of exclusiveness, each one rejoicing in the happiness of the others." The biblical injunction to love thy neighbor was taken as paramount, not to be cut short by such a restrictive practice as marriage.

Monogamy was held responsible for adultery, for forcing mismatched couples into lives of unhappiness. It hindered close relationships, fostered skimpy and monotonous tastes in sexual pleasure, and denied sex to adolescents, who had the greatest yearnings for it. Similar arguments were advanced at the time by advocates of easier divorce and "free love," and like Noyes they also blamed monogamy for prostitution, wife beatings, masturbation, and venereal disease.

As word got out, the Perfectionists came under heavy attack from their neighbors and were forced to move to Oneida, New York, where they were more tolerated and could expand. Here complex marriage was worked out on a grand scale, with everyone married to everyone else in a community that approached 250 members. They built a large mansion in which nearly everyone lived, with most people assigned to a room of their own, although some lived in dormitories and used small rooms off the parlor for "social purposes," as bedding down was called.

When complex marriage started at Putney, Noyes decided who could couple with whom; but at Oneida any man or woman was at first permitted to approach any other woman or man and ask to have sexual relations, although flirting was frowned upon. Men tended to be more aggressive, but women had the right to refuse anyone they did not want. In order to minimize the difficulties of saying "no" and to check the more amative men, the system was changed to require the seeker to make the request through an older woman who wrote down in a ledger who was sleeping with whom. Later a committee of elders took on the match-watcher role.

There were pressures to choose partners according to a theory of "ascending fellowship," which basically meant that anyone who was in the lower ranks of the spiritual hierarchy (normally including young people) was encouraged to gain the spiritual blessing of sex with those who were spiritually higher, those saintly souls losing nothing by stooping to share their bodies with the less holy. Also, young men were initiated into sex by older women, who taught them "male continence" but could, since they were past menopause, take the chance with accidental squirts of semen. Young girls, usually around age thirteen, although as young as ten, were introduced to sex by the central, older continent men, almost always having as "first husband," John Humphrey Noyes.

Even worse than spilling one's seed, the capital offense in the pantagamous sexual order of the Perfectionists was exclusive attachment, criticized in the regular "mutual criticism" sessions as a lack of "public spirit." Any couple who saw too much of each other too regularly would be prevented from having sex until they regained the communal spirit. At dances Oneidans avoided taking two turns in a row with the same partner. Couples did not sleep the night together since that could encourage exclusive attachment.

In an atmosphere which praised sexual pleasure, this led to great variety. Most women averaged four different men per month, with relations on the average of once every two to four days, although some especially attractive young women did it seven or more times a week. Most reports agree that both women and men greatly enjoyed sex at Oneida, and there was a constant air of courtship, especially since men and women mixed together in nearly all their work, as well as in playing chess, putting on theatricals for the neighbors, or holding evening discussions on topics of the day, including sex.

The counterpart to the art of amative intercourse was stirpiculture (derived from the Latin for "root"), a planned coupling of Oneidans who submitted themselves in service to God and his messenger, Noyes, to reproduce the community. Every man who applied was ultimately given the right to produce one child, largely to avoid badly hurt feelings. But Noyes (who headed the committee) was, quite predictably, elected to father nine of the fifty-eight "stirps" born from 1869 to 1879. This was the major internal increase in the community, since male continence produced only thirty-one "upsets" during twenty-one years of active use. Informal studies of the results of Oneida's breeding were similar to studies of the mental and physical health of the inhabitants while the community flourished. In all cases, the well-being of the individuals was significantly above average, although the reasons may be found more in economic stability, good food, and satisfying work than in anything genetic.

In 1879 the Oneida community was ripped apart in a conflict over the assumption of leadership by one of Noyes's sons and by the delegation by Noyes of rights to "first husband" to the young female virgins. An opposition faction formed, and pressure was added by an attack from a Hamilton College professor. Noyes left the community in the midst of the conflict, and wrote back that complex marriage should be abandoned. As soon as everyone shuffled themselves out into suitable couples, the communal property was also dissolved and the Oneida

Utopian Sex

corporation formed, bringing an end to one of the most remarkable small-scale social and sexual experiments of the nineteenth century.

Despite their notoriety, none of the secular socialist communities was as experimental with regard to sexual relations as the religious communities at times were, but their impact was probably far greater since their pamphleteering merged with broader social protests which wove together calls for emancipation of slaves and women, abolition of capitalism, and free speech. Frequently the utopian socialist theories were far more radical than their community practice.

There were three great waves of socialist community building in the United States, each basically inspired by a European writer. By far the most influential were the first two, in the 1820s under the banner of Robert Owen, and in the 1840s following the inspiration of Charles Fourier.(The Icarians, mainly Frenchmen led by Etienne Cabet, author of the fantasy *Voyage en Icarie,* started their less successful colonies in the late 1840s).

Robert Owen had succeeded in transforming the industrial town of New Lanark in Scotland from a cesspool of early capitalist evil into a harmonious, thriving village. He generated wide interest, if not the overwhelming support he wanted, from his writings on the new society. In 1824 he called on followers to join him at the site of the Rappites' Harmony colony in Indiana. More than 900 people came to New Harmony, where tolerance and understanding were the guiding principles and bickering and contention the early reality, especially since Owen did not stick around to act as master builder as well as architect. Although Owen excoriated marriage, most New Harmony residents got married.

Actually Owen was less concerned with marriage as such than he was with the social problems of existing marriage relations. Marriage was simple and secular at New Harmony, without churchly contagion, and premarital sex was approved if the couple declared intent to marry. Owen was concerned to guarantee community responsibility for children and equal rights for women, but he was not an advocate of any radical new sexual associations. Divorce should be possible (and Owen's influence led Indiana to take an avant-garde position on divorce for the time) and family ties, which were linked to private property and were seen as often even more divisive than social classes, should be dampened by participation in the large community family. Above all, Owen urged husbands and wives to be truthful and live together only if, in truth, they still felt mutual attraction.

New Harmony did not last long enough to take up many of Owen's ideas, and the sixteen groups inspired by it didn't even last as long. Toward the end of its third and last year, however, enemies were accusing New Harmony of being a haven of free love, but there is no evidence of sexual behavior much out of the ordinary for married couples. Despite its short tenure, New Harmony had a lasting impact on American social movements and utopian communities, not only through its example and Robert Owen's writings, but also through its influence of Owen's son, Robert Dale Owen, Frances Wright, and Josiah Warren, all of whom were instrumental in the more anarchistic wave of communalism which formed a new current in the secular stream of utopian settlements.

About twenty years after the New Harmony experiment Albert Brisbane, an American disci-

Frances Wright, founder of the Nashoba
Community, where things took place "in
good taste and good feeling."

Utopian Sex

ple of Charles Fourier, so excited Horace Gree-ley with a vision of a new society that he was given a regular column in the *New York Herald Tribune*. There he voiced the frequently wild and sometimes mad inspirations of Charles Fourier, which triggered a new wave of utopian socialist communities in the 1840s. A self-taught, socially isolated, sometime cloth merchant, Fourier de-vised a plan for the next stages of social evolu-tion. The main unit of his new world was the phalanx, an association of 1,620 people living, working, and loving together in a shifting com-bination of various groups designed to satisfy all the basic passions of the individual and to pro-mote social harmony. Although there would be a definite hierarchy and even a division between capital and labor within the phalanx, Fourier thought he had established proportions which would guarantee happiness.

In his published writings he criticized the monogamous family, and in his unpublished writings he sketched out a *New World of Love* in which every sexual and erotic amusement which did not abuse someone else against his or her will would be admitted, and even organized into clubs. Although his notion of a "sexual mini-mum" guaranteed to all members of the phalanx would be as popular now as his proposals for a minimum income and physical standard of liv-ing, his antirepressive theories were less impor-tant in the early nineteenth century than his theories of attractive labor and communal, al-though competitive, effort.

With gushing ebullience thousands of Ameri-cans swarmed into the forty or so experimental phalanxes established in the mid-1840s, all with fewer people and less capital than Fourier or his interpreters deemed necessary. The rosy hopes were soon clouded with irritants of disorganiza-tion, inadequate supplies, dishonesty, and quar-reling. Only three phalanxes lasted more than two years (although two were ended by disas-trous fires). None began even the milder experi-ments with association by passionate attraction which might have some day replaced marriage in the Associationist scheme. Families, often with separate cabins and at least with separate rooms, were maintained. In the case of Brook Farm, the Transcendentalist school-farm popu-lated by Boston intelligentsia which converted to a Fourier phalanx, romances were common among the many young students who carried courtship to the kitchen and fields as well as to the dances and witty evening salon conversa-tions. Many marriages were spawned by Brook Farm, but the sex life there appears to have been restricted to the minority of married couples. Brook Farmers were quite happy to show simply that men and women could live together in social settings other than the marital household.

The few, fleeting efforts at anarchistic com-munities in the nineteenth century came some-what closer to embodying the sexual theories of Owen and Fourier, although they, too, were much less radical than the theories often sug-gested. Soon after New Harmony was started, Frances Wright initiated the Nashoba communi-ty near Memphis, Tennessee, influenced by New Harmony but with a plan to emphasize both sexual and racial emancipation. She bought slaves, who were to have participated in the cooperative work of the colony and eventually repay their purchase price, leading not only to freedom but also to education of blacks and whites to be unprejudiced and equal. Robert Dale Owen, who remained a friend of Wright's for years and published articles on marriage among the Tonga, Turks, and various African tribes as well as a book, *Moral Physiology,* advocating birth control, joined in the Nashoba enterprise. Religion, the family, private property, and social class were sharply attacked and the criterion of life at Nashoba was that things "take place in good taste and good feeling."

Free thought was elevated to the highest place of honor, "inasmuch as the liberty of the mind . . . can alone constitute a free man," but freedom of publication got the community in hot water. Some extracts from a diary of one member were published in the *Genius of Universal Emancipation.* One passage described a dispute among some of the ex-slaves over the unwanted entry of a man into a woman's bedroom. The community view on sex was reiterated—"that we consider the proper basis of the sexual intercourse to be the unconstrained and unrestrained choice of *both* parties." The right to say "yes," or "no," and thus be "free" to choose was abhorrent to the common, official morality which saw sex as prohibited outside marriage, obliged inside. Another diary entry read: "Met the slaves—James Richardson (a white man) informed them that last night, Mamselle Josephine (a black woman) and he began to live together; and he took this occasion of repeating to them our views on color and on the sexual relation." It was hardly the first time that white men and black women had sex together in the South, but especially since it was in a context at least theoretically equal, there was a great outcry. Soon afterwards the community ran into organizational and economic problems as well and folded after two years, in 1828. The blacks in the group were transported to Haiti.

The other prominent anarchist communitarian, who had joined briefly in support of the experiments at both New Harmony and Brook Farm, was Josiah Warren, son of a respected, old-line New England family. After following Owen to New Harmony, he became a critic of the attempts to mold new people for the new society through environmental controls. That was the start of his doctrine of Individual Sovereignty, that "every man and every woman has a perfect and inalienable right to do and perform, all and singular, just exactly as he or she may choose, now and hereafter."

When he moved to Ohio, Warren developed his second watchword—"Cost the limit of price." He founded the Time Store, with clock prices reflecting the hours of work the producer put into it plus the amount of time Warren spent handling it. (When a man borrowed a couple of hundred dollars from him, he did not charge interest but simply the labor cost of five minutes handling time.)

His major communal enterprise was Modern Times, on Long Island, founded in 1851. Based on his two great principles, the community soon drew its share of people exercising their inalienable rights to be nudists, polygamists, evangelists, food freaks (one woman died after trying to live on a diet of nothing but beans), and odd dressers (such as the scandalous woman who insisted on wearing men's suits). Warren never had a clear position on marriage, although he eventually thought one man for one woman was probably a fairly good scheme (as long as they specified the period of time for living together), but he did oppose promiscuity. Some of his strong supporters were much more vociferously anti-marriage but even though "mutual love"

Utopian Sex

was declared the only sound basis for the sexes to physically link, there was nothing terribly sexually outrageous at Modern Times. One man did live with three women for a short period, but most of the scandal was in the talk.

One member was quoted as saying, "families arranged themselves according to the law of attraction. Those lived together who chose to do so, and people parted without giving any trouble to the courts of common pleas. The right of the law either to unite or separate was denied and free love was placed in the same category with all other freedom. A man might have one wife or ten or more if he could take upon himself the proper cost or burthen, and the same freedom was asserted to women."

"Institutions will be made for man, not man for institutions," they proudly declared, then went bankrupt in the crash of 1857.

Utopian communities always bump up against the reality of that larger social world. Communitarians' desire to escape and carry on their transformations of social and sexual behavior in a smaller, more manageable realm is understandable but illusory. Those communities which could best succeed were those which, like the celibates or the Hutterites, did not threaten the social-sexual patterns around them. Survival usually required internal solidarity maintained through very strong leadership, usually with divine sanction, and thoroughgoing ideological consensus, including sharp distinctions drawn by members between "us" and "them." American utopian communities had to contend not only with the periodic panics and depressions that overturned their economies, but also with American opportunity, or at least the belief in it. Wealth as well as poverty was an enemy of the communal experiment. "Buffeted by the gales of laissez faire," William Appleman Williams wrote, "utopian experiments sank in the sea of continental property. They appeared irrelevant, if not stupid or dangerous, to men who assumed that welfare, and wealth, were a matter of time and labor. Albert Brisbane's image of an America organized in self-sufficient communities of 1,600 souls had little appeal to men whose immediate problem was to dispose of cotton and wheat surpluses. And while John Humphrey Noyes was undoubtedly correct in arguing that the jealousy provoked by property and sex caused a good share of men's troubles, the majority preferred the competition to preempt such rights over a disciplined struggle to sublimate their impulses in a cooperative commonwealth."

The early religious communities were often appealing to their European peasant members because of the economic independence and self-reliance they could only achieve communally. The socialist experiments following the inspirations of Owen and Fourier drew more independent farmers, mechanics, and artisans, as well as a brisk seasoning of intellectuals, and for them the possibilities of success elsewhere were closer to Williams's description. The intellectuals, craftsmen, and petit bourgeois drawn to the Oneida community prospered from the sale of traps, silk cord, and silverware, produced largely by wage-earning employees, and were successful enough with their business not to want anything different. The social class of those who joined also clearly affected the type of appeal which would be persuasive.

The socialist programs of the nineteenth-century communities were both criticized and incorporated by the mass political movements and parties which were forming. Marx and Engels found great inspiration in the writings of Fourier and Owen but considered them dreamers with totally unworkable strategies which did not take into account power struggles and relied solely on good faith and reason to overcome deeply clashing material interests. Divorce, women's suffrage, and the general emancipation of women increasingly moved on to the main stage of national politics, although the utopian communities and their publicity helped dramatize the issues. It is ironic that those who defended the family also defended the main agent of its progressive dissolution, capitalism. Those who attacked capitalism and the family brought about reforms which helped to legally rationalize the tendencies of the breakup of the family and the introduction of women into the labor force which was the historic direction of the social and economic system which the reformers so despised.

The dream of a free, communal, egalitarian, and nonrepressive life of attractive labor and sexual satisfaction never died. Neither did the efforts to actually build such communities. There has been not only the dramatic resurgence in the late 1960s, but also a wide variety of socialist, anarchist, religious, and sexually revolutionary communes throughout the twentieth century. Each new wave of popular rebellion has produced a yearning for a less repressive sexuality and, as Frances Wright hoped for Nashoba, institutions which serve human needs rather than humans serving institutional needs. That hope leads some to try to transform the whole society, others to start living the better life right now, forming their own communities and believing others will follow their example. In the mass political movement, despite the constantly erupting pressures toward total human emancipation, the realities of politics lead many people to mistake seizing state power for the whole of revolution, and questions of sexual conduct get shunted aside. Josiah Warren concluded in his old age that the "labor question" was central, and that reformers would just draw public wrath for turning to questions of sex and marriage, however important those might be.

The issues of life are not so easily separated, however. Utopian sex demands utopian economics. And the resolution of the anarchic, self-destructive economy of present-day America through the collective exercise of labor will require as well what Fourier described as "the collective exercise of love."

DAVID MOBERG

A Note on Sources

The best survey of sex and utopias is Raymond Muncy, *Sex and Marriage in Utopian Societies,* (Bloomington: Indiana University Press, 1973, also a Penguin paperback, 1974) source of much of the material in this chapter. The earlier surveys by Noyes and by Charles Nordhoff, *Communistic Societies of the United States,* (New York: Harper and Brothers, 1875, also a Dover paperback reprint), as well as histories of particular phases or communities by Mark Holloway, *Heavens on Earth,* (New York: Library Publishers, 1951). Maren Lockwood Carden, *Oneida,* (Baltimore: The Johns Hopkins Press, 1969); and Arthur Bestor, *Backwoods Utopias,* (Philadelphia: University of Pennsylvania Press, 1950), are standard. Laurence Veysey, *The Communal Experience,* (New York: Harper and Row, 1973); Rosabeth Moss Kanter, *Commitment and Community,* (Cambridge: Harvard University Press, 1972); and John Hostetler, *Communitarian Societies,* (New York: Holt, Rinehart and Winston, 1974), provide both valuable general views and reports on recent communities.

Prostitution in the U.S.

6

In seventeenth- and eighteenth-century New England, very few women had the time to be full-time whores. There were too many jobs for too few people, and since women were even scarcer than men, nearly every marriageable woman found a husband. If she didn't, the occasional spinster or widow could easily find a job as an innkeeper, blacksmith, publisher, butcher, jailer, teacher, or midwife.

There are records of women who "walked disorderly," who committed adultery (and for married women this was a far worse crime than for men), and who bore illegitimate children. There were servant girls who slept with their masters or with other servants; there were betrothed couples who strayed before the ceremony. Church documents and diaries are full of confessions of fornication and premature births, but commercialized prostitution was not a problem.

The early American communities were rural and closely knit. There was much work to be done, and people married young in a spirit of partnership and practicality. The family was a "little commonwealth"—the smaller paradigm of the community. The worst sexual transgressions, then, were those that threatened to destroy the cohesiveness of the social unit—adultery was far more dangerous than premarital sex, and bastardy more of a problem than simple inconsequential fornication.

If some women were linked, Eve-like, to special evils and dangers, they were more likely to be categorized as shrews or witches than as prostitutes. And those wayward saints who presented danger in the sexual sphere by acting seductive or by birthing bastards were welcomed back into the fold rather easily, upon confession, with mild punishment.

In the South the structure of the community established an altogether different basis for the family, for the relationships between the sexes, and thus for illicit sex. In a class society based on landholding, property-owning, and people-owning, sex roles and work roles in the family were much more distinct and formalized; all women—whether the untouchable white goddesses or the less-than-human but ultimately

more touchable black slaves—were in some way outcasts, isolated and alien to men. The black women had no choice: "Resistance is hopeless," wrote one slave woman. "The slave girl is reared in an atmosphere of licentiousness and fear. The lash and the foul talk of her master and his sons are her teachers."

For the upper-class white woman, sex was inevitably linked with slavery, passion with blacks, lust with infidelity. No surprise, then, that sex was repugnant to her. But her husband did not have to go far to gratify his sexual urges. In 1773, a Bostonian reported, after a trip to the Carolinas, "The enjoyment of a negro or mulatto woman is spoken of as quite a common thing; no reluctance, delicacy or shame is made about the matter. It is far from uncommon to see a gentleman at dinner and his reputed offspring a slave to the master of the table. I myself saw two instances of this, and the company very facetiously would trace the lines, lineaments and features of the father and mother in the child, and very accurately point out the characteristic resemblance. The fathers neither of them blushed or seemed disconcerted. They were called men of worth, politeness and humanity."

A stringent double standard said that for rich white men promiscuity was acceptable—indeed, expected—and quite easily accomplished. And who needed to pay for prostitutes when the price of a slave—a permanent receptacle for the "radical insatiability of the Southern male"—was not much more than a few visits to a whore would cost? Even for white men of lower classes black women were fair game. But the name of the game was closer to concubinage or rape than prostitution.

It was not until the nineteenth century—with the rise of industrialization, the growth of the city, the loosening of family ties, and that strange phenomenon which ensconced women in the center of the home, the "Cult of True Womanhood"—that prostitution as an industry began to flourish openly.

While masses of men and women moved away from home industries to cities and factory work, the new mass media spread the image of "the lady"—whose leisure was her status symbol, and whose "piety, purity, submissiveness, and domesticity" were her chief virtues. The icon of the True Woman was the model for middle-class and working women alike.

For women, dignity was oddly imbedded in economics—if True Women stayed home, women who worked must be suspect, even in the realm of sexual purity. And virtuous women—True Women—did not enjoy sex. It was important to be a virtuous woman, since the world of feminine sexuality had only two categories: good women and fallen women. Male sexuality was an ugly monster that demanded satisfaction and lurked even in gentlemen; but sex was fundamentally dirty and not to be done with ladies except to procreate.

Contraception was primitive, and abortion out of the question for most women (it was illegal, immoral, and terribly dangerous). Sex in marriage meant pregnancy, an uncomfortable and physically dangerous condition—given the gynecological ignorance of doctors at the time—that was as repugnant as the original act itself.

So sex played a complicated part in the Victorian family, in spite of its obsession with domesticity. And women who gave in to the monstrosity of male passion, or (worse) enjoyed it, or who had to work for a living, or who in any

Time, Midnight. *Place,* not very far from the Academy of Music.

SERIOUS YOUNG LADY. "Ah! Fanny, *you* coming from the Opera! How long have you been *gay?*"

In the nineteenth century "gay" was a euphemism for "immoral." Note *La Traviata* on playbill.

Prostitution in the U.S.

103

"Go to a brothel and fester in crime; or
to a factory and die of consumption . . ."

Prostitution in the U.S.

other way violated the attributes of True Womanhood, were stigmatized—often even by themselves—as whores.

Prostitutes, as the agents of vice, could also conveniently serve as the guardians of virtue by removing sex from the Victorian home.

The view among the masses of middle-class people and reformers (and a convenient one it was) was that women were *naturally* chaste and virtuous. And although the line between chastity and "soiled dove"-hood was a fragile one indeed, falls from grace were explained away by the principle of victimization. No woman would become a whore unless she had first been raped or seduced or drugged or deserted. The solution, then, was to purify everyone past the point of no return, to arm everyone morally to the teeth so that while even the best of men were hurling their passion everywhere, even the worst of women could resist. Because, of course, once a fallen woman, always a fallen woman; there was no regaining the state of grace.

In the northeastern United States the women by far outnumbered the men by the middle of the nineteenth century; single women had the sexual options of either celibacy or prostitution, since there was no middle ground. They had the economic choice of one kind of degrading work or another kind of degrading work. As Horace Greeley pointed out, public sentiment practically said to women:

Go to a brothel, and fester in crime; or to a factory and die of consumption; or work sixteen hours a day, sewing shirts at ten cents apiece. You may have intellect, scholarship, judgment; you can know as much or more than we . . . but it matters not. You are a woman—so hence to a brothel, or a factory, or a garret!

In 1855 Dr. William Sanger, the physician in residence at a New York women's prison, surveyed 2,000 prostitutes. Only 309 of the 2,000 attributed the origins of their careers to seduction or rape. About half said they entered the life because they were attracted to it, whether because of "inclination," "bad companions," "drink," or "too idle to work." The victimization theory was fast coming unhinged, as was the Victorian idea that sex was only interesting to men. About one-fourth of the women were motivated by "destitution;" 164 claimed "ill-treatment by family" as the prime reason.

Sanger tried to use his study to show that prostitution should be legalized to prevent the spread of venereal disease. By 1870, debates raged in all the state legislatures on the issue of legalization or registration. During the Civil War, Nashville had registered prostitutes for a short time, but as soon as the army moved out, the system was abandoned. In 1870, the Missouri legislature authorized the city of St. Louis to implement a system of registration. The prostitutes were divided into three classes—those who lived in brothels, those who operated outside of brothels, and "kept women." All were visited periodically by doctors, and no registered woman could move without telling the authorities. After four years of constant pressure by outraged citizens, the law was repealed, but prostitution, of course, continued. In all states except Louisiana, Arkansas, and New Mexico, legalization attempts failed. But most cities began to use a sub-official system of registration that kept prostitutes segregated in red-light districts where they could be distanced from and ignored by the rest of the community; this made it easier, too, for police to keep track of prostitutes and to collect protection money regularly.

By the end of the nineteenth century, prostitution in the expanding West had developed from the hordes of women—imported from Mexico, Central and South America—setting up tents and shacks in the mining towns, to a two-class system: the crib girl and the parlor girl. "By the time I got to San Francisco [in 1898]," one madam reminisced, "the rich cocksmen were demanding class." But a strange kind of class it was. The parlor houses in the East were part of a whole system of upper-class excess and opulence; the men who frequented them also went with their wives to the Astor House, and aspired to be millionaires. But in the West, the parlor house was an anomaly, an oasis of gentility and splendor in a world of crudity, hardship, and recklessness.

The cribs were little shacks where the prostitutes worked but did not live. "A crib girl on a weekend night could take on a hundred studs or they'd say she wasn't trying. There was a color line—cost for a Mexican two bits. A nigrah whore, Chinese or Japanese asked fifty cents. All those who claimed they were French, seventy-five. A Yankee girl cost a dollar."

San Francisco's Barbary Coast, the scene of the cribs, bordered on Chinatown where Chinese women—imported as slaves by men, and madams like the infamous Ah Toy (who started out as a slave herself and ended up supplying Chinese whores to the entire country)—operated out of cribs and parlors. The rumor was that "Chinese girls they have cunt go east-west, not north-south like white girls." This was a

stroke of merchandising genius, because then they could charge two bits to look, four bits to feel, and then when the white johns were positive that anatomy was ignorant of color, six bits to do it. In the cribs, "everything was for speed and bed. . . . A crib drew no color line; men of all tints were serviced." There were different parlor houses for rich Chinese men—some of them supplied only with white women—and for white men, catering to an imaginary "idea of China, all in musk, sandlewood, teak, silk hangings, gods, scrolls and wall paintings . . . girls in Oriental costume, hair piled up and shiny, ready to be treated as a slave or toy."

Outside Barbary Coast and Chinatown, and located discreetly on respectable streets, were the fancy parlor houses run almost like finishing schools, with the madams presiding over elegant stables: educating their girls to be polite company for the lawyers, politicians, and businessmen who were their clients, and serving sumptuous meals and good liquor in luxurious settings. The ambience of a private club and the company of other men was as important here as the business that went on upstairs. "Were it not for the previous knowledge of the character of the house the visitor would never know but that he was in the private parlor of a wealthy gentleman, and his beautiful and affable companions were the brightest stars in the most respectable society—so chaste are their manners and conversation," one commentator mused, pointing out that "in Eastern cities the prostitute tried to imitate in manner and dress the fashionable respectable ladies, but in San Francisco the rule was reversed—the latter copying after the former."

Storyville, New Orleans, where Nell Kimball

Parlor girls on the Barbary Coast in the 1890s.
"Were it not for the previous knowledge of the character of the house the visitor would never know but that he was in the private parlor of a wealthy gentleman . . ."

Prostitution in the U.S.

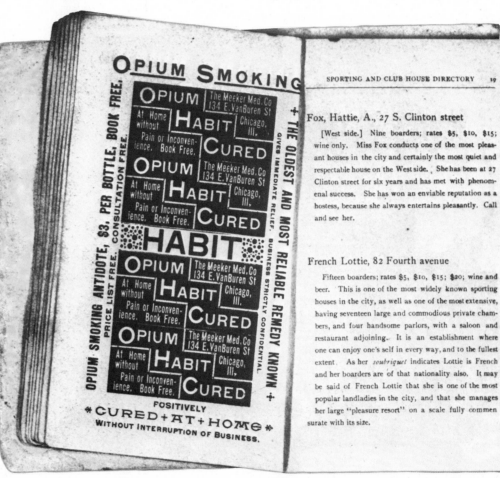

Fox, Hattie, A., 27 S. Clinton street

[West side.] Nine boarders; rates $5, $10, $15; wine only. Miss Fox conducts one of the most pleasant houses in the city and certainly the most quiet and respectable house on the West side. She has been at 27 Clinton street for six years and has met with phenomenal success. She has won an enviable reputation as a hostess, because she always entertains pleasantly. Call and see her.

French Lottie, 82 Fourth avenue

Fifteen boarders; rates $5, $10, $15; $20; wine and beer. This is one of the most widely known sporting houses in the city, as well as one of the most extensive, having seventeen large and commodious private chambers, and four handsome parlors, with a saloon and restaurant adjoining. It is an establishment where one can enjoy one's self in every way, and to the fullest extent. As her *soubriquet* indicates Lottie is French and her boarders are of that nationality also. It may be said of French Lottie that she is one of the most popular landladies in the city, and that she manages her large "pleasure resort" on a scale fully commensurate with its size.

A nineteenth-century guide to Chicago's houses of prostitution. (Courtesy Chicago Historical Society.)

spent twenty years as a madam, was famous as a red-light district. Here the houses were so ubiquitous and so competitive that yearly guidebooks with elaborate descriptions were printed for prospective customers. In Storyville prostitution was legalized in 1897, although madams still had to pay protection, since "the graft went on just the same and they could close you up for leaky plumbing or keeping old newspapers out back as a fire hazard."

Prostitution in the U.S.

Nell Kimball advised in her autobiography, *The Life of An American Madam by Herself:*

Furnishing a sporting house called for some sense and a lot of feeling for the customer's comfort, habits, and little tricks. . . . I had put in a lot of Venice glass over the gas jets and drapes of blood-red velvet reaching to the floor and had eight girls I had picked out myself, some from as far away as St. Louie, San Francisco, and two high yellows I called Spanish, and nobody gave a damn what they were, after they went upstairs for wick dipping or *neuf-soixant.* . . . Girls and gentlemen ate the best. The silver and the dishes were heavy and good. Wine came in dirty bottles with the right labels for the johns who knew what they wanted. Not all men who come to a cathouse are cunt-crazy. . . . Linen is a big item, and a house can go busted if that isn't watched, counted, marked, and sent to the best wash-tub mammy in town who had the top whorehouse trade. I always changed linen after every customer, but some houses only did it every day. And the cribs, they just had a gray sheet on a pallet and maybe never changed it, just threw it away when nobody would lie down on it.

I never had truck with the idea whores had hearts of gold, and I never turned a girl down because she was rabbity and jumpy, what they later called neurotic. They made the best whores sometimes. If a madam can't handle girls, she's better out of the business. The girls make or break a house, and they need a solid hand. You had to watch out for lesbians among them, and while I didn't mind the girls doing a bit of chumming and coupling up for clitoris-bumping, if I found a dildoe, I knew it had gone too far. Girls that become libertines with each other don't satisfy the johns because they are involved with themselves. . . . The guest must always be protected from anything that could cause a ruckus and expose him to scandal. It's amazing how much peace of mind a man needs, after a certain age, to fuck properly. . . . I paid the girls one third of what they earned and never held back, and I didn't shark them with interest on loans I made them, or get them on drugs or have them mulcted by fancy men like some houses did. I never cottoned to the sweet daddies that attached themselves to a girl's earnings and lived off her twat. There is nothing in life lower than a pimp, unless it's some politicians I've known.

Nell Kimball "never liked procurers but used them when I had to."

. . . I didn't take or want drugged girls, heavy drinkers, or girls with bruises all over them. A good whore has to *want* to be a whore, or she's no credit to the place. The trouble with forced girls is they usually lead to trouble. Besides, there was never any real shortage of willing girls who wanted to be whores. . . . It's true the Italians and the Eastern European ponces have an underground railroad to bring in girls attracted by promises of honest jobs and so are lured into the trade, but I never dealt much with them. At least not until the rage for red-headed Jew girls took on in the town.

Of course, the madams of high-class parlor houses never dealt much with procurers, but in fact white slavery was a burgeoning problem all over the world in the early twentieth century. While the parlor house madams were conducting their genteel business, pimps and cadets (procurers) were going into small towns, offering jobs as governesses, maids, actresses, and singers to country girls. "Once in a city, they were made drunk, drugged, and woke up in a whore house, raped, their clothes gone, and they were beaten if they didn't go to work accepting all comers."

Meanwhile, the general attitude toward prostitution had shifted from the victimization theory, with an emphasis on individual responsibility, to a more complex assessment of all the sociological factors that affect behavior. Abraham Flexner's report on vice, published in 1914, stressed that urban life, with all its complications, was the perfect breeding ground for commercialized prostitution. And this was the rallying cry of the reformers who set out to eradicate prostitution and the white slave traffic, along with their apparent causes—poverty, bad working conditions, liquor, drug addiction, dance halls, and a lack of sex education.

In Chicago, while the notorious Everleigh sisters were running their exclusive club, publishing brochures to advertise their Southern hospitality at $50 a throw plus food and drink, Jane Addams was rehabilitating immigrants and country girls at Hull House. In her writings she recounted story after story of the young innocent who had been welcomed at Ellis Island by a fellow countryman, only to be lured off to a brothel; or who had met a young man at a dance, fallen in love, come to the city to marry him, and found herself instead one of a pimp's stable. These girls could not return home, in many cases could not escape the dilapidated brothels, and certainly never saw the money they earned.

Vice commissions in various cities took up the problem, and found that as Jane Addams had warned, immigrant women were "as valuable to a white trafficker as a girl imported directly for the trade." Sanger's report had shown that 1,238 of the 2,000 prostitutes interviewed were foreign-born. Public sentiment toward immigrants was confused for a variety of reasons, and nativists were convinced that aliens were not simply victims of the white slave trade—that in fact international networks of vice, mostly run by Russian Jews and southern Italians, were the victimizers; foreigners were all either whores or whoremongers. The whoremongers ostensibly operated according to the Ellis Island scheme, or through private employment agencies which "were used as markets for selling girls for prices varying from $3 to $50 or as procuring places where immoral women and men came and selected their victims."

Organizations like the Immigrant's Protective League, the National Young Women's Christian Association, and the National Council of Jewish Women began to do preventive social work, visiting the docks with leaflets warning, "Beware of those who give you addresses, offer you easy, well-paid work, or even marriage. There are many evil men and women who have in this way led girls to destruction."

It seemed as if prostitution and the white slave trade had become synonymous; if the latter could be eradicated, surely the former would be also.

More radical social thinkers, like anarchist Emma Goldman and her circle of friends, believed that the problem of prostitution went

Prostitution in the U.S.

deeper than the cadet system, and was older than the current white slavery scare. Goldman herself had once resorted to walking the streets to raise money for an assassination scheme—unsuccessfully, since "when I looked at the passing men and saw their vulgar glances and their manner of approaching the women, my heart sank. . . . Something stronger than my reason would compel me to increase my pace the moment a man came near me."

"To the moralist," Goldman commented bitterly in "The Traffic in Women," an essay she published in her journal, *Mother Earth:*

> prostitution does not consist so much in the fact that the woman sells her body, but rather that she sells it out of wedlock. . . . Yet a prostitute, if properly defined, means nothing else than 'any person for whom sexual relationships are subordinated to gain'. . . . Not that the gratification of sex must needs lead to prostitution; it is the cruel, heartless, criminal persecution of those who dare divert from the beaten track, which is responsible for it. . . . Whether our reformers admit it or not, the economic and social inferiority of woman is responsible for prostitution.

Goldman was convinced that the cadet system which caused such a sudden furor was "the direct outgrowth of police persecution, graft, and attempted suppression of prostitution." She warned that further suppression would only increase the degradation of the prostitute and do little to eliminate the institution as a business. For her the problem of the immigrant woman—which had captured the Progressive imagination—was superfluous.

There is no reason to believe that any set of men would go to the risk and expense of getting foreign products, when American conditions are overflooding the market with thousands of girls.

But the exportation of American women was a much graver issue; she cited the shipping of New England girls to Panama "for the express use of men in the employ of Uncle Sam" and she charged that

> in Hong Kong, Shanghai, and Yokohama, the Augean stables of American vice are located. There American prostitutes have made themselves so conspicuous that in the Orient 'American girl' is synonymous with prostitute.

For Goldman sexual happiness was not possible in marriage either, as long as capitalism shaped people's lives and relationships. Both prostitutes and wives were victims of the thoroughly degrading conditions imposed by "Property Morality"—and the only way to abolish prostitution was to abolish industrial slavery and to absolutely restructure all accepted values. She was no prude, but dreamed of a world where "the rapture of love, the ecstacy of passion which reaches its culminating expression in the sex embrace," could take place in dignity and freedom.

Havelock Ellis, one of the earliest sex researchers, pointed out that "the wife who married for money, compared with the prostitute, is the true scab. She is paid less, gives much more in return in labor and care, and is absolutely bound to her master. The prostitute never signs away the right over her own person, she retains her freedom and personal rights, nor is she always compelled to submit to man's embrace."

But these were lone voices, speaking before the world was ready to listen.

The Mann Act of 1910, which outlawed the transportation of women across state lines for immoral purposes, and subsequent state laws prohibiting pandering and compulsory prostitution, effected the closing of most red-light districts before World War I. With U.S. involvement in the war, the government prohibited prostitution within five miles of army camps and naval stations. Storyville, the last legal red-light district, was finally closed down in 1917. Here "every man wanted to have one last fling of screwing before the real war got him. Every farm boy wanted to have one big fuck in a real house before he went off and maybe was killed. . . . It wasn't really pleasure at times but a kind of nervous breakdown that could be treated only with a girl between him and his mattress. Some were insatiable and wrecked themselves, and some just went on like the barnyard rooster after every hen in sight," Kimball said. "I dreamed one night the whole city was sinking into a lake of sperm."

After the red-light districts were closed, prostitutes began to operate increasingly through call houses—where dates were arranged, but not consummated—and out of bars, dance halls, and on the streets. The transaction could culminate in a hotel room or a car. Bordellos still existed but had to make their presence less felt than ever before. Madams moved around frequently to avoid police harassment; periodic arrests and protection payments were the requisite dues for madams and whores.

The advent of the freewheeling flapper shook

the business very little. And the Depression, like the Great War, improved business by leaps and bounds. Polly Adler, a notorious New York madam, wrote of the stock market crash, "I had almost more customers than I could take care of. . . . Some men who had been terrific womanizers now came to the house solely to drink, and no longer showed the slightest interest in my girls. . . . Others, who had been casual customers, now came in nightly and behaved like satyrs. The atmosphere, at times, was more that of an insane asylum than a bordello."

Adler was an unwilling witness during the investigation of New York City corruption led by Judge Seabury in 1930-31, which exposed an extortion ring earning profits off prostitutes and alleged prostitutes. Lawyers, policemen, judges, and bondsmen, who had been blackmailing women accused of prostitution—whether they were actually whores or not—were investigated, fined, fired, and jailed. "Whatever else it may have accomplished, ironically enough, the Seabury investigation turned New York into a wide-open town," Adler commented. "The police no longer were a headache; there was no more kowtowing to double-crossing Vice Squad men, no more hundred-dollar handshakes, no more phony raids to up the month's quota. In fact, thanks to Judge Seabury and his not-very-merry men, I was able to operate for three years without breaking a lease."

Even though sex outside of and before marriage was becoming less and less stigmatized; even though women who enjoyed sex were no longer automatically considered whores (and so practically destined to become whores); even though boys could increasingly "get their cherries copped" by their girlfriends, prostitution

Prostitution in the U.S.

In *Tricks of the Trade* a call girl explained:

Very few men want ordinary sexual intercourse from a call girl. . . . If you don't encourage them, they'll settle for ordinary sex because they don't want to offend you. There are men who want me to go down on them but who are very nervous about suggesting it. This is mostly the case with men who don't have much experience as johns and who don't realize that the average girl has some sort of oral sex with—oh—the vast majority of her tricks. . . . Almost every john wants this at least some of the time, and there are regulars who never want anything else but.

Not to mention vibrators, dildoes, whippings, fetishes, and therapy sessions. The whore's room is a fantasy realm where anything can be suggested, said, or done, and whether or not the john can truly get what he thinks he wants, he has purchased the whore's time and body to try.

All a man has to do is hear of something new and you know he wants to try it. For instance, the expression *sleeve job.* Do you know the expression? Well, as far as I know, it all comes from an old joke. A man wants a sleeve job and no one will give it to him or even tell him what it is, and finally he finds a desperate old streetwalker who agrees to do it, but on the way to her place he slips on a banana peel and dies and so he never does find out what a sleeve job is. And that's the punch line, because there is no such thing.

At least, I don't think there's any such thing, but wouldn't you know that every couple of months someone asks, in all seriousness, for a sleeve job, and sometimes they have an idea of what it is that they want, and other times all they know is the name, 'a sleeve job,' and have no idea.

Men continue to make prostitution an economically profitable profession, and women, who still—in 1975—are undervalued and underpaid in every profession, continue to opt for those profits. As one hooker explained, "It's very *hard* for women to earn an adequate living and so we do not have much economic choice—even the call girl. And the minority woman on the street—the poor woman—she has no choice at all.

"For white women you usually can't say that there's no choice between working for somebody else and going into business for yourself. . . . Prostitution on those terms is a kind of laissez-faire capitalism. But it's also slavery."

It is also currently a crime in every state but Nevada; a crime committed by two people, only one of whom is usually punished. Policemen arrest the prostitute but not the client, since, as sociologist Kingsley Davis put it, "Though the service is illegitimate, the citizen cannot be held guilty, for it is both impossible and inadvisable to punish half the populace for a crime. Each citizen participates in vital institutional relationships—family, business, church, and state. To disrupt all of these by throwing him in jail for a mere vice would be, on a large scale, to disrupt society." But prostitutes are already outcasts, and streetwalkers (usually minority women), who are the most outcast, are arrested more often than call girls. The enforcement of this particular law reflects a glaring discrimination according to sex, class, and race.

But it's not as if the legalization of prostitution would do anything to eliminate the business,

A call girl in a madam's apartment in New York City.

Prostitution in the U.S.

nor the degradation that comes along with it. It would simply legitimize pimps as brothel owners, or transfer the role of pimp directly to the state. It would not, contrary to what Sanger said more than a hundred years ago, eliminate the spread of venereal disease, since a new customer could reinfect a prostitute at any time; in fact, prostitutes who receive low doses of penicillin every day to curb infection find that new resistant strains of the disease develop which are immune to the dose.

The feminist movement of the 1960s gave birth to a new consciousness of the whore as a paradigm of, even the epitome of, the exploited woman. It has also, for the first time, created a common ground where the hookers and reformers work *together* to change things. The feminist who feels that all women are whores in a sexist society is right in one sense. We are all economically dependent on men (although less and less so), whether we are wives, employees, girlfriends, call girls, or streetwalkers. But it's important not to let the metaphor cloud the realities of the real prostitute's actual experiences. The woman who accepts dinner from a man in return for a quick lay is a world away from the hooker who daily faces arrest; violence from clients, police, and pimps; venereal disease; and the prospect of twenty tricks to turn by morning.

In 1973 an ex-hooker from San Francisco, Margo St. James, formed a coalition of women—housewives, hookers, feminists, lawyers—who work at decriminalizing prostitution and provide legal aid, medical help, and job counseling for prostitutes. This "loose woman's organization" is called COYOTE (Call Off Your Old Tired Ethics). "To be able to fulfill a need of a fellow human being, and profit by it, is good

business, besides being an act of faith and sometimes charity," St. James avers.

The point is that ultimately it is every woman's right to decide what to do with her body in private. In a society where sex is considered a normal, healthy human activity, and where women can easily get well-paying, satisfying jobs, women are less likely to choose to sell their bodies. Prostitution—like working in a factory—is degrading and horrible, but all the more so because the prostitute, as victim of economic and sexual conditions, is also the one who is held legally responsible for those conditions. Neither illegalization nor legalization changes the status of the prostitute; neither eliminates prostitution. But decriminalization would at least eliminate the most oppressive aspects for the prostitute—the harassment, the brutalization, the stigma—as long as "good business" is the basis for human interactions.

SALLY BANES

Far left: a working girl; *left:* Margo St. James.
"Call off Your Old Tired Ethics!"

Prostitution in the U.S.

Solange—a call girl.

Prostitution in the U.S.

A Note on Sources

John Demos, "The American Family in Past Time," *American Scholar* 43 (1974): 422-46 was the source for colonial sexual behavior, as was Edmund S. Morgan, "The Puritans and Sex," *New England Quarterly* 15 (December 1942): 591-607. Useful accounts of relationships in the South include Linda Brent, *Incidents in the Life of a Slave Girl,* edited by L. Maria Child (New York: Harcourt Brace Jovanovich, 1973; originally published privately, 1861); Winthrop D. Jordan, *White Over Black: American Attitudes Toward the Negro, 1550-1812* (Chapel Hill: University of North Carolina Press, 1968); Anne Firor Scott, *The Southern Lady: From Pedestal to Politics 1830-1930* (Chicago: University of Chicago Press, 1970); and Julia Cherry Spruill, *Women's Life and Work in the Southern Colonies* (Chapel Hill: University of North Carolina Press, 1938; reprinted New York: W. W. Norton, 1972). For attitudes toward women and work in the nineteenth century, I have relied on Barbara Welter, "The Cult of True Womanhood 1820-1860," *American Quarterly* 18 (1966): 151-74; Gerda Lerner, "The Lady and the Mill Girl: Changes in the Status of Women in the Age of Jackson," *Midcontinent American Studies Journal* 10 (1969): 5-14; and Robert W. Smuts, *Women and Work in America* (New York: Columbia University Press, 1959; Schocken Books, 1971). Vern Bullough, *The History of Prostitution* (New Hyde Park, N.Y.: University Books, 1964) gives a short but thorough overview of American prostitution, and Curt Gentry, *The Madams of San Francisco: An Irreverent History of the City By the Golden Gate* (Garden City, N.Y.: Doubleday, 1969) provides an account of prostitution in the West. For nineteenth-century whoring, William W. Sanger, *The History of Prostitution: Its Extent, Causes and Effects Throughout the World* (New York: Harper and Brothers, 1858) gives data and analysis of his survey of New York prostitutes;

Robert E. Riegel, "Changing American Attitudes Toward Prostitution (1800-1920)," *Journal of the History of Ideas* 29 (1968): 437-52 traces shifts in public opinion, while Nell Kimball, *Nell Kimball: The Life of an American Madam by Herself,* edited by Stephen Longstreet (New York: Macmillan, 1970) gives a lively account of an inside view. For material on the Progressive fervor to stanch prostitution and white slavery, I am indebted to Riegel and to Egal Feldman, "Prostitution, the Alien Woman and the Progressive Imagination, 1910-1915," *American Quarterly* 19 (1967): 192-206. Also useful were Jane Addams, *A New Conscience and an Ancient Evil* (New York: Macmillan, 1912); The Vice Commission of Chicago, *The Social Evil in Chicago* (Chicago, 1911; reprinted New York: Arno, 1970); *International Agreement for the Suppression of the White Slave Traffic, Signed at Paris on 18 May 1904, Amended by the Protocol Signed at Lake Success, New York, 4 May 1949* (Lake Success, New York: United Nations Publications, 1950). The best source for Emma Goldman's life and work is her autobiography, *Living My Life* (New York: Knopf, 1931; Dover reprint, 1970). "The Traffic in Women" is included with other important essays in Alix Kates Shulman, ed., *Red Emma Speaks* (New York: Random House, 1972). Polly Adler, *A House Is Not a Home* (New York: Rinehart, 1953) is the autobiography of a madam, a chatty look at the New York scene in the 1920s and 1930s. John Warren Wells, *Tricks of the Trade* (New York: New American Library, 1970) is a salacious but illuminating series of interviews with modern call girls and streetwalkers; for a sensitive study with feminist commentary, see Kate Millett, *The Prostitution Papers: A Candid Dialogue* (New York: Avon Books, 1973; also in Vivian Gornick and Barbara K. Moran, eds., *Woman in a Sexist Society,* New York: Basic Books, 1971).

Wishbones, Condoms, Pessaries, and the Pill

A History of Birth Control

7

Even now, in 1975, with enormous quantities of literature on birth control and an endless assortment of birth control devices, gadgets, and techniques, women still have pregnancies that lead to abortions, "shotgun" marriages, and unwanted children. For many of us the questions of whose responsibility it is and what techniques to use are a highly volatile part of our sexual relationships; but the easy availability of effective contraceptives as well as the frankness with which many of us discuss the subject are new phenomena. We are led to wonder what our grandmothers and grandfathers—and their grandmothers and grandfathers—knew about birth control. Just how much control *did* they have over when they were going to have children and how many children they were going to have? Where did they find out about birth control? Where did they get their contraceptives? These are not easy questions to answer when asking about generations which tended to deal with sexuality—publicly at least—by denying that it existed. In looking to public sources

we have to remember that before 1938 it was illegal—even for physicians—to import, mail, or prescribe birth control devices. It is easy to see why our knowledge about the history of birth control has been so limited; particularly so when its past has been filled with misinformation, moral and religious speculation, and outright quackery.

A well-informed, eighteenth-century authority on birth control, Musitanus, could write the following on the subject:

> Passionate coitus is to be avoided, for it is unfruitful. Sometimes the woman does not draw back her buttocks, and conquers as is the custom of Spanish women who move their whole body while they have intercourse, from an excess of voluptuousness (they are extraordinarily passionate), and perform the Phrygian dance, and some of them passionately sing a song . . . and on account of this Spanish women are sterile.

Apart from his genuine interest in the sexual

charms of Spanish women, about which he wrote with some authority, Musitanus was doing nothing more than echoing the sentiments of the father of gynecology, Soranos, who had written more than 1,700 years earlier that too much passion in women resulted in sterility. This belief persisted in medieval Christian thought and could be written about not as belief or speculation but as fact by Musitanus.

Contraception is so intimately tied to the baffling question of sexuality that it has fallen heir to everyone's ambivalence, squeamishness, and fantasies, and this has resulted in some curious practices. German folk medicine prescribed willow tea for women to prevent conception; drunk boiling hot it would drive away all unchaste desires. This prescription was inherited from the Romans and was commonly used until the beginning of the twentieth century. Other folk cures required suspending hare dung and mules' hides and hanging children's teeth arranged in silver platters over women's beds to prevent pregnancy. Polish immigrants in this country used a technique specifying that

> A young girl in order to prevent children, takes a few drops of her menstrual blood and lets it flow into a hole in the first egg of a young hen. She then buries the egg near the table in the room. There the egg remains for nine days and nine nights. When the egg is taken up it will be found to contain worms with black heads. She will have as many children as the egg contains worms. If she throws the egg with the worms in it into the water she will have the children; if she throws it into the fire, they will burn up once and for all.

One of the curiosities in the history of birth control is the frequency with which women's fingers appear in contraceptive rituals. Serbian women in this country placed "as many fingers in a child's first bath as they desire years of freedom from pregnancy." Another culture attributed the years of childlessness to the number of fingers that the bride sat on in her wedding coach. Bosnian brides put their hands in their wedding girdles when mounting their horses, one finger for each year without children; putting both hands in simultaneously induced sterility. Another folk belief had it that "if a woman carries on herself the finger of a premature child, or if she drinks the urine of a ram or of a hare, she will not conceive. The same is the case if a thorn is extracted from the foot of a living weasel and a woman wears it."

There is a certain whimsy in these practices that Dr. Freud would have appreciated, but some techniques imported to this country were surprisingly sophisticated. Cervical caps made of beeswax—precursors of the modern diaphragm—were used by German and Hungarian women. Each one was individually made from an impression taken from the woman's cervix, insuring a perfect fit. Another common practice was to insert a sponge, or in some cases a small linen rag, into the vagina to stop the sperm from traveling any farther up into the female reproductive organs. Frequently these were soaked in solutions, such as lemon juice, that were highly effective; at other times ineffectual, even poisonous, solutions were used.

Prior to the twentieth century the most sophisticated contraceptive device in common use was the condom, commonly referred to as a "rubber," "safe," or "French letter." As early as the sixteenth century articles of this sort were

Wishbones, Condoms, Pessaries, and the Pill

A nineteenth-century
gynecological examination.
Just how much did our
grandmothers know?

Wishbones, Condoms, Pessaries, and the Pill

used in Europe for the prevention of venereal disease and, from the eighteenth century on, for birth control. The first mention of condoms is found in the work of the sixteenth-century Italian scientist, Fallopius, who claimed that he had invented a linen sheath which was custom-fitted to the male member and provided effective protection against syphilis. Fallopius, apparently a practical man, cited as one of the advantages of his invention that it could be carried around in the pocket and produced instantaneously when the need arose.

Another theory as to the origin of the condom is that it was discovered by a slaughterhouse worker in medieval times who first used the membranes of animal organs to protect himself against disease.

By the seventeenth century the article was in common use in France where Mme. de Sévigné, in a letter to her daughter, counseled her on the use of the condom and described it as "armor against enjoyment, and spider web against danger."

By the eighteenth century it had become a common item of trade in whorehouses all over Europe; it was known in France as an English Riding Coat and in England as a French device. And as early as the eighteenth century we read about men rankling at the idea of having to use a condom. Casanova wrote in his memoirs that he was not inclined "to shut myself up in a piece of dead skin in order to prove that I am perfectly alive."

The first mention of the condom in English appears in the eighteenth century in the work of a London doctor, Daniel Turner, who wrote ". . . the *Condom* being the best if not the only Preservative our Libertines have found out at present; and yet by reason of its blunting the Sensation, I have heard some of them acknowledge, that they had often chose to risk a *Clap* rather than engage *cum Hastis sic clypeatis* [with spears thus sheathed]."

The condom boom, however, awaited the technological advances of the nineteenth century and the successful vulcanizing of rubber by Goodyear in 1843. Almost instantaneously a large industry sprang up in the production and distribution of condoms. The next major advance in condom production was the introduction of liquid latex to the industry and the use of fully automated assembly lines—both in the 1930s. Condom production soared and mass marketing and distribution made it an item as common in gas stations and coffee shops as Coca-Cola. Currently, close to one billion condoms are sold every year in this country, and it is now possible to get pastel condoms; extra thin ones for greater sensitivity; tips; and lubricated condoms.

But where did Americans before the turn of the century get their information about birth control? The earliest American writings on the subject date from the second quarter of the nineteenth century. The first published tract was Robert Dale Owen's *Moral Physiology,* published in 1830. Judging from the numerous editions that appeared, it was a well-read book (75,000 copies had been sold by the time of Owen's death in 1877). Owen's advice was at times questionable, but he covered most of the forms of birth control common at the middle of the century. His first recommendation was "coitus interruptus," or male withdrawal prior to

Wishbones, Condoms, Pessaries, and the Pill

orgasm, which he felt was practical and feasible for all but the most hot-blooded of the male sex.* Owen mentioned the sponge, which he thought was ineffective and uncomfortable. Finally, he wrote about condoms, which he had heard were perfectly effective, though he found them, for reasons which he didn't elaborate on, "inconvenient." Owen's writing becomes lyrical when he talks of the future of birth control, of which he wrote with uncontained optimism.

> In the silent, but resistless progress of human improvement, such a change [the widespread use of birth control] is fortunately inevitable. We are gradually emerging from the night of blind prejudice and of brutal force; rational liberty and cultivated refinement win an accession of power. . . . It is not a question whether such reforms will come: no human power can arrest its progress.

In 1832 Dr. Charles Knowlton anonymously published the *Fruits of Philosophy,* a book which was considered to be the first major work on contraception since the classical texts of Soranos and Aetios. In it he recommended douching as the most effective form of birth control. He listed elaborate douching solutions composed of "astringent vegetables such as white oak bark, hemlock bark, rose leaves, green tea, rasberry leaves, sulphate of zinc, baking soda." On the other hand he was "quite confident that a liberal use of pretty cold water would be a never-failing

preventative." He advised douching two or three times within five minutes after coitus. Knowlton was convinced that he had invented douching and praised it for its sureness, cheapness, simplicity, and because it did not interfere with the sexual act itself. Knowlton was one of the few writers at the time who showed much sensitivity to vaginal problems. He and Owen were also the first to argue that birth control should be in the hands of women, rather than men.

Of his work Knowlton wrote that he felt he was "rendering a signal service to a frail and suffering humanity;" and to do both Knowlton and Owen justice, it must be said that they wrote with a good deal of integrity, limited though they were by a lack of information about effective birth control methods. Both men argued for a measured and dispassionate examination of the subject, and consequently both stand out against much of the popular literature on birth control in the nineteenth century which was filled with exaggeration, mystification, and misinformation.

One very popular work published in 1847 by A.M. Mauriceau entitled a *Married Woman's Private Medical Companion* contained this bit of questionable puffing for the author's own technique. "Its efficacy is beyond question," he wrote, "as in Europe among the higher classes, especially, it is universally used . . . of late among all classes. Thousands of married persons have for years used it with invariable success . . . it preserves and conduces to the health of the female, by eradicating all predispositions to sexual weakness, fluor-albus or whites, the falling of the womb, and restores and maintains elasticity and firmness of the

---

* It is now known that since only 50 percent of men ejaculate in one powerful gush, and for the rest semen flows out in small quantities before and after climax, this method is not reliable.

Wishbones, Condoms, Pessaries, and the Pill

generative function." Unfortunately, Mauriceau was the exclusive distributor of this "French Secret," and we can't send in our check or money order for the ten dollars that he charged to find out what his technique was. Probably it was some form of douche or vaginal suppository.

Some of the advice given in these nineteenth-century birth control manuals was quite dangerous. In a well-known pamphlet published in 1856, J. Soule recommended the following for destroying sperm: opium, prussic acid, strychnine, iodine, and alcohol. No advice was given on proper doses or possible side effects resulting from the use of these drugs. Numerous pamphlets erroneously testified that during the middle part of the woman's menstrual cycle she was infertile. Though most writers didn't claim infallibility for this technique, it was highly recommended in many texts.

Other commonly suggested, and novel, contraceptive techniques that appeared in the nineteenth century include jumping, running, stomping, sneezing, coughing, and belching. Referred to as "movement cures," these techniques were alleged to cause quick contractions of the uterus after sexual intercourse, thus preventing pregnancy. One writer declared:

> Some women have that flexibility and vigor of the whole muscular system that they can, by an effort of will, prevent conception.
> They can by a voluntary bearing-down effort compress the abdominal muscles upon the pelvic viscera as the cause of the uterus to contract with a degree of force that expels the impregnated egg or at least causes it to be moved from the point where the impregnation occurred.

Though not a major force in the contraceptive history of this country, John Humphrey Noyes of the Oneida community practiced a method of male control known variously as Male Continence, Karezza, Magnetation Method—in Latin, *coitus reservatus*. This technique allows for full sexual intercourse, without ejaculation, however, so that the penis gradually shrinks inside the vagina without spilling any seed. The Oneida community used this technique very successfully. An essential part of their method, however, was training young men in the company of experienced women who, in case of an accident, couldn't conceive.

Noyes was well-informed about birth control and chose this method over all of the other possibilities, consciously rejecting condoms, douches, and sponges as "unnatural, unhealthy, and indecent, and of course, destructive to love." The Oneida community was notorious in the nineteenth century for the attention that it paid to sexual satisfaction for both sexes.

By the middle of the nineteenth century, at least among the middle and upper-middle classes, birth control information was widespread. A New England doctor in 1867 could write that "there is scarcely a young lady in New England—and probably it is so throughout the land—whose marriage can be announced in the paper without her being insulted within a week by receiving through the mail a printed circular offering information and instrumentalities, and all needed facilities by which the laws of heaven in regard to the increase of the family may be thwarted." Other nineteenth-century doctors corroborated this fact, and judging from the quantities of birth control devices confiscated by Anthony Comstock (a professional crusader

Wishbones, Condoms, Pessaries, and the Pill

Anthony Comstock.
In 1880 alone he confiscated over 64,000
"articles for immoral use of rubber, etc."
and over 700 pounds of "lead moulds for
making Obscene Matter."

Wishbones, Condoms, Pessaries, and the Pill

127

against obscene literature) it would seem that these articles were widely circulated. In 1880 alone he confiscated over 64,000 "articles for immoral use of rubber, etc." and over 700 pounds of "lead moulds for making Obscene Matter."

The medical profession in the nineteenth century was determined to make itself look good while working both sides of the street; publicly doctors claimed that birth control wasn't any of their business, while privately they collected fees from grateful clients. All in all it was a very neat job of public relations. It is worth remembering, though, that public confidence in medicine reached an all-time low in the early nineteenth century. It had been an uphill fight for doctors to solidify their status as professionals, and in the course of it, they learned to be shifty about questions as controversial as birth control. They were also quick to dissociate themselves from anything that smacked of quackery—and birth control in the nineteenth century smacked of just that. So, on the whole, a better-safe-than-sorry philosophy prevailed.

Articles on birth control finally did begin to appear in medical journals in the last quarter of the century. Some of these articles were remarkably "enlightened." In 1882 an article in the *Michigan Medical News* by O.E. Herrick argued that since people were going to find out about and practice birth control anyway, it might as well be in the hands of professionals—to wit, doctors. The author went on to argue that self-induced abortions, frequently fatal, could be eliminated by widespread dissemination of information about birth control. Finally, he argued that no woman should be a mother unwillingly. He attacked the medical profession and wrote

that "medical teachers and writers have pandered to the notion spread among the people by the priesthood, that it is their [women's] duty to raise many children." The article generated replies from doctors which tended to support his arguments.

Six years later, in 1888, the first symposium on birth control took place in the *Medical and Surgical Reporter*. The editors' justification for having the symposium is of interest. First, they argued, contraception was important because of the relationship between population size and the economic well-being of the nation. Second, it was essential for women to be healthy in order to be good mothers and wives. Finally, the editors wrote:

> No medical man of any experience can fail to know that the propriety and feasibility of preventing conception engages, at one time or other, the attention of a large proportion of married people in civilized lands . . . there is a danger that an undue dread of discussing it frankly in medical circles may deprive medical men of the means of properly directing a disposition which cannot be ignored and which, in the present state of human nature and civilization, it seems impossible to eradicate.

The medical profession was in a quiet and belabored way screwing up the courage to talk about birth control.

They weren't about to rush into anything, though. The American Medical Association ignored the whole business until 1912 when its president, the renowned pediatrician Abraham Jacobi, citing the rising costs of welfare, the high birth rate of the immigrant communities, and the hardships of poverty, concluded that "only a certain number of babies should be born into the world."

It wasn't until the late 1930s that the AMA finally took a position in favor of birth control. Until the mid-sixties the government, too, had not been willing to support birth control. As recently as 1959 President Eisenhower could say, when asked about the federal government's relationship to birth control: "I cannot imagine anything more emphatically a subject that is not a proper or political or governmental action or function or responsibility. . . . That's not our business."

With a government that vacillated between self-righteousness and squeamishness, and with a medical profession that was at best wishy-washy, the task of forcing changes in legislation, popularizing the movement, and making birth control information widely available fell upon a group of nonprofessional, politically conscious women.

The foremost of these was Margaret Sanger who was part of a left-wing, highly visible group of New Yorkers at the turn of the century. Sanger turned out to be the perfect messiah for this mission: she had a revolutionary zeal about birth control which she was capable of turning into stirring appeals; she had a good strategic sense which she was able to refine with each succeeding battle; and she was a splendid organizer. One gets a vivid sense of her personality from the description in her autobiography of how she got involved in the birth control movement. Working as a nurse, she had visited a patient who was recovering from a near-fatal, self-induced abortion. The doctor had warned her not to get pregnant as this would seriously endanger her health; the only contraceptive that

he would recommend was that her husband sleep on the roof. Sadie Sachs got pregnant again, and died in 1912 from the effects of another self-induced abortion. Sanger left her patient's house deeply upset and

walked and walked and walked through the hushed streets. When I finally arrived home and let myself quietly in, all the household was sleeping. I looked out my window and down upon the dimly lighted city. Its pains and grief crowded in upon me, a moving picture rolled before my eyes with photographic clearness: women writhing in travail to bring forth little babies; the babies themselves naked and hungry, wrapped in newspapers to keep them from the cold; six-year-old children with pinched, pale, wrinkled faces, old in concentrated wretchedness, pushed into gray and fetid cellars, crouching on stone floors, their small scrawny hands scuttling through the rags, making lamp shades, artificial flowers; white coffins, black coffins, coffins, coffins interminably passing in never-ending succession. The scenes piled one upon another. I could bear it no longer.

As I stood there the darkness faded. The sun came up and threw its reflection over the house tops. It was the dawn of a new day in my life also. . . .

I was resolved to seek out the root of the evil, to do something to change the destiny of mothers whose miseries were as vast as the sky.

Margaret Sanger's initial battle was to make birth control a subject that could be discussed openly and publicly. It was a battle that was to go on for decades. Her first confrontation with the government came after the publication of

BIRTH CONTROL REVIEW

Edited by Margaret Sanger

NOVEMBER, 1923

Official Organ of
THE AMERICAN BIRTH CONTROL LEAGUE, INC., 104 FIFTH AVENUE, NEW YORK CITY

Family Limitation, a birth control pamphlet which was released in 1914 in an edition of 100,000 copies. In the pamphlet she talked about the need for birth control intelligently and unapologetically. Unfortunately, as far as offering practical advice, she could do no more than rehash nineteenth-century information on the subject.

It wasn't until the twenties that Sanger was to find out about and begin to smuggle Mensinga diaphragms into this country. These diaphragms were the invention of a German doctor in the 1880s. Used in conjunction with a spermicidal jelly, they constituted a genuine advance in contraception—the *only* major advance in the first part of the century.

In the early part of the century the movement began to get support from unexpected quarters. It had become known that the native American —WASP—birthrate was less than half that of the immigrant birthrate. "Race Suicide!" President Teddy Roosevelt screamed in 1903. "Among human beings, as among all other living creatures, if the best specimens do not, and the poorer specimens do, propagate, the type [race] will go down." Put more directly, "doubtless there are communities which it would be in the interest of the world to have die out." Chilling; but birth control—for the masses—was becoming acceptable to a certain class of Americans.

Under Sanger's leadership the birth control movement changed from a movement of feminists, anarchists, and communists—or so the press had it—to a cause directed by upper-middle-class women. More and more the rhetoric became that of the upper-middle class. In 1918 Sanger wrote that "all our problems are the

Wishbones, Condoms, Pessaries, and the Pill

Margaret Sanger—diaphragm smuggler.

result of overbreeding among the working class." One of the leaders of her national committee put it even more clearly. "My family on both sides were early Colonial and pioneer stock and I have long worked with the American Coalition of Patriotic Societies to prevent the American people from being replaced by alien or Negro stock, whether it be by immigration or by overly high birthrates among others in this country." A little dose of racism was to do the cause of birth control a world of good, making it at last a "respectable" American activity in the

Wishbones, Condoms, Pessaries, and the Pill

METHOD	Constant User Rate	Average User Rate
Pill	99.5%	—
I.U.D.	98 %	94%
Diaphragm	97.5%	86%
Condom & Foam	99 %	95%
Condom	97 %	86%
Foam or Creams	97 %	71 %
Rhythm	86 %	61 %

Contraceptive technology 1973–1974,
Emory University.

company of what came to be called population control.

But some of the real problems of contraception were just beginning to come into focus. The Mensinga diaphragm, douches, and various types of intravaginal and intrauterine devices, when properly used, were reasonably effective in preventing pregnancies; but all of these created their own problems. Wishbones, stems (two types of intrauterine devices), and cervical caps caused infections. The common practice of leaving the Mensinga diaphragm in for weeks at a time created another host of problems. Douching solutions frequently caused irritations that led to infections.

By the mid-twenties the pace of medical research into these questions and research on new contraceptive techniques was stepped up; experiments were made with vitamin treatments, X rays, diathermy of the testicles, subcutaneous injections of sperm, and the use of hormones. But as late as 1946 a medical authority looking back over the preceding decades could report that "no striking discoveries" had been made.

There were a few good tries though. In the 1920s two independent researchers discovered that ovulation occurred twelve to sixteen days before the beginning of menstruation. They concluded that by avoiding intercourse during that period pregnancy could be averted. Their work was popularized by Leo Lautz in *The Rhythm of Sterility and Fertility in Women.* Finally, after years of work, a technique had been found which was believed to be effective and which was acceptable to almost everyone. The American Medical Association, in a show of uncommon ebullience, lauded it and proclaimed that it was, moreover, "free from criticism on

Wishbones, Condoms, Pessaries, and the Pill

religious and social grounds." After the initial brouhaha it became clear by the end of the thirties that most women's cycles were not regular enough for this method to work effectively. By the 1940s doctors had reversed their position on rhythm and resigned themselves to prescribing the diaphragm and contraceptive jelly.

It is one of the curiosities of the history of contraception that one of the oldest and most effective devices was to be one of the last ones "discovered" by modern medicine. For thousands of years people have known that small objects left in the uterus prevent pregnancy. Camel drivers in the Middle East for centuries have placed small stones in the uteri of their camels on long trips to prevent pregnancies, and Hippocrates, an ancient Greek physician, described an early intrauterine device (IUD) which was inserted through a lead pipe.

In 1909 a German doctor, Richard Richter, made a device of silk wrapped around a ring and secured by a very fine bronze wire. The IUD was then fitted in the patient's uterus, and proved very successful. For reasons which are hard to fathom, his discovery went unnoticed. In the following decade numerous bulky and poorly made devices of this sort were made and prescribed. These frequently caused serious uterine infections, and the more responsible part of the medical profession stopped prescribing them. In the 1930s another German doctor rediscovered Richter's ring and began making a highly effective device out of silk for his private patients. There was still no response from the rest of the profession until the late 1950s when an Israeli and a Japanese doctor independently rediscovered the device.

Though IUDs are now commonly used no one really knows how they work. They affect neither ovulation nor fertilization. What *is* known is that when an IUD is used, fertilized eggs are dead when they reach the uterus. Though effective, IUDs are frequently difficult to insert and for many women difficult to retain. Other side effects include severe cramps, heavy menstrual bleeding, and irregular bleeding.

The only major advance that has been made by medical science in this century is the development of the Pill, an easy to use oral contraceptive that is virtually 100 percent effective. In the early 1950s Margaret Sanger and the Planned Parenthood Federation encouraged a biologist—Dr. Gregory Pincus—working at the Worcester Foundation of Experimental Biology to develop a new contraceptive. Pincus came up with the idea of using two artificially produced female hormones—estrogen and progesterone—to regulate ovulation. Taken in twenty or twenty-one day cycles the Pill works by imitating the functions of the female body during pregnancy. When an egg has been fertilized, progesterone and estrogen are produced in large quantities preventing the pituitary gland from releasing two chemicals, FSH and LH, which are necessary for the production of new eggs. The Pill mimics the body's defenses against overlapping pregnancies by preventing the pituitary gland from releasing FHS and LH, thus preventing ovulation. In addition, the synthetic progesterone prevents conception by thickening the mucus at the opening of the uterus to such an extent that sperm cannot penetrate this barrier.

The Pill was further researched and eventually marketed by G.D. Searle Co. In 1956 tests were made on the first human guinea pigs, 256 Puerto

I.U.D.

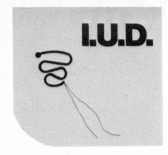

JELLY

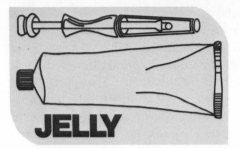

FOAM

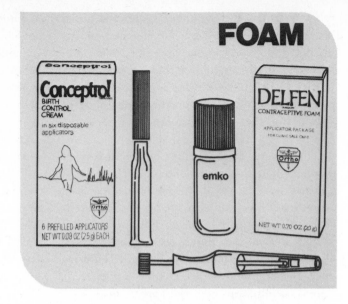

RHYTHM

DIAPHRAGM

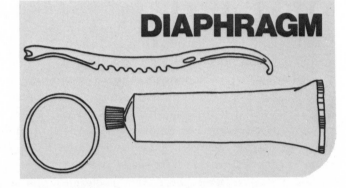

CONDOM

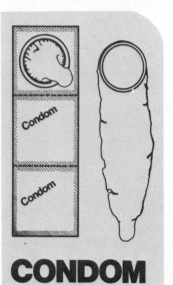

For many of us the questions of whose responsibility birth control is and what techniques to use are a highly volatile part of our sexual relationships—our world is clearly different from our grandparents'.

PILLS

Wishbones, Condoms, Pessaries, and the Pill

Rican volunteers "from the low income population living in a housing development project in a slum clearance."

Though nearly 100 percent effective as a birth control device, it turned out that the Pill had some nasty side effects: fluid retention, nausea, blood clotting, and a greater likelihood of getting certain kinds of cancer. For women who have had cancer, thromboembolism, heart disease, sickle cell anemia, or a stroke the Pill is prohibited. So even the Pill has not solved the problem of birth control.

Ours is clearly a different world from our grandparents'—these days lavender condoms are advertised in family magazines; fourteen-year-old girls take birth control pills that they get on prescription from their family doctors; and the government and medical profession are outspoken supporters of birth control. We do have more control over our bodies because of advances in contraceptive techniques, and greater freedom to decide if and when we want children. And for large numbers of us there is less and less conscious connection between sex and children—which marks a revolutionary change in our consciousness. But, with all of this, until there is a benign contraceptive that is foolproof, and until we resolve some of our own ambivalence about sex, the troublesome question of birth control and its relationship to sex and babies remains very much an open one.

TEM HORWITZ

A Note on Sources

The *Birth Control Handbook* published by the Montreal Health Press, Inc. in 1973 contains a great deal of information on the current state of contraception, as well as some information on the history of birth control. David M. Kennedy, *Birth Control in America: The Career of Margaret Sanger,* (New Haven and London: Yale University Press, 1970), is an excellent biography of Margaret Sanger as well as a highly informative history of the birth control movement. This book also contains an excellent bibliography. *A History of Public Health* by George Rosen, (New York: M.D. Publications, 1958), contains some good material on the birth control movement. Norman E. Himes, *Medical History of Contraception,* (Baltimore: Williams and Wilkins, 1936), is the best work on this subject, and the source of much of the material in this essay on early contraceptive techniques in this country. Margaret Sanger and Hannah Stone, eds., *The Practice of Contraception,* (Baltimore: Williams and Wilkins, 1931), contains much information on contraception in the first third of this century. *Complaints and Disorders: The Sexual Politics of Sickness,* by Barbara Ehrenreich and Deirdre English, (Old Westbury, N. Y.: The Feminist Press, 1973), is a good study of women and the medical profession in the nineteenth and early twentieth centuries.

Sex in Two Dimensions

Erotic Movies

8

Once upon a time, there was an exotic dancer named Fatima whose popularity led to the naming of a cigarette after her. And one of the reasons for this popularity was that she had shaken her ample proportions in front of Edison's primitive motion picture camera, thus becoming the world's first acknowledged erotic film star. The short film of Fatima's dance is available from the Museum of Modern Art, as is Edison's notorious film of John Rice and May Irwin recreating their torrid kiss from a long-forgotten Broadway success of 1896. Neither film, after eighty years, is very arousing but histories have to begin somewhere. Even if May and John were not the first lovemakers on screen, they were indeed the first to be singled out by moralists as corruptors of movie audiences.

Prints of Fatima's dance circulated with black bars printed across the offending portions of her anatomy, but the Rice-Irwin smooch played the hinterlands uncut and unretouched. It was not until 1908 that municipal censorship of movies came into existence, and not until a year later that the National Board of Review was born. Surprisingly, the board appears to have been formed not specifically to execute wholesale repression of films, but to protect filmmakers from unwarranted censorship by singling out not only films unworthy of public exhibition but also films eminently worth seeing. Still, perhaps the dual nature of America's first censorship agency is not so surprising, given the ethic of Progressivism, a dedication to the proposition that well-intentioned professionals could systematically reorder the habits and the morality of the American public and thus free the way for incalculable progress.

As Progressivism brought the United States the income tax, settlement houses, popular election of senators, time-and-motion study, Prohibition, and a war to make the world safe for democracy, so too the film review movement brought some imposed form of prior censorship to most communities by the beginning of the 1920s. The first decade of the century had already seen the emergence of relatively risque peep-show films, like *One Way of Taking a*

Girl's Picture and *Her Morning Exercise* (in which, for a penny, a viewer could peer into a slot and watch a woman clad in undergarments or tights walk about, undress, or exercise). And in the teens filmmakers took on such subjects as white slavery, prostitution, drug addiction, venereal disease, sex education, birth control, and abortion.

In 1913, for example, Universal Pictures released a film based on the Rockefeller White Slavery Commission report, *Traffic in Souls,* which grossed a quarter of a million dollars and led many other companies to follow Universal's lead. Films like *The Serpent of the Slums* and *Port of Missing Women* picked up the white slavery theme; and elements of this trend can even be seen in D. W. Griffith's *The Musketeers of Pig Alley* and *Intolerance.*

Apart from Universal, none of the companies producing films on sex-related themes, in that pre-1920 era of seemingly endless legal battles and outbreaks of open warfare among rival film crews, grew to major status. By 1920, the movies had grown into a respectable industry, and only the small, independent companies seemed willing to supply the franker, more explicit product that the majors couldn't get away with in marketing. The Hays Office, created by the industry itself in 1922 to force film production companies to adhere to rigid guidelines regarding what could or could not be depicted on screen, forced the production of sex-exploitation films virtually underground. Of course, this had always been true of genuinely dirty movies, which had begun to circulate only a few years after the birth of the film industry.

Stag films, like *A Free Ride* (*circa* 1915), which is housed in the Kinsey Institute Collection, were never actually distributed, but were shown locally by itinerant showmen whose existence was neither officially sanctioned nor recognized. Surely a good many more films like *A Free Ride* were made to be shown at club smokers and private parties and were subsequently lost, given the fragility of the nitrate film stock used at that time. Judging from the evidence of this particular relic, the plotless, graphic format of the stag film is as old as the movies themselves.

Though established filmmakers like Cecil B. De Mille and Erich von Stroheim employed nudity and perversion in their works in the early years of the 1920s, the Hays Code, and later the Motion Picture Production Code of 1934, kept American films fairly tame. De Mille's films, as Gerald Mast rightly points out, exploit naughtiness in order to sell conventionality, and religion in order to dwell on lewdness; but neither his biblical nor his reportorial films display enough conviction or dwell forthrightly enough on their sexual content to warrant the label exploitative. Von Stroheim is another case. His films are always wonderfully perverse, as much in their naturalism as in their subject matter. But Von Stroheim's career as a Hollywood director, first at Universal and later at Metro, was virtually over by 1924. (Irving Thalberg, who worked at both studios in the 1920s, had the unique and, in retrospect, disastrous opportunity to fire Von Stroheim twice.)

As long as films were silent, exploitation features and shorts could be produced fairly cheaply; but with the introduction of sound, producers were forced to take technical factors more into account, and hence to upgrade their product. Working under studio conditions, producers of exploitation features were turning out films by 1930 that were virtually indistinguishable technically from the typical low-budget Hollywood feature. *Child Bride,* one of the more interesting films of this period, was made by Harry Revier (whose earlier film *The Slaver,* made in 1927, dealt with the selling of a white girl to an African chieftain by a dissolute sea captain). Revier's film was typical of the sort of film that played the exploitation market. Its somber theme, the evils of child marriage in the backwoods of Kentucky, gave the director many opportunities to depict the evil he was supposed to be attacking. Though the young girl suffers one humiliation after another in *Child Bride,* the audience is clearly meant more to be enticed by the frequent shots of her bared bosom than touched by the seriousness of her plight.

During the thirties and forties, the pattern set by the early exploitation features persisted. Most of the handful of pictures released each year were cheap melodramas (*Wages of Sin, Forbidden Oats, Honky Tonk Girls*) little different from the nineteenth-century stage melodramas or the confessional literature of the 1850s. All three forms offered sufficient voyeuristic delights to make up for the Victorian moral (a woman once fallen can never entirely redeem herself) that invariably ended the piece. Even the few films with obviously serious intentions fell into this pattern. Kroger Babb, one of the producers of exploitation features in the late forties, made two such films, one a sex-education feature called *Mom and Dad* (which featured the on screen birth of a baby and grossed $40 million, according to one of its owners); and the other, an anti-drug film called *Wild Weed,* that starred Lila Leeds, an actress who was arrested along with Robert Mitchum in that infamous drug bust in 1948. Both *Mom and Dad* and *Wild Weed* (as well as a later Babb feature, *One Too Many,* an anti-alcoholism film that starred Ruth Warrick) preached the thesis that ignorance of the facts of life could lead to addiction, disease, and destitution.

For the most part, the exploitation market throughout the thirties and forties was ruled by a small group of independent producers known collectively as the "Forty Thieves." The films they produced, like the race pictures that played the segregated theaters throughout the South and in the Northern ghettos, played in theaters specializing in exploitation films. The number of these theaters was small relative to the number of legitimate houses (though some theaters, like the grind houses on Forty-second Street, made little distinction in their programming policies between Hollywood B-pictures and exploitation pictures); so any given exploitation picture might make the circuit of exploitation houses more than once. The advent of drive-in theaters helped the exploitation market a bit, but for the most part the supply of films never seriously threatened to exceed the demand. Where a typical Hollywood film would run a week or two in a first-run house, close and reopen in a second-run house two weeks later and run for two or three weeks more, close and reappear on the third-run circuit four weeks later, the typical exploitation product would play a theater for a week and reopen in the same theater six months later.

The advent of television posed as great a threat to the exploitation industry in the late forties and early fifties as it did to the mainstream Hollywood product. While the major studios searched for gimmicks like 3-D and

Burlesque films never enjoyed
much of a vogue.

Sex in Two Dimensions

widescreen processes to convince waning audiences that "movies were better than ever," exploitation filmmakers responded with burlesque films (among them *Strip Tease Girls,* starring the incomparable Tempest Storm) and "nature" films. Burlesque films never enjoyed much of a vogue; but the nature films represent a significant change of direction, both legal and thematic, in the exploitation industry.

The *cause célèbre* of 1955 was a nudist camp film called *Garden of Eden,* which purported to be a documentary record of the activities of a nudist colony in a remote part of Florida. *Garden of Eden* had been denied an exhibitor's license by the Motion Picture Division of the New York State Education Department, and the decision was upheld on appeal to the Regents of the University of the State of New York (the final arbiter of all censorship cases involving movies shown in the state). By the middle of 1957, the case of the distributor *Excelsior Pictures* vs. *the Board of Regents* had reached the Court of Appeals of the State of New York; and in an opinion handed down by Judge Charles Desmond (July 3, 1957), the court found that nudity *per se* was not indecent, and that the film *Garden of Eden* could therefore be exhibited. "There is nothing sexy or suggestive about [the film]," Desmond wrote. "Nudists are shown as wholesome, happy people in family groups practicing their sincere but misguided theory that clothing, when climate does not require it, is deleterious to mental health by promoting an attitude of shame with regard to natural attributes and functions of the body." There was no suggestion of sexual activity in the film, no purposeful contact, no references at all to the "private"

parts of the body—apart from the obvious fact that everyone in the film had them. Male and female genitalia were never actually shown.

Family magazines like the *National Geographic,* Desmond went on, regularly portrayed nudity (a fact nearly every pre-adolescent schoolboy in America was grateful to confirm); and besides, the Supreme Court, in the matter of *Joseph Burstyn, Inc.* vs. *Wilson,* had found that "expression by means of motion pictures is included within the free speech and free press guarantees of the First and Fourteenth Amendments to the Constitution." The issue had been clouded, of course, by the fact that nude women in *National Geographic,* as Kenneth Turan and Stephen Zito accurately pointed out, were "primitive" and, most important, nonwhite; but Desmond ignored this distinction and concluded simply that nudity on film was not by itself the definition of pornography.

The Desmond decision, needless to say, was greeted ecstatically by the producers and would-be producers of nudist camp movies. As long as the films openly advocated nudism, and as long as thousands of respectable people practiced its tenets, the nudist films could never be accused of lacking redeeming social value. And since decisions of New York censors were looked upon as informal national guidelines, nudist films seemed to be perfectly legal throughout the country. So after 1957, and continuing well into the mid-sixties, nudist films like *My Bare Lady, Hollywood Nudes Report, 1,000 Shapes of the Female,* and *The Nude and the Prude* came rolling regularly off the exploitation production line.

The principal figures in the exploitation industry in the late fifties were David F. Friedman, director of the nudist musical *Goldilocks and the Three Bares,* who operated out of Chicago; William Mishkin and Joseph Brenner in New York; and Daniel Sonney in Los Angeles. The total output in the nudist market, Friedman reminisced recently, was about eight or ten pictures a year in 1957.

> The fifty or sixty theaters that had to play this stuff played each one of these pictures ten or twelve weeks, gave you a fair percentage, and you made a fortune with it. I bought a drive-in in Joliet and I had one of the first nudie houses in Chicago back when Chicago had a very tough police censorship board and everything had to be submitted to that board. And I dare say that it was more profitable then than it is today when you don't have to submit anything and they're playing hard-core in Chicago.

Like virtually every other area of American popular art, the nudist films were rigidly formulaic. There are always conventions in a country's culture, but popular culture is almost *totally* conventional. So it was with the nudist films: the plots were limited to a few favorites, the characters were stereotyped, the ideas espoused were simplistic, and the metaphors, images, and values were highly conventionalized. Male and female genitalia were never shown, only implied by the bare breasts and buttocks of the actors. And nearly every performer in a nudie film was a professional actor—audiences would not tolerate authentic, unphotogenic nudists in nudist films.

Since nudity and occasional bodily contact (generally in the course of some wholesome activity like a volleyball match or touch football game) were the films' major selling points, the highly formulaic plots were only serviceable vehicles. Typically, a nudie film related the story of how a sweet young girl is initiated into nudism by an experienced man. Within this context, the filmmaker could show scenes of brutality (the girl being undressed forcibly for the first time), voyeurism (a reporter or detective venturing into a nudist camp in search of a missing person or criminal), and seduction (implied but never depicted). All the while, the narrator was assuring the audience that it was watching a genuine documentary extolling the virtues of nudism.

Frontal nudity finally made it into the nudist films with John Lamb's *The Raw Ones* (1966), a nonerotic though cleverly promoted tribute to nudism and attack on censorship, that included as part of its narration quotations from Bertrand Russell and Thomas Jefferson. The film was an astonishing success ($3,400 in one night at one Los Angeles theater); and, though it ran into severe legal complications for its depiction of the male penis and female pubic hair, *The Raw Ones* was eventually cleared for public exhibition under the Supreme Court guideline that nudity, even full frontal nudity, was not of itself obscene. In October of 1967, the film received an exhibition clearance from the notoriously severe Maryland State Board of Censors.

Lamb followed *The Raw Ones* with *She Did It His Way,* starring Kellie Everts, Miss Nude Universe; but by the early sixties American audiences had already discovered the films of Russ Meyer, films that displayed a technical resourcefulness far beyond the capacity of most makers of sex-oriented films. And the Meyer product had something that the simple pictorial records of well-endowed actors-*qua*-nudists frolicking and avoiding contact with one another didn't have—they had humor.

Russ Meyer's *The Immoral Mr. Teas* (1959) is arguably the most important sex film ever released in the United States. "The public was waiting for something new," Meyer recalls. "I think they were becoming disenchanted with the so-called European sex films, like some of the early Lollobrigida pictures in which there's a lot of promise but never any kind of real fulfillment. . . . There were a number of secondary art houses that were floundering and they were looking for product. It was this field that we were able to jump into."

The "real fulfillment" that Meyer offered was hardly more than that of the nudist films. What he did offer was a frank portrayal of nudity as a sensual delight. Meyer was not interested in rationalizing nudity, nor was he out deliberately to play down the purely entertaining aspects of his film in order to give it that air of social uplift that producers thought was essential in order to slip their work past the censors. *The Immoral Mr. Teas* was a comedy about sex, whimsically structured, expertly photographed, and enormously successful. It set the course for erotic films for years to come.

Mr. Teas was the second collaboration between Russ Meyer and Peter DeCenzie, owner of a burlesque house in Oakland, California, the El Rey Theater. Several years previous to 1959, the two had completed *The French Peep Show,* a burlesque film starring Tempest Storm and shot on the stage of DeCenzie's theater. Out of this initial collaboration grew *The Immoral Mr. Teas,* which was largely improvised over a period of four days in 1959, on a budget of just over $24,000. The film realized a profit of over $1 million.

In the role of Mr. Teas, Meyer cast Bill Teas, a friend from their army days (where Meyer had learned his trade as a combat cameraman traveling with Patton's Third Army). Meyer acted both as director and cinematographer; Edward Lasko contributed the screenplay and accordion accompaniment. The plot of the film is episodic, a feature that persists in nearly all erotic features. Teas is a delivery man for a dental supply house; he delivers false teeth and mentally undresses virtually every girl he sees. In his pink overalls and straw hat, riding around town on his bicycle, Teas is the archetypal girl-watcher whose fantasies match the fantasies of most of the males in the audience. All women appear to him in the nude; and in this sense, Meyer's visual techniques presage by more than a decade the devices used by Ernest Lehman in his wretchedly "serious" adaptation of Philip Roth's *Portnoy's Complaint.*

Though controversial—and an enormous financial success—*The Immoral Mr. Teas* was anything but hard-core pornography. Leslie Fiedler noted in a review for *Show* magazine that the film displayed

no passion . . . no contact, no flesh
touching flesh, no consummation shown or
suggested. For pornography the woman's
angle of vision is necessary, but there were
no women outside of Bill Teas's head; and
Bill Teas was nobody's dreamed lover, but
only a dreamer, with his half-modest,
half-comical beard, his sagging pectoral
muscles, his little lump of a belly creased by

Aroused. ". . . a frank portrayal of nudity
as a sensual delight. . . ."

baggy shorts or hidden by overalls. . . . Mr. Teas conducts his odd business and carries his frustrated dreams through a world of noncontact and noncommunication. [The film's] makers have not attempted to surmount the difficulties which confront the American moviemaker who desires to make nakedness his theme; but they have, with absolute good humor, managed at once to bypass and to illuminate those difficulties. The end result is a kind of imperturbable comedy, with overtones of real pathos.

Still, given the innovative use of nudity in the film, *Mr. Teas* was destined to create a new image for the sex-exploitation film. It played theaters that had never before shown exploitation films; it made Russ Meyer both a celebrity and a millionaire, and according to one estimate spawned more than 150 imitations in the three years following its release. Though, "when we finished it," Meyer reminisces, "we couldn't get a release anywhere. . . . Six months went by, and Pete DeCenzie found himself in Seattle, Washington, with a print of the film. Seattle had a censor board, and Pete met a fellow *paisan* who was one of the board members. And he said, 'Well, why don't we come up to my room and bring the board up there and I'll get a lot of wine and we'll eat some raviolis and I'll show you the film,' which was a most unusual way for a censor board to review a picture. So the fellow *paisan* says 'Atsa nice,' and they all went up there and they passed the picture in a hotel room." *The Immoral Mr. Teas* played three years in Seattle.

After *Mr. Teas,* Meyer "immediately made another film with a lot of nudity and big tits and all that stuff. I copied myself maybe ten, eleven more times." Some of these copies included *Eve and the Handyman, Erotica, Europe in the Raw,* and *Heavenly Bodies.* David Friedman, one of the top producers of nudist films, now entered this new market with *The Adventures of Lucky Pierre;* other entries in the field included *Not Tonight, Henry* (Ted Paramore), *The Prude and the Parisienne* (Robert Gurney, Jr.), and *Sinderella and the Golden Bra* (Paul Mart). All the films tried to copy the *Mr. Teas* formula: voluptuous women in varying stages of undress and a wry approach to the battle of the sexes. If nothing else, the era of Russ Meyer produced a style of exploitation film that was technically proficient and often quite funny, a style that presented nudity with all its sexual overtones, but without explicit sexual content.

Arthur Knight and Hollis Alpert, in their *Playboy* "History of Sex in the Cinema," wrote that "the Nudie-Cuties of the early sixties offered a broad burlesque of sex—purveying asexual nudity and depicting the male as a bumbling buffoon rather than a lover. . . . The voyeuristic nature of these early nudies is perhaps the most striking thing about them. The hero does not crave sex; he just wants to look."

This went on for nearly five years; and between 1959 and 1964, the Meyer-inspired exploitation features dominated the sex film market. As with most developments in American popular culture, one genuine innovation was enough. Those who followed in Meyer's footsteps kept well within the boundaries of the genre. *Not Tonight, Henry,* a broad, slapstick comedy by Ted Paramore and Bob Heidrich, grossed more than $500,000 on an initial investment of $40,000 (a fairly high production budget for an exploita-

From the film
The Corporate Queen.

Sex in Two Dimensions

tion feature, but one necessitated by the fact that Paramore used union crews and some fairly established performers). The star of the film was Hank Henry, a nightclub comic and close friend of Frank Sinatra (with whom he had appeared in *Pal Joey, Ocean's Eleven,* and *The Joker Is Wild*).

The plot concerns a fat, sexually frustrated husband who daydreams of erotic escapades with notorious women of history, among them Cleopatra, Empress Josephine, Delilah, and Pocahontas. The nudity in the film was unexceptional, though the prolongation of some of the nude shots got the film into trouble both with the California courts where it was cleared of obscenity charges, and the New York State Board of Censors where all but eleven minutes of the film, according to *Variety,* would have been eliminated by the cuts the board ordered. In the New York case, even the opening credit sequence had to go.

John McCarthy's *The Ruined Bruin* and *Pardon My Brush* combined nudity without sex and knockabout comedy, and are among the best examples of the genre. Barry Mahon's *Nude Scrapbook, Naughty, Naughty Nudes,* and *Nude Las Vegas* are more typical: nudity, no sex, burlesque humor, a certain technical gloss which cannot, however, disguise the trimmed scenes, makeshift sets, and inexperienced actors that indicate severe cost-cutting, and a few obvious (though useless) stabs at dramatic involvement. The average budget for a Mahon feature was ~und $15,000; and by 1962, he was producing veen fifteen and twenty films a year.

an interview with *Film Comment,* Mahon rked that his was not the kind of business e one looked for "the single picture that is to make us rich. We are looking for the

business that's like turning out Ford cars or anything else. If there is a certain profit per picture, and we make so many pictures, then we have established a business that is on a basis that is economical." On a $15,000 investment, Mahon generally realized between $40,000 and $60,000; his total output was over sixty films by 1964.

But by then the public's appetite had been sufficiently whetted—and the question of nudity in movies sufficiently tested in the courts—that mere nudity on film was no longer enough. One of the directions in which exploitation films began to move was toward the sex-and-violence features, movies that exploited dismemberment, torture, flagellation, defloration of the most brutal variety, sexual humiliation, and wholesale slaughter. David F. Friedman, one of the men who had easily made the transition from nudist films to nudie films, now turned his talents to what the trade referred to as roughies.

Friedman's first roughie was released in 1963 and entitled *Blood Feast.* Doubling as producer and screenwriter, Friedman and director/cinematographer Herschell G. Lewis managed to finish the film in four days and realize, ultimately, a $1.2 million profit over their initial cost of $20,000. But *Blood Feast* was only the first title in what was to become Friedman's "Blood Trilogy."

Friedman and Lewis shot *Two Thousand Maniacs* the next year in St. Cloud, Florida. This time Friedman designed the film and did the sound, while Lewis acted as writer, director, cinematographer, and composer of the theme music. A variation on the *Brigadoon* theme, *Two Thousand Maniacs* starred Connie Mason,

Sex in Two Dimensions

whose appearance in *Blood Feast* had led to a *Playboy* centerfold and, of course, a good deal of publicity for the film.

Friedman's approach to violence was much more direct than his approach to sex, indicating perhaps that the portrayal of violence in films—whether in exploitation movies or in "serious" films—has always seemed easier to filmmakers, both legally and artistically, than the portrayal of sex. *Two Thousand Maniacs* featured an amputation of a woman's thumb, an axe murder, a drawing-and-quartering, and assorted rapes. And all this in the context of the story of a group of Northern vacationers who are victimized by the inhabitants of a Southern town during the course of a Civil War centennial celebration. As the film ends, and the two survivors return to the site of the town with the state police, it becomes clear that the town (now vanished) materializes once every 100 years for the celebration of ritual murders of unwitting Northerners.

Color Me Blood Red, the third installment in the Friedman-Lewis trilogy, tells the story of a demented artist who murders his models and uses their bright blood for the red in his canvases. The "Blood" films of David Friedman are his most grotesque; but all his roughies contain elements of bizarre, cruel sex. *The Defilers,* loosely based on John Fowles's novel *The Collector* and directed and photographed by R. Lee Frost, parodies the novel while at the same time capturing some of its tensions. *She Freak,* another Friedman roughie, is based on Tod Browning's classic film *Freaks;* while subsequent Friedman efforts incorporated the characters of Fanny Hill, Zorro, and Trader Horn.

Two Thousand Maniacs was considered too

rough by the Kansas State Board of Censors; and numerous cuts—including one of a horse running with an amputated leg trailing behind it on a rope—were ordered. Though no actual amputations, decapitations, or other species of physical defilement were actually shown in the Friedman roughies, enough was implied and enough close-ups of victims screaming in agony were included to make the grotesque points with absolute clarity.

Even Russ Meyer negotiated the transition into roughies with *Lorna, Mud Honey, Motor Psycho, Common Law Cabin,* and *Faster, Pussycat! Kill! Kill! Kill!* Meyer's action films were less lush than his sex-exploitationers, generally in black and white and incorporating whippings, hangings, beatings, fist fights, lust, hate, and realistically motivated sex and nudity.

Lorna was typical of this group. Sex definitely plays a strong supportive role to violence here, as Meyer recounts the tale of a voluptuous young woman (Lorna Maitland) whose rape by an escaped convict leads first to unexpected sexual liberation, but then to violence and death. Lorna is married to a naive young man who is unable to satisfy her lusts. After the rape, she brings her assailant back with her to the couple's shack; and when the husband interrupts their ensuing lovemaking, a fight ensues during which both Lorna and the convict are killed.

Elemental in its morality, unexceptional in its nudity (despite the mammoth physical proportions of Ms. Maitland), *Lorna* proved a sound investment for Meyer and expanded the circle of theaters willing to book exploitation features. The reviews for the film were good; even the traditionally cautious Richard Schickel called it "a film of preachment against hypocrisy, exhib-

A scene from
the motion picture
*The Female:
Seventy Times Seven.*

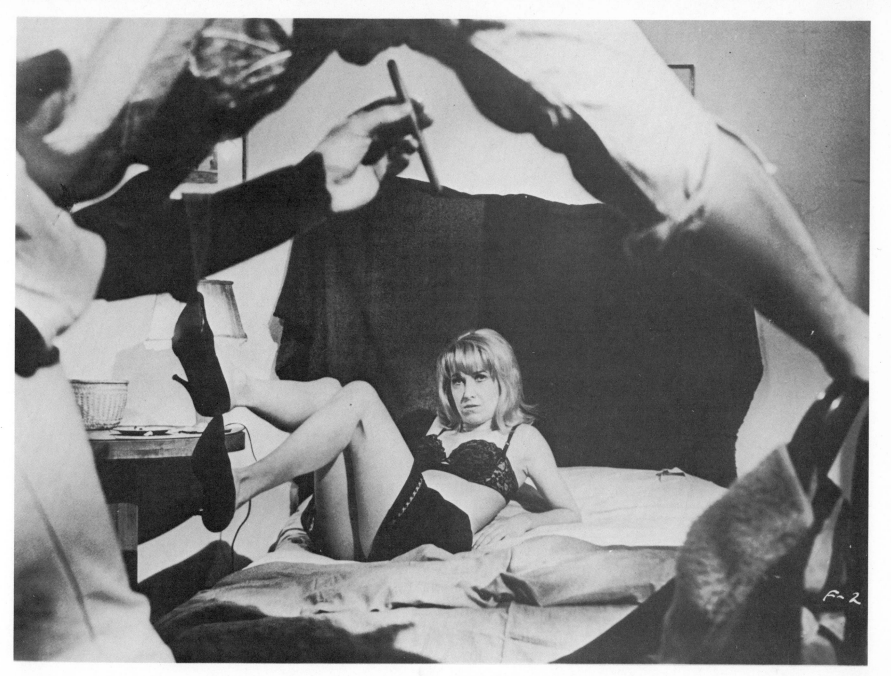

Sex in Two Dimensions

Sex in Two Dimensions

iting no more skin than the plot requires . . . crudely vigorous in development."

"It's a style, it moves very fast," Meyer has commented on these violence-and-sex features, "they're not overly long. I like violence in films. I think it's highly entertaining." So did audiences, judging from the number of films that followed the early Friedman and Meyer successes. By the mid-sixties, over 750 such films were in general release. Most kept to the perennial themes of sex leading to revenge and/or sadism. Most exhibited a marked hostility to women, casting them as bitch-castrators, objects to be feared and therefore subdued.

Indicative of this theme are *Invitation to Ruin, The Sadistic Lover, The Touch of Her Flesh,* and *The Curse of the Flesh. Invitation to Ruin,* directed by Kurt Richter, casts 300-pound Bertha Bigg as Mama Lupo, proprietress of a brothel into which young girls are lured in order to be imprisoned and trained as high-class whores. Apart from the film's portrayal of bondage and whipping, the high points are the insertion of a red-hot poker into a tortured girl's vagina and the castration of Mama Lupo's chief procurer. All of this is implied; but the implications are, if anything, stronger than similar portrayals of torture in Ken Russell's *The Devils.*

Anna Riva and Julian Marsh's *The Touch of Her Flesh* is a revenge drama in which an insane young man contrives the deaths of several people, in one case murdering a girl he has just married by shooting her with a harpoon gun after watching a pornographic movie in which she masturbates with a squash. There is also a scene in which two women make love and one is killed by a spring knife concealed in the dildo the other is wearing. Again the film ends with the castration, by machete, of the hero.

Olga's Girls, Olga's Massage Parlor, and *White Slaves of Chinatown,* all produced by George Weiss and directed by Joseph A. Mawra, represent perhaps the apotheosis of the roughies. The latter features water torture, bondage, whipping, beatings with rubber hoses, hanging, and thumb-screwing. *The Daughters of Lesbos* deals directly with the subject of female dominance and castration-as-revenge against men who rape defenseless women, as does Barry Mahon's *Prostitute's Protective Society.*

The hostility that these films exhibit toward women takes the form of a self-fulfilling prophecy. Women worship the male phallus, envy the man his virility, and make every effort to rob him of both. Yet this phallus-envy is mixed with a legitimate hatred for men, for men make women objects of lust and dominance. Hence, like the slaves of the Old South who were treated both as objects of contempt and as potentially murderous avengers of their race, women in the roughies are treated both as objects to be abused for male pleasure and as instruments of revenge for that abuse. Whipping and bondage are thus rationalized.

We should not be too surprised to learn that the roughies experienced little interference from the censors. Violence, particularly violence against women, has been a staple of American popular art since the end of the American Revolution. Thus, countless erotic films made in America—from the teens of this century through the latest hard-core loops available in Super-8 for home projection—use the themes of rape, white slavery, prostitution, bondage, flag-

A tense moment
from *All the Loving Couples.*

Sex in Two Dimensions

ellation, and simple brutality as their take-off points.

Nor is the theme of violence against women purely the preserve of the exploiters of American popular art. Alfred Hitchcock's *Psycho,* an enormously popular film of immense subtlety and erotic daring, explores the nature of this notion of woman as victim and castrator. The hero, Anthony Perkins, is dominated sexually, intellectually, and physically, by an overbearing woman (his mother) for whom he professes fanatical devotion. When she betrays his incestuous love by bedding down with another man after the death of her husband, he kills her. Yet, once she is dead, he resurrects her and casts her *in the role he has always secretly imagined for her*—a murderess wielding a gigantic, phallic butcher knife. In this guise, he/she murders the young girl (Janet Leigh) who has aroused his lusts and acted unknowingly as the object of his voyeurism. Hitchcock has taken great pains to underscore the sense of identity Perkins and Leigh feel for each other. Hence the fallen-woman-as-castrator destroys the woman-as-sexual-victim; Perkins-as-mother castrates Leigh-as-Perkins. The circle is complete.

Hitchcock's film, made in 1959, the same year as Meyer's *The Immoral Mr. Teas,* casts a good deal of light on the nature of the exploitation films employing violence against women as their chief impetus, both the early erotic films and the explicitly violent roughies of the sixties. Typically, the early erotic films portrayed women as innocent, passive victims of domineering, violent men. Or else the women are carnal creatures, whose lusts can never be adequately satisfied by men and who eventually destroy any man who is unlucky enough to become their partner in sex. Both images of women are the obvious male fantasies, and both fantasies are variations on the persistent notion that a woman, once fallen into sin, can never be redeemed. Throughout the nineteenth and twentieth centuries, men in popular art could sin and, by an act of sacrifice or public humiliation, atone for their sin and return to the community. But a woman once fallen was a creature for whom redemption was impossible.

Clearly this was a convenient way for a male-dominated society to rationalize its relegation of women to an inferior status in society. For, if women were endowed with a special "moral sense," then their fall had to be total and irrevocable. They were different from men; it was not in their "nature" to lust or to think about sex at all; thus, if their natures were corrupted by initiation into the male preserves of lust, there was no way back.

The early erotic films played on the theme of lost innocence; the later roughies emphasized the theme of female corruption. In the early years, a woman seduced was a woman lost; later on, a woman who lusted was not a woman at all, but a monster who would destroy any man. And the male role in erotic films emphasized both views. Men in the early years of American erotic cinema were aggressors. They beat and violated defenseless women who whimpered and protested, but who eventually responded and became "real" women. By the early sixties, men were reduced to voyeurs like Bill Teas or defenseless candidates for castration like the hero of *The Touch of Her Flesh* or *Prostitute's Protective Society.* In *Psycho,* Anthony Perkins as-

Sex in Two Dimensions

sumes both roles, the first as the withdrawn son of a domineering mother, the second by proxy as Janet Leigh, a kindred spirit who, he discovers, is as lonely, defenseless, and frightened as himself.

But either way, the erotic cinema in the years 1895 through 1965 carried on a tradition in American popular art, a tradition that stressed sexual violence against woman as the expression of man's natural instincts and as little better than she deserved. Exploitation movies seem to be just another area in which, more blatantly perhaps than in other areas of American culture, men can have it both ways.

DON DRUKER

I Lost It in the Back Seat

A Personalized History
of America's Auto Romance

9

Surely one of the most important reasons for America's love affair *with* the automobile is the tremendous number of love affairs that have been conducted *in* the automobile . . .[1]

My family was quite wealthy. I led a very sheltered life. In public school I met a boy fifteen years old about whom I became wild. My family did not think much of him because his family wasn't prominent. My family would not allow me to go out with him except on a few occasions. This did not stop us. He had a car. So every afternoon, or nearly every afternoon, we went to the woods to make love. . . .[2]

On the other hand, many boys who did not have access to a car did not even try to get dates. They presupposed . . . that girls would snub them for this reason. . . .[3]

The Early Years

The idea probably makes the old man double up in his grave. But if we were to point out a single

person as *the* parent of modern sexual standards, the one who got the old ball rolling, it probably wouldn't be your first guess.

It wouldn't be Sigmund Freud who brought children into the game. It wouldn't be Elvis Presley who brought rotating hips to WASP America. It certainly wouldn't be the stapled navel man, Hugh Hefner. It would be the man who put America on wheels, Henry Ford. Because if there is one *thing* that above all other things paved the way for the democratic orgasm, it has to be that energy-guzzling, pollution-proliferating, luxurious necessity—the American automobile.

Of course, even before the automobile took over the American landscape, whale-boned Victorian moral codes were strangling themselves to death. The twentieth-century realities of industrialization and urbanization meant that fundamental change was inevitable. People—bosses and workers, men and women, parents and children, etc., etc.—were going to have to evolve new ways of dealing with one another. But when Henry Ford came along in 1908 with a

I Lost It in the Back Seat

horseless carriage that everyone, not just the rich, could afford, he shifted the whole process into overdrive.

A few numbers will illustrate the revolutionary impact of Ford's assembly-line method of mass-producing his Model T. In 1908, when it went on sale, the car cost $850. Eight years later Ford had streamlined his technique so thoroughly that the price dropped to $400. In 1926 the price was an incredible $290. So contrasted with the $1,000 price tags on other makes, Ford's flivver was a grand bargain. And when he discontinued the Model T in 1927 in favor of the Model A, Ford had sold more than 15,000,000 cars—more than half the total of all automobiles sold in this country during those twenty years.

For our purpose, the single most liberating effect of Ford's auto was that for a whole new class of suddenly mobile Americans it threw the old, accepted rules of courtship out the window. It meant that, for the first time, America's ever-growing numbers of urban young didn't have to get to know one another in the parlor or on the front porch swing. They could go for a ride.

And if you think, perhaps, that the real consequence of this new freedom is exaggerated, simply consider the reaction of that era's moral watchdogs. Even before cars were enclosed, red-eyed ministers were pounding pulpits and denouncing the "devil wagons" and the "profligate young heirs" who drove them. One juvenile court judge gained a kind of immortality when he branded the family car "a house of prostitution on wheels."

By 1920, America's annual auto production reached the 2 million unit mark. Nine years later the total jumped to 5.5 million. And if we compare that number to the record 9.5 million that Detroit produced in 1973, the statistic looks very impressive. In fact, by 1929—some very clever slide rule pusher discovered—there were enough registered autos in the country that it was mathematically possible to transport the entire U.S. population at the same time.

In that same year Walter Lippman observed that "the whole revolution in the field of sexual mores turns upon the fact that the external control of the chastity of women is becoming impossible." And Kinsey's research, with premarital intercourse as the key index, demonstrates that sexual freedom made a statistically significant leap in the late twenties and into the thirties.

Now obviously, no one would argue seriously that the automobile was the sole reason for this upsurge in sexual activity. But it should be evident that what the pulpit pounders had been saying was quite true. The automobile was providing the vehicle—literally as well as figuratively—for the great change in courting standards.

And naturally, at the same time during those key years the auto manufacturers were making their cars ever more comfortable places to conduct sexual experiments. In 1919, 90 percent of all cars were open vehicles. In 1926 safety glass was developed, and so by 1929 90 percent of all cars were enclosed. Heaters and radios became available during the same decade. . . . And voila! an enclosed space, heat, and a mood adjustment device—the basic ingredients of urban romance.

Curiously enough, while the great stock market crash and the advent of depression did bring an abrupt halt to a lot of Roaring Twenties craziness, and certainly did stagger the auto

Henry Ford and his son, Edsel, in a Model F Ford in front of their home in Detroit, 1905.
The old man would probably double up in his grave.

". . . the external control of the chastity of women is becoming impossible."

manufacturers, it didn't stop young people from getting to know one another. Even if no one—or hardly anyone—was buying a new car in the early thirties, the total number of auto registrations declined only slightly. By 1930, the car—and everything that came along with it—was a fixture of American life.

Yet, while that Great Flow Chart of sexual activity continued upwards from the twenties to the thirties, there were some important psychological differences in the quality of the sex.

Tristam Coffin, author of *The Sex Kick,* suggests that there was a general naivete in the twenties that had a lot to do with the giddiness of a new kind of industrial prosperity. There was a pervasive sense of toying with the old rules, and trying to see what you could get away with.

But in the thirties sex changed. An element of desperation appeared. There was a feeling among the young that the world of their parents was crumbling, and that they had better enjoy the available pleasures while they were still

I Lost It in the Back Seat

There was a feeling among the young that the world of their parents was crumbling.

available. As Coffin put it: "So the adventurous young felt a need to try the forbidden. . . . They got drunk and sick on bad liquor. They petted furiously in rumble seats. This was known as necking, and it left the boys aching and the girls vaguely elated."[4]

Well, I'll tell you. Getting anything in a rumble seat was a challenge. The good part was that a rumble seat was so compact and concealed that you probably could be partaking of sex with the girl on your lap

and nobody would know. The bad part was that I could never get anybody to sit on my lap like that—at least I couldn't get 'em to give me the whole thing.

To tell you the truth, I never did much more than just parking and necking, you know? See, you were always taking the risk that the cops would come along. Usually they would be kind of vulgar, and, you know, looking for a bribe or something. And if any gal ever got caught in a real predicament, the cops would be pretty

I Lost It in the Back Seat

rough on 'em. They would threaten 'em and scare 'em. And some cops, I guess, would try to get the girl to go all the way with them. They'd threaten to tell her folks unless she did it. And they could be pretty mean on the guys, too, threatening to take you down and book you for statutory rape. It was something that had to be on your mind, you know? Still, I suppose there was many a cherry lost in those old cars. . . .

The Fifties

During the war commercial auto production was suspended in favor of military equipment needs. And back home the cars on the street were not only getting old, but gasoline was rationed.

So after the war, the big manufacturers were eager to get back to the ripe home market. They began studying consumer buying tables, and they came up with some surprising conclusions. Primary among them was that the typical car buyer was not—and probably still is not—a rational beast. He did not buy, the manufacturers concluded, on the bases of performance and practicability. He bought for any number of reasons other than the ones that simple intuition would suggest are most reasonable. And one of the main other reasons was sexual. The car itself had become a sex object.

As the corner to the fifties was turned, the selling of cars began to depend on escalating doses of sex-sell. The auto designers built all manner of sexually symbolic and would-be-sexually symbolic shapes into their cars, hoping that the effect would somehow connect with the potential buyer's sexual proclivities. And the advertising people, also aware that it was men who signed checks, slid red-lipped, high-heeled,

up-thrust-bosomed dream girls into their ads. If they couldn't get 'em by hook, they'd get 'em by crook.

Proof enough of the buyer's lack of rationality was driven home by a near fatal blunder made by the Chrysler Corporation. In 1953 Chrysler announced that it would come out with an all re-designed fleet of shorter, less gaudy, more efficient and practical cars. Chrysler's decision-makers thought that a line of demonstrably superior cars would be a grand way to boost sales. Two years later, though, Chrysler gave up on the whole noble experiment. Sales had dropped sharply, and to stay in business the company had little choice but to follow the lead of Chevrolet and Ford. In the following year Chrysler returned to the market with a bunch of huge, finned, gaudy-colored bathtubmobiles. And sure enough, sales immediately climbed.

In *The Hidden Persuaders* Vance Packard tells a most revealing tale of the manufacturers' decision to go all out for the sex-sell. It stems in large part, Packard says, from a study titled "Mistress Versus Wife," which Chrysler commissioned from Dr. Ernst Dichter.

Dr. Dichter was called upon to explain a fact puzzling marketers. While most men bought sedans and rarely bought convertibles they evidently were more attracted to convertibles. Dealers had found they could draw more males into their showrooms by putting convertibles in the window. . . . Dr. Dichter concluded that men saw the convertible as a possible symbolic mistress. The man knows he is not going to gratify his wish for a mistress, but it is pleasant to daydream. The daydreaming drew the man to the auto

I Lost It in the Back Seat

salesroom. Once there he finally chose a four-door sedan just as he once married a plain girl who, he knew, would make a fine wife and mother.[5]

From Dichter's study came the not un-clever idea of mating the sedan *with* the convertible. The hybrid was the hardtop, which may or may not have been a conscious pun (soft underneath?). But the hardtop did become the most successful new car style in several years—jaunty enough to tickle the fancy, yet sedate enough to pass for normal.

Obviously, new car buyers made up only a fraction of the total number of car owners in the fifties. But further proof of the extent to which cars were becoming sexual symbols was plainly observable out on the street—where all those rebels without causes were cruising for burgers and smoking Lucky Strikes. Youth car culture was coming into its own.

The kids didn't have money to burn, but with some wrenches and a little know-how they built their own custom rods. The motivation was simple and direct: with a tough car, you were a big shot at the drive-in. As one woman who was there at the time put it, "Back in the fifties, your car was really *you*. You were riding around the high-school parking lot in your own self-definition, or as near to it as time and money would allow."[6]

For most, the self-definition didn't mean much more than hanging a graduation tassel or furry dice from the rearview mirror. Or maybe adding a plastic grip nob to the steering wheel. But for others, it meant all sorts of tampering with the structure and power of the car. Rods were chopped, channeled, and raked. Engines were rebored, rebuilt, and generally souped-up as much as traffic would allow.

Maybe the grandest of all examples of fifties customizing is a hot little number called Baby Bullet, which is on display at the Chicago Historical Antique Auto Museum in Highland Park, Illinois. It's a 1940 Ford frame stuffed with a 1957 three-carb Corvette engine. The front fenders are from a 1947 Buick. The rear fenders and fender skirts are from a 1947 Lincoln Continental. The tire wells are from a 1958 Kaiser Manhattan. The side panels are from a 1948 Buick. The windshield is from a 1956 Olds. The taillights from a 1953 Olds, and the hood from a 1950 Mercury. As a final touch of elegance, the wire wheels are from a 1957 Thunderbird.

If such a beast is an undeniably exotic specimen, an even more engaging question is what, exactly, were the kids doing to one another in those customized cars? The answer is that if they weren't doing anything more than the young people of a decade or two earlier, they were at least doing a lot more of it. Car-sex, by the mid-fifties, was an omnipresent element of youth culture.

In high school, which for me was between 1953 and 1957, I never had my own car. In fact, my parents didn't have one either, and that was a problem. If I wanted a date I had to arrange a double with someone who could drive. What a car was for, naturally, was parking.

What did you do when you parked?
A lot of petting.
Details please.

Well, there was a lot of moving the hands over all areas of the body. There was

I Lost It in the Back Seat

petting above the waist, and below the waist. Over the sweater, and under the sweater. Unhooking the bra, and feeling underneath it . . . that was a pretty heavy number.

On double dates there was no screwing. But one very heavy thing was finger insertion. And mutual masturbation. That was a really big deal. I can remember many times going home with wet pants, and wondering what I would do with my soiled underwear. I didn't want my mother to find them.

The heaviest thing of all, though, was the dry hump. Mostly this didn't go on in the car. I mean, not with another couple present. It happened usually after an evening of heavy petting—when you took your date to her door.

But sometimes there would be a little dry humping in the back seat. And a few times it was accomplished with key articles of clothing pushed out of the way. One of the really nice things about winter was that you wore so many heavy clothes. With your coat on, you were covered enough so you had the feeling of some privacy. Of course, anybody who got into heavy panting was subjected to a lot of giggling and bad jokes.

Hearing a healthy male discuss fifties car-sex in such glowing terms shouldn't be surprising. It was a hip thing (for those lucky few who actually "scored"). But the following comments suggest that for the girls, car-sex experiences may have had another kind of meaning beyond the purely physically pleasurable. As a conscious choice—to have sex, or not to have sex—the decision to proceed was a rather heavy existential leap toward personal independence.

My mother's attitude toward sex has given me a terrible guilt complex. I often get in trouble because I tell her the truth. Sometimes when I've been out parking with a boy, my mother has asked me what he did, and I have told her. She has scolded me, and wouldn't let me go out again for several days. My mother claims that she does this because my father doesn't want me to go parking. But I know this isn't so.

It's all my mother's doing. My mother has said it's all right for me to kiss 'a little' when we're in front of the house or saying good night. But she says that I must not park or go any further than that. Although I feel close to her, I have decided I must stop telling her everything I do . . . .[7]

Of all the auto styles and models of the fifties the one *Motor Trend* selected as "The Most Obvious Makeout Car of All Time," is "the bathtub that turned into a bed," the 1951 Nash Ambassador. It wasn't sleek. It wasn't fast. And it didn't look sexy. But its front seats did something very interesting—they reclined, instantly converting the humble Nash into an auto-boudoir.[8]

Maybe it's because the car's potential was so obvious. Or maybe it was because Nash was worried that a hot car image would damage sales. But whatever the real reason, Nash made sure its advertising for the recliners was yawnfully sedate (which may be one good reason why Nash no longer makes automobiles). Usually the ads featured an All-American husband and wife of middle age. While he drove with a contented smile, the wife was comfortably napping her way through the long drive to grandmother's house.

But is he really looking for a nice girl to marry?

I Lost It in the Back Seat

Out on the street, however, recliner Nashes were a rolling joke. Girls who were seen in them suddenly developed bad reputations. A friend whose parents owned one says that the car was indeed a Don Juan's delight, but that its very convenience sometimes led to problems. One minor drawback was that when the seat went down it was easy for small articles to slide into the gap between upper and lower cushions. Then, when the seat was returned to upright, the thing disappeared. Usually it was money. But once, when the friend's father was cleaning the car's interior, a Tampax materialized. Fortunately, it was still in the wrapper, and my friend wriggled off the hook.

But he wasn't quite so lucky on the morning he climbed into the car and noticed the distinct outline of a girl's bare foot on the windshield. With classic nonchalance, he flipped on the defroster—hoping it would erase the evidence. But his father saw. So for the next two months his only dates were secret doubles in the back of someone else's car.

The Sixties

One good way to measure the extent to which car-sex became institutionalized is to explore the car-sex code of behavior. To be sure, the code was unwritten. But it did exist, and it did provide rules for playing the parking game.

> It was all so routine. It was a routine, you know. Your date picked you up, you went to a movie, you got something to eat, and then you went and made out for a while in the car. Now the whole thing strikes me as being very . . . self-limiting. It wasn't like there was something that was going to happen, and I had to stop it. Like the guy

was going to put his hand in my pants or something. The boys knew how far they could go. Occasionally you got some joker who was all over you, but not too often.

What you are saying is that going on a date almost inevitably ended up with the car parked somewhere?

Yes. That is, if you were 'going out' with someone.

That means someone you went out with more than once, right?

Yeah. On the first date you usually didn't park. It was the third date. (laughs) First date you could kiss them. I don't know what you did on the second date—kiss them a little longer, maybe.

To tell you the truth, I don't remember that I ever got *that* turned on when the car got parked. Also, in those days we wore a lot of clothes: skirt, sweater, blouse, slip, bra, panty girdle . . . and on the right days of the month there was a Kotex belt, too. In order to get under all that stuff he had to go through incredible contortions. His hand could go numb from the pressure.

Along with The Rules another important aspect of institutionalization was peer group pressures. By the early sixties, any person who didn't at least go through the motions of "going to see the submarine races" was considered a little peculiar:

> I can remember going out with this guy, Midget. He was very short . . . anyway, we were doubling with another couple. And this was the ritual sort of thing. The four of us went to a movie. Then we went to eat. And then, without anybody saying anything, we drove to Mozart Park. We just went there. Nobody said, 'Hey, let's go

park.' We just went there. The moment the car was stopped, you turned to your date, and started kissing. Mary and Vince were in the back. Midget and I were in front. Occasionally we would, you know, peek into the back to see how they were doing.

You did?

Sure, wouldn't you? (laughs)

Did you do it in a joking way?

Oh no. It was all very serious. I mean you were proving your whole . . . your whole thing.

What whole thing?

Well, in my case . . . I was there with Midget, right? I wasn't that crazy about him, but I had to prove to Vince and Mary that I could make out.

When you made out, what did you do?

It depended on what kind of girl you were. Some girls would go all the way. Others might French kiss. It all depended, you know? But usually the rules were like . . . if you doubled with a couple, you never went all the way. But you might pet a lot. This is in like freshman and sophomore years in high school, and you weren't getting undressed yet. Mostly it was just a lot of rubbing and kissing. See, you had to prove yourself, because . . . well, it was a thing you had to do.

When Midget pulled his car over, even if I didn't want to park with him, I couldn't have said, 'No, take me home.' I couldn't show my friends that I didn't know how to make out. I just had to sit there and make out for maybe two hours. I guess I just didn't want to look like a sissy.

Did you ever park with any boys you did like?

Oh sure, there was this one guy . . . I would go make out with him a lot, but I was afraid to fuck him. A girl friend of mine would, though, so naturally he went out with her instead of me.

As I think about it, I guess I did go pretty far with him, even if I didn't ever go all the way. My girl friends and I used to call ourselves half virgins. That meant you would finger fuck. Of course, that was pretty serious . . . I mean, it was serious for some girls. Others were more, you know, loose. Like the Catholic girls were more loose. I guess it was because they were locked up in those Catholic schools all day. Some of those chicks were really tough. Maybe it's because once they'd Frenched for the first time they'd already committed a mortal sin. So after one time it didn't matter much what else they did.

Although the two preceding recollections are very busy—there was a lot of activity, at least—they are strangely devoid of pleasure content. The girls sound as if they simply were going through motions; doing what the other kids did, but only because it was expected. Not because they were having an especially good time. But it would be wrong to assume that all young women thought of parking as nothing more than a social obligation. There were some who clearly enjoyed it as much as the boys.

I remember very well being in my mother's car, and getting very hot and heavy. Dry humping was a favorite sport. All of a sudden you'd feel that hard (laughs) lump in your groin. The thing that amazed me the most was when the guy suddenly got wet and sticky. Obviously it was the phenomenon of coming. But in those days I didn't know exactly what was happening. I mean, biologically I knew what 'to come' meant, but in the flesh (laughs) I didn't really get it yet.

This type of business was all happening when I was about fifteen or sixteen. I remember back even before that, that the big thing was to compare how your date kissed. My girl friends and I would sit around saying things like 'Oh he was so *great*! MMmmmmMMh! Those lips!' It wasn't hip then to be a slobbery kisser, but good tongue action was one of the fine points.

Once my boyfriend said to me that so-and-so had told him about something he should do that was a real turn-on. And he kissed my breast. (giggles) I mean, that was the first time that had ever happened to me. You know . . . like playing with the nipple with his mouth, and . . . I liked that a lot. I guess I liked anything he did to me. Just waving at him across the room would get me hot enough to juice up.

When we got a little older, like senior year in high school and early in college, we used to go out, find a place to park, and then start taking our clothes off . . . very slowly. I would end up with this sloppy wet . . . I mean, I was wet beyond belief. I mean, I was seventeen years old at the time, and you know how the juices were flowing then. If a guy would so much as brush my arm, I'd immediately start pulsating. It was all pent up.

I literally remember those flashes. That's the only word I can use to describe the feeling. They were electrically charged flashes that would flow through my body, and when he would take me home my underpants would be wringing wet . . .

Just as in earlier years, the great bogeymen of car-sex, the people who made it all so difficult, were the police. Right when things would be getting comfortable, they had a nasty habit of appearing from nowhere with blazing flashlights and leering grins. At least, that's the way it always seemed. A typical scenario went something like this:

One time my boyfriend and I were parked in front of my parents' house. I was in my junior year of college, which must have been about 1968. And it was probably about 2:30 in the morning. We were just making out, nothing special really, just kissing a lot. But just at the point where I was starting to get into it, a bright light suddenly came shining in on us, and a voice said, 'All right, both of you get out of the car.'

It was a cop, naturally, who wanted to see our identification. In a way it was sort of comical because poor Jim was trying really hard to cover the tremendous bulge he had in the front of his pants, and act like nothing had been going on. The cop was talking really loud, and I kept trying to get him to talk quieter, because, well, there we were right in front of my parents' house.

When the cop finally saw from my driver's license that I was twenty, he looked disappointed. Like it pained him that I wasn't so young he could arrest us. When he couldn't think of anything better to say, he finally just said, 'If you're going to park here, then put on your parking lights.'

While the kids almost universally considered the cops creeps, they also carried around some curious misconceptions about what was legal and what wasn't. One woman told me that when she was younger she thought that if her head went below the window level her boyfriend could be arrested for statutory rape. Another

I Lost It in the Back Seat

remembered that a friend had told her that the way to avoid arrest while engaging in auto-intercourse was to keep your shoes and socks on. As long as shoes and socks were in place, they wouldn't arrest you.

Fortunately, the coppers usually didn't live up to their reputation—they'd been kids once themselves, after all. But occasionally things could take an ugly turn. This happened in Dayton, Ohio:

Jeffi and I were parked in the woods one night. We had been going together for about three years. She was still a virgin, but we were pretty free with one another's bodies by then. So anyway, on this particular night all of her clothes were off. I was dressed, but we were being pretty passionate when whammo, out of nowhere these two flashlights were shining in on us. It was two cops. One was about forty and really fat. The other was much younger. He didn't say too much, but the older one, the fat one, started yelling at us. At first I thought he was just mad that we were there, you know. . . . But there was something in the tone of his voice that got me scared.

He yelled at us to get out of the car. He tried to open my door, but it was locked. Jeffi started getting dressed, but he screamed, 'Don't do that.' We started to get nervous . . . like, what should we do? Then the cop says, 'You heard me, bitch, get out of that car. If you're so interested in sex, I'm gonna show you what a real man can do.' Jeffi, by this time, is really freaked. The asshole is pounding on the car, and everything. I didn't know what to do. If we tried to get away, would he shoot us?

Then the cop changes tactics. He stops shouting, and says, 'You two are in big trouble. The only way you're going to get out of it is to open the door, and give me what I want.' That did it. I got so mad I wanted to kill the son of a bitch. But what I did instead was start the car, throw it into gear, and drive the hell out of there. For the first few seconds I was sure he was gonna shoot us. I thought I was kissing the world goodbye. But he didn't do anything. He didn't even chase us, thank God. If he had, I don't know what I would have done. . . .

Meanwhile, back in Detroit, the automobile as sex symbol was going through quite a few heavy changes of its own. Foreign sports cars like the Triumph and MG, with their obvious pointy hoods, sculptured rear ends, and fancy maneuverability were beginning to attract a large chunk of America's youth market. So Detroit, which knows a trend when one kicks it in the wallet, responded with its own line of sporty cars. Ford gave us the Mustang; Chevy introduced the Camaro; American Motors tried the Javelin . . . etc.

With their optional whopper V-8 engines (which transformed these sports cars into "Muscle Cars") and relatively low prices, these cars meant that not only the kid with the greasy fingernails and torque wrench, but also even the boob who didn't know a piston from a spittoon could careen down the expressway in a very hot car. Suddenly everybody could have a hot car, and play king of the road.

The undisputed champion of the "Muscle Cars" was the GTO, which Pontiac introduced in 1964. It was an immediate hit; not only on the street, but also on the car radio—because a group called Ronnie and the Daytonas had a big

Top 40 hit with their own version of "GTO."

Actually the GTO wasn't much of a connoisseur's car. It didn't corner at all well. In fact, its only distinctive quality was acceleration. The stock 325 hp V-8 was spectacular. But the optional Tri-Power 348 hp V-8 was pure fantasy:

> The visceral excitement of driving a Tri-Power GTO was unparalleled for the time. The sounds—the harsh rumble of the exhaust, the howling of the U.S. Rubber Tiger Paw red-line tires on the pavement, and the unearthly sucking noise of the air being gulped through the carburetors, coupled with the raw sensation of being bashed into the seat back by the forward thrust of the car—were enough to make every kid in America think he was the fastest, toughest driver in the world. The car was pure macho filled to the brim with hokey gadgets like bucket seats, tachometer, hood scoops, wood-rimmed steering wheel, etc., to enhance the Mittyesque urgings of the grocery boys behind the wheel . . .
> "Let's face it," said one industry observer of the day, "buying a GTO is like adding two inches to your cock."[9]

The Seventies

To get the feel of the full extent to which the automobile plays a sexual role in the everyday life of contemporary America, all you have to do is drive around in any city. In our time sex roles are turning inside out—which means there is a lot of emotional confusion out there on the street. And for an embarrassingly large number of people—mostly men—the car serves as sexual reassurance. The symbolism is obvious and ubiquitous. It cuts across all the economic and ethno-cultural divisions of America.

In white America the class differences between the middle-aged WASP who tools down the expressway to work every morning in a flaming red sports car, and the greaser who flashes an equally expensive hand-painted, chrome-engined Camaro at a custom car show are clear. Yet both types are expressing the same basic urge. Tromping down on that accelerator is ego-massaging evidence of virulent masculinity.

In minority communities, too, the car plays the same role. Chinese kids in and around San Francisco's Chinatown have a blooming car culture that outwardly, anyway, bears striking resemblance to the white teen style of a decade ago. They like their cars to have a super-forward-tilt look with the rear ends jacked up sky-high, and balanced above those extra-fat, red-lined, oversized tires.

In Black America the most obvious head turner is the Pimp-mobile look—a Cadillac Eldorado with a chromed front end, those wide-eyed headlamp holders (yellow lights, of course), and a gargoyle hood ornament, a velour Landau top, ultra-wide whitewall tires, and a diamond-shaped rear window. Inside there is a phone, TV, and bar service.

One particular Los Angeles eye-catcher may not have that Superfly cool, but it does express itself very clearly. The car is an aging Caddy that's been refinished with a multicolor paint job. The focal point is the rear end which bears, in large letters, the legend "I married a white woman," and photos of the happy couple.

Latino communities, too, find machismo in the auto. One classic, spotted in Chicago, is a raked, lime-green '57 Chevy. The interior features oversized dice (dangling from the rearview

California glue artist Dickens Bascom and his incredible car.
There is a lot of emotional confusion out there on the street.

I Lost It in the Back Seat

I Lost It in the Back Seat

mirror), a pink fake-fur-covered steering wheel, a matching fake-fur rear window deck cover, red tassel fringe around each window, gold-flecked vinyl upholstery, and a bouncing hula girl in the rear window. In case there were any doubts about the intended effect, the driver had stenciled "The Sex Car" on both doors.

However, even as street level autoeroticism reaches new heights in fantasy, powerful outside forces are signaling a great change—a change that may be the greatest since Ford introduced his Model T. Environmental worries, the energy crisis, soaring prices, and the great mid-seventies stagflation indicate that the seventies are probably a turning point in the history of American auto use.

So far, the manufacturers' hurried response has been to think smaller and smaller:

> DETROIT (AP)—The standard-size family car, the eighteen-foot, 2.5 ton American species of automobile, is on the verge of extinction.
>
> Detroit automakers are designing cars for the late 1970s which will be shorter, 500 to 1,000 pounds lighter, and several inches taller than today's full-size cars . . . .[10]

And besides shortening the standard autos, Detroit has also created a series of midget and even sub-midget cars.

Now, all of the new, smaller automobiles may make a successful compromise with the new economic-environmental realities, but clearly, as sexual symbols, these new little jobs do not measure up to the old macho-mobiles. And what is even more important is that the new cars are so small, and so rigged with anti-sexual booby traps (bucket seats, shoulder harnesses, floor-mounted gear shifts, consoles, and practically no back seat) that they make *actual* car-sex very difficult. In fact, the new so-called "sub-compact" models have less free space than the average bathtub.

One indicator that the decline of the standard American car as a *place* already has set in is the rise of an alternative auto-sex culture in (where else?) Southern California. Utilizing Detroit's basic delivery van as the vehicle, an estimated 30,000 "vanners" are rolling around in a new kind of bedroom on wheels. For example, witness the "Love Machine" created by Hollywood's customizer to the stars, George Barris. Starting with a standard Dodge Sportsman, Barris refinished the exterior with forty coats of lacquer—burnt orange sunset pearls-of-essence blended to a bright sun-ray yellow. The inside features lighting from a crystal chandelier, which is mounted between two gold frame mirrors (to give the feeling of greater space), a stereo music system (coordinated, of course, with a colored light effect), a sterling silver cocktail service, a color TV, and a revolving, six-foot "boudoir" sofa.

Another good indication that the times are a-changing is a sudden gush of auto-sex nostalgia. One classic example, if slightly before its time, is Edward Kienholz's sculpture, "Back-Seat Dodge," featuring a rather grotesque couple copulating in the back seat. Another, very different for-instance comes from *Rolling Stone* magazine. Mixed in among the music biz gossip was this pearl:

> Motown Records, in the midst of a diversification gambit, is considering a new band called Country Porn. Their first tune list includes "Dry Humpin in the Back of a '55 Ford," and "Feelin' You Feelin' Me." A

I Lost It in the Back Seat

spokesman for Motown says, "We're starting to get a lot of off-the-wall stuff while we diversify. Either they're legit, or somebody is putting us on very skillfully."[11]

Not surprisingly, the skin magazines are into the act, too. *Viva* ("The International Magazine for Women") has used old cars in several of its supposedly female-fantasy-oriented seduction layouts. But what must be the ultimate elbow-in-the-ribs auto-sex spread is in the February 1975 issue of *Oui* ("For the Man of the World"). Its title, no kidding, is "Back Seat Love: In Which Seaman Hornblower Meets Edna St. Louis Missouri, Famed Gonzo Philosopher, and a Conclusion Is Reached."[12] That the twenty-photo sequence is candy-coated for heavy-handed guffaws (several faces peer in on the scene through the rear window) doesn't negate the long-lost-fantasy effect. The car has a back seat large enough to comfortably accommodate the models' athletic contortions.

The greatest car-sex put-on of them all, however, is the hand-crafted vision of Steven Hastings Paige of Los Angeles. Paige calls his sculpture The Dickmobile. And it is.

The body of the full-size, two-seater convertible is an elongated, distinctly penile pink tube. It is tipped by a purple, clearly circumcised head, and vein-like pipes run along the sides. The rear end is shaped like a pair of testicles. Paige describes his Dickmobile:

Nightmare of love, pistons ripping at hot cylinders in frenzied confusion, speed noise laughing at sappy deals along smoggy boulevards; our power packed machismo American meatmaker. Optional equipment at no extra cost: Tires (four). Steering wheel. Motor. Handmade body. Windshield. Upholstery 'n' paint. Front end. Chassis. Sides (two). Doors (two) . . . and more.[13]

And Then What?

So what does it mean that Detroit's new cars no longer look as sexual, and that they are, in fact, much less sexually functional as well? Well . . . at this stage in American history, the meaning of a traveling pun like Paige's hot rod is perfectly transparent. And it makes us snicker.

But remember, in earlier years so ballsy a display would have raised more outrage than snickers. We laugh because our attitudes toward sex are a lot different from say . . . Henry Ford's. (Ford was such a swinger that one of the most colorful things he ever did was to remark that a customer could get his Model T in any color he wanted—as long as it was black.)

In other words, there are, these days, more people who are more open, more free, and more willing to tolerate the notion that sex is a normal, human, physical function than at any other time in the last 200 years. And one very good reason *why* our collective attitude has come this far is that the automobile has carried us down the sexual liberation road. Right now, at this particular moment in our national history, almost everyone between the ages of five and sixty-five has had some kind of sexual experience in a car. If you find that hard to swallow, ask around. You might be very surprised at the variety and originality of the replies you'll get. I was.

One very quiet, conservatively dressed banker confided that one summer when he and his wife had been married five years—and were begin-

"Nice body styling, huh?" says the UPI
caption for this ME 3000 sports car from
AC Cars.

I Lost It in the Back Seat

ning to lose interest in one another's sexual needs—they suddenly decided to drive to the beach and make love.

It was a lark. We just drove down there in broad daylight, parked in the lot and began kissing like we hadn't done in years. It was fantastic. We could not wait to pull our pants off. Jane sat on my lap facing me, and just sort of lowered herself onto me. We were terribly worried that someone would come along. And in fact, some guy did sort of walk back and forth in front of the car about three or four times. But somehow, even that just added to the excitement. That little trip to the beach fueled our fantasies for months. Now, whenever we find we're getting bored with each other, we hop in the car and drive somewhere where we can do it.

Sometimes it doesn't even take two to boogie. A young woman writer told me that occasionally on warm summer nights she likes to roll herself an illegal cigarette, climb into her car, and go for a ride.

This isn't something I'd normally admit to. But what I do is get stoned, find a nice quiet stretch of road, turn the radio up really loud, and then . . . uh, I masturbate. Sometimes I use a vibrator, but mostly I just use my fingers. But I must say that I do enjoy it, and . . . well, it is a great way to get rid of tensions.

Sometimes it happens to people who least expect it:

Here's one for the book. I'll bet this doesn't happen very often. Once when I was

hitchhiking home for the weekend, a girl who was driving alone gave me a ride. She was on her way from someplace up north to someplace downstate for a vacation. . . . She may have been married. . . . We immediately struck up a conversation. After a while she gave me the 'come on' signal. So I showed her a good place to drive into the woods . . . Technically, I suppose she seduced me.[14]

This too is an engaging tale:

Actually, I haven't really fucked in a car since high school, which was seven years ago. Ever since I've had my own place there wasn't much need. But even now there is a lot of hand sex that goes on in the car. I have a friend that I used to go on a lot of driving trips with, and several times I went down on him while he was driving.
    At first the idea sort of freaked me out because I was afraid we'd have an accident and the bodies would be found in a rather compromising position. . . . But of course, it works the other way, too. I mean, I can remember lots of times driving home up the Dan Ryan expressway with his fingers up my cunt. This is something you can do, and not have to worry about people seeing you. Unless, that is, a truck or a bus pulls alongside. Or at least he's told me that people can't see. I really don't know. . . . People probably have been watching us all the time. . . .

The main point to all this is that nearly everyone has had some sort of sexual experience in a car—encouraged by the fact that the car has been such a convenient place to do it. But what of the future? If the auto manufacturers are indeed going through a major, lasting change in emphasis—from big and roomy to small and cramped, what effect will it have on the youth of the seventies and eighties? How will it change their orientation to sex? Will it make them different from us?

These are not flip questions. The subject never has received much serious attention, but car-sex experiences have played a very vital role in making us the people we are. For instance, one of the few published studies shows that 40 percent of all American males who propose marriage do it from behind the wheel.

The auto-descendants of Henry Ford's flivver have brought changes of the most profound nature to the shape and quality of American society. Many of those changes have been appraised. But we are only beginning to get a picture of the impact car-sex has had on our national psyche. In fact, a good measure of the *lack* of understanding of the social importance of auto-sex—by people who ought to know better—is revealed in a remark Marshall McLuhan once made. "The car," said the philosopher, "is no more of a sex object than the wheel or the hammer."

But McLuhan is wrong. The car *is* a sex object—and more. And even as we begin to think about just how much more, the car itself is changing radically. In the days of the big, fat hogmobiles, America's young had real opportunities to make firsthand discoveries about themselves and the opposite sex. That may well be what the so-called Sexual Revolution is all about.

But if the automobile becomes something other than what it has been for the last fifty-odd years, where will America's children go to find out about the opposite sex, and about *themselves*? Is anyone so foolish to argue that a semester of sex education in some stuffy, uptight classroom could possibly replace the real learning experience of a night in the back seat of a 1964 Chevrolet?

JACK HAFFERKAMP

Notes

[1]David E. Davis, Jr., "50 Years of Back Seats" in "Love and the Automobile," *Motor Trend,* February, 1973, p. 70.

[2]Winston Ehrmann, *Premarital Dating Behavior* (New York, Henry Holt & Co., 1959), p. 108.

[3]*Ibid.,* p. 43.

[4]Tristam Coffin, *The Sex Kick* (New York, The Macmillan Company, 1966), p. 32.

[5]Vance Packard, *The Hidden Persuaders* (New York, David McKay Co., 1957), p. 87.

[6]Carol Troy, "Confessions of a Back Seat Girl," in "Love and the Automobile," *Motor Trend,* February, 1973, p. 75.

[7]Ehrmann, p. 106.

[8]Steve Spence, "1951 Nash Airflyte Ambassador Custom," in "Love and the Automobile," *Motor Trend,* February, 1973, p. 96.

[9]Brock Yates, "The Macho Machines," *Playboy,* April, 1974, p. 193.

[10]*Chicago Tribune,* January 18, 1975.

[11]*Rolling Stone,* January 2, 1975, p. 24.

[12]"Back Seat Love in which Seaman Hornblower Meets Edna St. Louis Missouri, Famed Gonzo Philosopher, and a Conclusion Is Reached," *Oui,* February, 1975, pp. 51–55.

[13]*Oui,* June, 1973, p. 18.

[14]Ehrmann, p. 215.

A Note on Sources

Cartnel, Allan. "Love Vans," in "Love and the Automobile." *Motor Trend,* February, 1973, pp. 85–88.

Coffin, Tristam. *The Sex Kick.* New York: The Macmillan Company, 1966.

Davis, David E. "Fifty Years of Back Seats," in "Love and the Automobile," *Motor Trend,* February, 1973, pp. 69–72.

Ehrmann, Winston. *Premarital Dating Behavior.* New York: Henry Holt & Co., 1959.

Joseph, James. "Sex and the Single Car," *Motor Trend,* April, 1967, pp. 44–47.

Keats, John. *The Insolent Chariots.* Philadelphia: J.B. Lippincott, 1958.

"Love and the Automobile." *Motor Trend,* February, 1973, pp. 69–104.

Packard, Vance. *The Hidden Persuaders.* New York: David McKay Co., 1957.

Rae, John B. *The American Automobile.* Chicago: University of Chicago Press, 1965.

Spence, Steve. "1951 Nash Airflyte Ambassador Custom," in "Love and the Automobile." *Motor Trend,* February, 1973, pp. 96–99.

Troy, Carol. "Confessions of a Backseat Girl," in "Love and the Automobile." *Motor Trend,* February, 1973, pp. 75–76.

Yates, Brock. "The Macho Machines." *Playboy,* April, 1974, pp. 159–162; pp. 188–194.

Manual Sex

From Kinsey to Comfort

10

"Is the love of man and woman merely an animal function?" asked an article in the June, 1948, issue of *Reader's Digest,* six months after the publication of the first Kinsey report. "Are spiritual ideals of mating, of fidelity and chastity no more than irrational and sentimental nonsense? Have our conventions and moralities—and what we have always held to be simple decency—been outmoded by findings of modern science?"

The *Digest's* concern was understandable, because Dr. Alfred C. Kinsey had discovered something that people like Norman Vincent Peale, J. Edgar Hoover, and the national commander of the Salvation Army—all of whom were quoted in the article—had a vested interest in keeping secret: American men liked sex. They liked it with their wives; with women who weren't their wives; with other men; and with themselves. A certain number of them (17 percent of the farm population, 4 percent of the urban population) even liked it with animals. Kinsey's second report, published six years later, revealed for the first time that American

women didn't mind sex either. "It is impossible to estimate the damage this book will do to the already deteriorating morals of America," the Rev. Billy Graham said—and time has proved him right.

It would be hard to imagine a more unlikely instigator of the "sexual revolution" than Dr. Kinsey. Born in 1894 in Hoboken, New Jersey, the oldest son of thrifty, respectable, working-class parents, he was a boy who never went out with girls until he was twenty-seven; who married the first woman he had ever dated; and who was trained in biology at Bowdoin and Harvard. He was a specialist in the life history of gall wasps (small insects found mostly in oak trees and rose bushes); an associate professor at Indiana University, distinguished only by his dogged capacity for work, his straightforward manner, considerable personal charm; and possessed a gall wasp collection which ultimately numbered 4 million specimens. . . . Why, in 1938, did the University choose this obscure faculty member to coordinate an interdisciplinary marriage course?

Nobody knows—but the marriage course, one of the first offered by an American university, proved immensely popular with the students and just the opposite with influential members of the Bloomington clergy who finally forced Kinsey to give it up two years later. In the meantime he had made a survey of available sex education literature, found it wholly inadequate, and begun his own research program by taking the sexual histories of his students. He had also begun making field trips to Chicago to extend the range of his sample. By the end of the marriage course, he had compiled 570 histories.

Three years later Kinsey received a small grant from the medical division of the Rockefeller Foundation. The Foundation's support continued and was increased each year, enabling him to hire three research associates and a clerical staff. A library of sex-related materials, which eventually became one of the largest collections of erotica in the world, was begun. Interviewing techniques were developed and standardized; and Kinsey devised an elaborate code, known only to himself and three other interviewers, in which all initial data was recorded. By 1948, when the first report appeared, more than 12,000 sexual histories had been collected.

Neither Kinsey nor the editors at W.B. Saunders, a respected medical publishing house, expected *Sexual Behavior in the Human Male* to be a best-seller. After all, it contained 678 pages of scientific prose, interspersed with 173 figures and graphs, followed by 163 clinical tables, a statistical appendix, and an index. Saunders ordered a modest first printing of 10,000 copies.

They had vastly underestimated both the public's curiosity about sex and the sensationalizing abilities of newspaper and magazine writers. Americans were dying to know who was doing what and with whom, and reporters concentrated on Kinsey's juiciest (and most general) findings: 90 percent of all American males over sixteen had masturbated to orgasm; 85 percent had premarital intercourse; something between 30 and 45 percent of the married population had sex outside of marriage; 37 percent of Kinsey's sample had participated in at least one homosexual contact. So multitudinous were the American male's sexual outlets, Kinsey concluded, that "only 45.9 percent of the total outlet of the total population is derived from marital intercourse." After figures like these were publicized, 200,000 copies of the book were snapped up in the first two months.

The book remained near the top of the best-seller lists for more than a year, and "hotter than the Kinsey report" became a national figure of speech. According to an article in the May 8, 1951, issue of *Look,*

> Since the first Kinsey report was published, many American communities have been pestered by imposters claiming to be Kinsey interviewers. . . . In Tacoma, Washington, a man posing as a Kinsey investigator managed to get the intimate sex histories of scores of women before he was exposed as a fraud. Some of his victims made complaints only after they failed to get the "nylon pretties" the man had promised them as a reward for their cooperation. . . . When a Boston psychiatrist with a penchant for writing poetry turned out a volume called *Clinical Sonnets,* it was described as a "Kinsey report in verse." A sober book on bird life was advertised as an "ornithological Kinsey report."

Manual Sex

Dr. Alfred C. Kinsey.
Americans were dying to know who was doing what with whom.

None of this pleased the editors of *Reader's Digest* or other guardians of American moral values who were convinced that the real motive behind Kinsey's report was to encourage wholesale immorality, up to and possibly including copulation in the streets. Kinsey and his associates replied that they had no desire to bring about a change in American "sex standards;" they had merely conducted a survey to determine what those standards really were in practice.

In one respect, though, Kinsey was an advocate of social change; he never missed an opportunity to argue for the liberalization or elimination of laws governing the sexual conduct of consenting adults. After adding up the types of activity that were illegal in most states (pre- and extra-marital intercourse, mouth-genital contacts, homosexuality, animal contacts, etc.) and the incidence of each as reported in his survey, he concluded that no less than 95 percent of the U.S. male population had violated at least one criminal statute. The few "sex offenders" who were caught and punished, he pointed out, probably had not committed any more serious offenses than the policemen who arrested them.

Kinsey was an early advocate of "gay rights" and of regarding homosexuality as nothing more than a variant form of sexual behavior, not a perversion. More broadly, it is clear from the tone of his reports that he regarded all common forms of sexual "contacts" and "outlets" as natural and healthy. He was, to put it indelicately, an advocate of fucking. The closest his reports ever come to poetry is in describing the period of relaxation that follows orgasm:

> The famous aphorism, *post coitum triste* [one is sad following coitus], is not only a

distortion of Galen's original statement, but an inadequate description of the usually quiescent state of a person who has experienced orgasm. There is neither regret nor conflict nor any tinge of sadness for most persons who have experienced orgasm. There is, on the contrary, a quiescence, a calm, a peace, a satisfaction with the world which, in the minds of many persons, is the most notable aspect of any type of sexual activity.

The above passage is atypical in the extreme; Kinsey usually described sexual activities without any reference to the emotions of the participants. This dryness of approach (Kinsey would have called it "objectivity") gave rise to the oft-repeated criticism that he made sex seem "mechanical." Sometimes this charge was made by self-styled "humanists" who resented the idea that human sexuality, previously the domain of philosophy and poetry, had become the subject of a "cold, detached" scientific survey. But scientists raised the "mechanical" objection, too. Geoffrey Gorer, the British anthropologist, for example, stated:

> The fundamental criticism which, to my mind, invalidates a remarkable amount of industry and perseverance, is that, by Dr. Kinsey's implicit standards, sex becomes a quite meaningless activity, save as a device for physical relaxation—something like a good sneeze, but involving the lower rather than the higher portions of the body. . . . The concept of love is completely omitted from the analysis of sexual behaviour; the word does not even figure in the admirably full 31-page index. All "outlets," all orgasms, are treated as equal

Manual Sex

and interchangeable; no qualitative difference is considered or discussed. . . .

It is easy to concede Gorer's point, but harder to say what Kinsey could have done about it. How do you include love in a statistical table?

When the second report, *Sexual Behavior in the Human Female,* appeared in 1953, there was nothing surprising about its conclusions—the males in the first study had obviously been having sex with somebody. Their partners, as Kinsey made abundantly clear, were America's wives and sweethearts.

Slightly over 60 percent of the total female sample had masturbated, 58 percent to the point of orgasm. Nearly half had had premarital intercourse, and 26 percent of the married sample had coitus with men other than their husbands. Nearly 20 percent had made physical, sexual contacts with other females.

The critics' response to the second report was far more outraged and vociferous than before. U. S. Representative Louis Heller of Brooklyn called it "the insult of the century against our mothers, wives, daughters, and sisters," and tried to get it banned from the mails. Dr. John W. Wimbish, minister of New York's Calvary Baptist Church, believed that "the professor from Bloomington would lead us, like deranged Nebuchadnezzar of old, out into the fields to mingle with the cattle and become one with the beasts of the jungle." And an Indianapolis minister, Dr. Jean S. Milner, found "a fundamental kinship" between Kinsey's research and Communism. Wardell B. Pomeroy, Kinsey's research associate and biographer, blamed this reaction on "the American double standard operating again. We might make disclosures about men

that were shocking to prevailing middle-class morality, but after all, they merely confirmed the conventional wisdom that men were no better than they should be. To talk of girls and women as sexual beings, however—that was too much."

Given the political atmosphere of the time, it was probably inevitable that Kinsey's research should become the object of a Congressional witch-hunt. In 1954 Representative B. Carroll Reece, an ultra-right-wing Republican from Tennessee, formed the House Committee to Investigate Tax-Exempt Foundations. In Reece's mind, the chief question before the committee was whether the Rockefeller Foundation should be allowed to give its financial support (and, by extension, its prestige) to research that encouraged immorality and besmirched the honor of American womanhood. After sixteen sessions, at which Kinsey and his supporters were not allowed to testify, Reece's committee filed a majority report which merely recapitulated his original charges. Congress took no further action, but two months later the Rockefeller Foundation quietly cut off its support of Kinsey's research, supposedly because he was "now in a position to obtain support from other sources."

Those "other sources" never materialized, but Kinsey was able to support his research for the next two years on royalties from the *Male* and *Female* volumes. He died of heart failure in August, 1956, at the age of sixty-four.

Now, nearly two decades and a sexual revolution later, Kinsey's reports gather dust on library shelves. They are read, if at all, as historical documents—products not just of an earlier generation, but of a different culture. The statistics which seemed most shocking then would hardly cause a raised eyebrow today; we are struck not

by how much sexual activity Kinsey unearthed, but by how boring most of it must have been.

In the *Male* volume deep kissing, nude intercourse, pre-coital petting, and mouth-genital activity were classified as "sophisticated" sexual techniques, since they were common only among the college-educated segment of the population. Most couples, married or not, used only one coital position (guess which one). "Universally, at all social levels in our Anglo-American culture, the opinion is held that there is one coital position which is biologically natural, and that all others are man-devised variants which become perversions when regularly engaged in." Furthermore, "for perhaps three-

quarters of all males, orgasm is reached within two minutes after the initiation of the sexual relation, and for a not inconsiderable number of males the climax may be reached within less than a minute or even within ten or twenty seconds after coital entrance."

"This quick performance of the typical male," Kinsey admitted, "may be most unsatisfactory to a wife who is inhibited or natively low in response, as many wives are; and such disparities in the speed of male and female response are frequent sources of marital conflict. . . . A portion of the upper level college educated males do deliberately learn to delay ejaculation, and it is probable that most males could learn to control

Manual Sex

"Have our conventions and moralities—and what we have always held to be simple decency—been outmoded by findings of modern science?"

urethral convulsions, primarily through a tightening of anal muscles, so they could prolong sexual activity before orgasm. But it is only a portion of the male population that would consider the acquirement of such an ability as a desirable substitute for direct and rapidly effected intercourse." In other words—tough luck, ladies.

Male readers, naturally enough, were greatly relieved. What they had been afraid was premature ejaculation turned out to be normal, and it was up to their female partners to make the best of things by somehow speeding up their "inhibited" responses. What seems incredible today is that there were no complaints from Kinsey's female readers; in 1948, even Betty Friedan was busy collecting casserole recipes.

If there had been any female revolutionaries around, the repercussions of Kinsey's second report would have been far greater. Unbeknown to the Congressional committee, he and his researchers had been secretly observing human intercourse and masturbation in their laboratory and recording it on film. Their conclusions—nearly all of which were later confirmed and elaborated by Masters and Johnson—turned established theories of female sexuality upside down.

There was "tremendous individual variation" in the speed and frequency of female response,

Manual Sex

Kinsey found. Ten percent of the married women in his sample had never reached orgasm during intercourse, even after fifteen years of marriage, while another fourteen percent demonstrated a "remarkable ability . . . to reach orgasm repeatedly within a short period of time." He was unable to discover any innate biological differences between the sexes: "Orgasm is a phenomenon which appears to be essentially the same in the human female and male. . . . Females appear to be as capable as males of being aroused by tactile stimuli; they appear as capable as males of responding to the point of orgasm. Their responses are not slower than those of the average male if there is any sufficiently continuous tactile stimulation."

This tactile stimulation had to be applied to the clitoris and labia, he declared, because "in most females the walls of the vagina are devoid of end organs of touch." The "vaginal orgasm," which Freud believed to be the sign of "sexual maturity" in women, was a myth: "the areas primarily involved in the female's sensory responses during coitus are exactly those which are primarily involved in masturbation, namely the clitoris and the labia." These findings, predictably enough, outraged orthodox Freudian psychiatrists, many of whom had built lucrative practices around weaning women away from "infantile" clitoral orgasms.

Dr. Edmund Bergler, a Freudian analyst, claimed in a book called *Kinsey's Myth of Female Sexuality* that Kinsey's data was based on "self-selected groups of neurotics," such as (vaginally) frigid women, prematurely ejaculating males, homosexuals, and masochists, who agreed to talk to him either because they were "pathologic exhibitionists, hunting for a thrill"

or because they were seeking his reassurance that their "neuroses" were normal. "Is sex but a 'mutual gratitude society' in which two neurotics join to negate their neuroses?" he asked, sounding not a little like the *Reader's Digest*.*

Marriage counselors were generally more receptive to Kinsey's findings than psychiatrists, but they were also puzzled about how to use them in therapy. "Kinsey's statement that all female orgasm is clitoral may serve to relieve some of the anxiety which many couples harbor," commented Abraham Stone. "They will perhaps come to accept clitoral stimulation to orgasm as a normal way of achieving satisfaction, if it cannot be obtained otherwise. Yet it in no way solves the problem. Most couples will still want to achieve a simultaneous, mutual, complete response during the sexual act and will not be satisfied, even with an authoritative explanation, with a so-called clitoral orgasm without penetration. . . . " The "problem" Stone referred to, of course, was his clients' desire for a "simultaneous, mutual, complete" orgasm, a goal that kept both partners frustrated and anxiety-ridden. The solution that seems so obvious today—forget about simultaneous performance, and use whatever techniques are nec-

---

*The clitoral-vs.-vaginal orgasm controversy raged in academic journals for the next decade and a half, and became a burning issue in the women's movement during the late 1960s. Masters and Johnson supported Kinsey's contention that all female orgasms are physiologically alike and depend on clitoral stimulation, but they also pointed out that the orgasm itself is always marked by contractions that are centered in the vagina. It now appears that Kinsey underestimated some women's capacity for vaginal sensations, and that there is no clear dichotomy between the two "kinds" of orgasms.

Manual Sex

essary to maximize each partner's sexual potential—apparently did not occur to most marriage counselors until Masters and Johnson suggested it thirteen years later.

Masters and Johnson—it sounds like a law firm or a brand of steak sauce—had not yet found each other when Kinsey died in 1956. William H. Masters, a forty-one-year-old gynecologist at Washington University in St. Louis, had wanted to specialize in the physiology of sex as early as 1943, but his academic advisors had told him that he was too young to put his career on the line by entering such an unorthodox field; he should make a name for himself first in some more respectable area of medical research. Masters heeded their warning and went on to do pioneering work in hormone replacement therapy for menopausal women. Finally, in July 1954, he returned to his primary interest and began studying female sexual response in a university laboratory, using prostitutes as subjects. In 1957 he hired Virginia E. Johnson as his research assistant. Johnson was an outgoing divorcee with two young children; she had no medical background or academic degree, although she had attended the University of Missouri.

By this time Masters had designed a laboratory specifically for the observation of sexual behavior, equipped with a bed, monitoring equipment (electrocardiograph, electroencephalograph, electromyograph, etc.), movie cameras, and an invention that was to cause more public indignation and curiosity than just about any other aspect of his research—a transparent plastic penis, or "artificial coition machine," as Masters preferred to call it, powered by an electric motor. Its length and diameter could be adjusted, as could the depth and the frequency of thrust, and an optical system inside the machine made it possible to observe internal changes in the user's vagina and record them in full color on motion picture film.

Masters soon came to the conclusion that prostitutes were unsuitable for a study on normal sexual responses, since they tended to develop a condition of chronic congestion in the pelvic region. Cautiously he began to recruit medical students, their wives, and other volunteers from the university community. Finding suitable and willing subjects proved easier than he had hoped; by the time *Human Sexual Response* appeared eight years later, 1,273 volunteers had been interviewed and 694 selected. These included 276 married couples who participated jointly, plus 106 single women and thirty-six single men.

Unlike Kinsey, Masters and Johnson didn't try to make their sample representative of the population as a whole. They did just the opposite, in fact, since participants in the program had to be physically normal and capable of reaching orgasm. Impotent men were excluded, as were non-orgasmic women: "Our rule of thumb is if they're not sure about it they probably haven't had it." Before the final selection was made, Masters and Johnson spent several hours taking each volunteer's sexual and medical history. When interviewing married couples they worked as a team; Masters would take the wife's history and Johnson the husband's, or vice versa, and then all four would meet together. This was the start of the "two on two" technique, which later became a hallmark of Masters and Johnson's work with sexually dysfunctional couples.

These initial history-taking sessions allowed

Manual Sex

volunteers who had second thoughts about participating to drop out gracefully, and enabled Masters and Johnson to eliminate obvious exhibitionists (whose impatience to "get on with it" gave them away) as well as those with physical abnormalities or histories of mental illness.

The final requirement for participation—ability to respond sexually under laboratory conditions, while hooked up to various machines and while being observed by scientists, lab technicians, and movie cameramen—did not turn out to be a major stumbling block. After an initial practice session in private, nearly all volunteers quickly lost their inhibitions. In eight years of research, only 118 failures by female participants to reach orgasm were recorded (out of 7,500 tries). The male failure rate was six times as high, but still less than ten percent: 220 failures out of 2,500 attempts.

The first and most persistent objection to Masters and Johnson's findings, of course, was that volunteers who agreed to participate in such a project must have been exhibitionists or perverts of some kind. Leslie H. Farber, a Washington, D.C. psychoanalyst, made this charge in its most subtle form in an article which appeared in *Commentary* magazine in November, 1964, eighteen months before *Human Sexual Response* appeared but after Masters and Johnson had published several preliminary reports in medical journals. For the volunteers, Farber speculated,

> . . . the erotic basis would have to be provided by the situation itself, in addition to the actual manipulation: that is, the prospect of arriving at the laboratory at 10:00 A.M., disrobing, stretching out on the table, and going to work in a somewhat businesslike manner while being measured

and photographed, would have to provide *its own peculiar excitement* [italics mine]. . . . [The female participant's] sexuality would be mechanically accessible or "on call"—under circumstances which would be, if not intimidating, at least distracting to most bodies. . . . In other words, her sexuality would be wholly subject to her will: whenever she determined—or the project determined—that she should have reached a climax, she would willingly begin those gestures that would lead to one. To use the modern idiom, all that would be unavailable to her sexological dexterity would be frigidity. Or, to speak more clearly, all that would be unavailable to her would be a real response to the laboratory situation.

It is obvious from this passage that Farber's real objection to Masters and Johnson's research was the one that had been raised so often against Kinsey's: it made sex seem mechanical, quantifiable, divorced from human emotions. Sex just wasn't sexy anymore.

Masters and Johnson refused to enter into an argument on these grounds; they had never claimed that the behavior they observed in their laboratory bore any resemblance, other than a purely biological one, to most peoples' sexual experiences. They were studying their volunteers' physiological responses, not their motivations. The underlying assumption of their research was that these physiological responses were universal, like those involved in digestion or any other bodily function. If this assumption is correct—and no one has proved otherwise—then the subjects' psychological makeup didn't really matter. Necrophiliacs, people who were

Dr. William H. Masters and Mrs. Virginia E. Johnson, 1970. "Our rule of thumb is if they're not sure about it, they probably haven't had it."

turned on by Shetland sheep dogs, and honey-mooning newlyweds would all presumably reach orgasm the same way.

Farber's article went on to blame the modern era of sexual discontent on "sexologists" who had convinced women that they, too, were entitled to orgasms. "As far as I know, little attention was paid to the female orgasm before the era of sexology. Where did the sexologists find it? Did they discover it or invent it? or both?" Farber longed for the good old days, when a woman's capacity to reach orgasm " . . . had not yet been abstracted and isolated from the totality of her pleasures and enshrined as the meaning and measure of her erotic life. She was content with the mystery and variety of her difference from man, and in fact would not have had it otherwise."

Apparently Farber's lament struck a responsive chord, at least among male readers; his article was so widely read and quoted that Masters and Johnson feared their upcoming book would be "buried in an avalanche of unfair publicity" and speeded up their preparation of the manuscript. *Human Sexual Response* finally appeared in April, 1966, and, like Kinsey's reports became an instantaneous best-seller. It is doubtful whether most buyers ever got past the first chapter—as Max Lerner said in a *New York Post* review, "the book's language . . . is so severely technical and barbarous as to make Kinsey seem a light essayist."

Briefly, Masters and Johnson divided the human "response cycle" into four phases: excitement, plateau, orgasm, and resolution. They agreed with Kinsey that male and female orgasms are nearly identical physiologically; in both sexes, the body's primary reactions to sexual stimuli are myotonia (increased muscle tension) and vasocongestion (engorgement of the blood vessels), particularly in the pelvic region.

The excitement phase begins with vasocongestion which causes erection of the penis in the male and a "sweating reaction" that lubricates the walls of the vagina in the female. The woman's clitoris, labia, and breasts also swell and the inner two-thirds of the vagina lengthens and becomes wider. The male's testes are pulled up further into the scrotal sac and the skin of the scrotum tenses and thickens. In both sexes the "sex flush," a reddish measles-like rash, may begin to spread over the abdomen and breasts; 75 percent of the female subjects and 25 percent of the males exhibited this rash at some point in their response cycle.

In the plateau phase, these reactions continue and become more marked. The male's testes become about 50 percent larger in diameter than in their unstimulated state and are pulled up even higher into the scrotum. In the female, the clitoris retracts to a position under the clitoral hood and the tissues around the outer third of the vagina swell, reducing the vagina's diameter by as much as 50 percent. Masters and Johnson call this engorgement the "orgasmic platform." Both sexes experience an increase in pulse rate, blood pressure, and rate of breathing, along with a general tightening of both voluntary and involuntary muscles throughout the body.

During orgasm, naturally, the entire process comes to a climax. In both sexes, orgasm begins with a series of intense rhythmic contractions at intervals of four-fifths of a second; after the first few contractions, the interval between them becomes longer and their intensity decreases. In

Manual Sex

women these contractions occur in the outer third of the vagina, or "orgasmic platform," and the uterus also contracts in a wavelike motion. In men, the contractions force semen and prostatic fluid through the urethra (the first stage of ejaculation) and then the urethral bulb, which has doubled or tripled in size, projects the semen outward (the second stage). Both sexes experience involuntary contractions, spasms, and contortions of various other muscles, most noticeably those of the face, hands, and feet.

During the resolution phase, these muscular tensions dissipate and the engorged blood vessels gradually release their excess fluid. The sex flush disappears, and pulse rate, blood pressure, and breathing rate gradually return to normal. In men, of course, the penis loses its erection and shrinks back to its unstimulated size; in women, the orgasmic platform relaxes, the clitoris returns to its ordinary position, and other genital tissues gradually return to normal.

The most significant difference between male and female sexual response cycles occurs during this final stage. Men experience a "refractory period" of greatly varying length during which they cannot have another erection, while women can begin the cycle again as soon as stimulation is resumed. Some women, when continuously stimulated, are capable of going from orgasm to orgasm repeatedly with practically no time lapse; they may "experience five to 20 recurrent orgasmic experiences with the sexual tension never allowed to drop below a plateau phase maintenance level until physical exhaustion terminates the session." Since Masters and Johnson were not studying a representative sample, they could not estimate what percentage of the female population is or can be multi-orgasmic—but they were convinced that it is much greater than Kinsey's reported 14 percent:

> If a woman who is capable of regular orgasms is properly stimulated within a short period after her first climax, she will in most instances be capable of having a second, third, fourth, and even fifth and sixth orgasm before she is fully satiated. As contrasted with the male's usual inability to have more than one orgasm in a short period, many females, especially when clitorally stimulated, can regularly have five or six full orgasms within a matter of minutes.

Masters and Johnson's laboratory techniques, especially full-color filming and use of the artificial penis, allowed many aspects of female sexual response to be observed for the first time. One of the most interesting of these was the retraction of the clitoris beneath the "hood" formed by the inner lips of the labia. This discovery made most marriage manuals of the time obsolete, since their advice to husbands of unresponsive or "frigid" women was to concentrate on direct stimulation of the clitoris throughout intercourse—a near impossibility, as countless frustrated men discovered as they fumbled around trying to locate their equally frustrated wives' elusive but all-important clitorises.

What actually happens during normal intercourse, Masters and Johnson concluded, is that the thrusting of the penis during intercourse causes the hood to slide rhythmically back and forth over the clitoris, thus stimulating it indirectly. If a woman fails to reach orgasm during intercourse, it is probably because this indirect clitoral stimulation is not continued long enough or rhythmically enough. Masters and Johnson found that their female subjects experienced their most intense orgasms (measured by the number of orgasmic contractions) during masturbation, when they were free to "concentrate on their own sexual demand without the distraction of a coital partner."

Predictably enough, this choice of words caused critics to raise the cry of "mechanization" once again—and not just male critics, either. "Distraction! Is that the meaning of a partner in sex?" wrote Dr. Natalie Shainess. "This points to a dehumanizing view . . . sex seems little more than a stimulus-response reflex cycle, devoid of intra-psychic or interpersonal meaning."

Masters and Johnson's second book, *Human Sexual Inadequacy,* can be seen as an indirect answer to such criticism. In 1958, just one year after their research program began, they had begun to study and treat individuals whose sexual response cycles failed to follow the normal pattern. They became sex counselors and therapists as well as scientific researchers, and this expansion of their role inevitably led them to consider the psychological and interpersonal aspects of sex.

Human Sexual Inadequacy, published in 1970, outlined Masters and Johnson's basic two-week therapy program and described the techniques they had developed to deal with seven kinds of sexual inadequacy: premature ejaculation, ejaculatory incompetence, and primary and secondary impotence in men, orgasmic dysfunction and vaginismus (involuntary vaginal spasms) in women, and dyspareunia (pain during intercourse) in both sexes. The overall success rate (measured by follow-up interviews conducted with 226 patients five years after treatment) was 74.5 percent—an astounding figure, considering the complexity of the problems and the shortness of the treatment period.

The most spectacular results were with prematurely ejaculating men: only four failures out of 186 patients. The "squeeze technique" these men and their partners were taught is so straightforward, easily learned, and effective that Masters and Johnson believe premature ejaculation "could be eliminated in a decade" if it were made widely available. The technique rarely works on a do-it-yourself basis, however, because the cooperation of both partners is needed, and many prematurely ejaculating men are unwilling to admit they have a problem. At least a minimum of communication between partners must be established first, which usually requires the services of a therapist or marriage counselor.

Communication is the key to Masters and Johnson's therapeutic approach, no matter which particular form of sexual dysfunction they are treating. They refuse to accept married patients without the full participation of both partners; one of their favorite clichés is "the relationship between the partners is the patient." After two days of initial interviews, four-way discussions between the two cotherapists and the couple begin. Each therapist acts from time to time as a "friend in court" for the partner of the same sex, while also trying in a nonjudgmental way to show both partners the destructiveness of their behavior patterns toward each other.

By the time they seek professional help, all dysfunctional individuals have developed a "fear of failure syndrome"; they are so worried about achieving an erection, an orgasm, or whatever that they're almost certain not to. Masters and

Johnson concentrate on removing these "goal-oriented performance anxieties" and substituting the concepts of "pleasuring" and "being pleasured" instead. After the third day of treatment, couples are instructed to choose a quiet, private place, remove their clothing, and—without touching each other's genitals or the woman's breasts—to "trace, massage, and fondle each other . . . to experience and appreciate the sensuous dimensions of hard and soft, smooth and rough, warm and cool, qualities of texture and, finally the somewhat indescribable aura of physical receptivity expressed by the partner being pleasured." As treatment progresses, patients are instructed to explore each other's genitals and to massage one another with scented lotions. They are not allowed to attempt intercourse until they have learned to communicate with each other, both verbally and nonverbally, about what gives them pleasure.

Once this "sensate focusing" has reawakened their capacity for sexual response, both partners are given instruction in specific techniques to correct their particular problem. Without going into these techniques in any detail, two general points are worth repeating. First, the traditional male-superior position in intercourse is just about the only one Masters and Johnson *don't* recommend. Second, simultaneous orgasms are one of the "goals" they advise their patients to forget. Sexual response is basically an involuntary physiological process; if the participants are preoccupied with trying to coordinate their orgasms, they are likely to "assume a spectator role" and lose their ability to respond naturally. Besides, why should the woman "hold herself back" if she is capable of several orgasms in a single session?

Masters and Johnson's failure rate in cases of "primary orgasmic dysfunction" in women (they refuse to use the term "frigidity") was 16.6 percent—or, to put it another way, more than 80 percent of these women, who had never experienced an orgasm of any kind before entering the treatment program, were having orgasms regularly with their husbands by the end of the second week. These patients were the products of entire lifetimes of negative conditioning toward sex, which Masters and Johnson believe all women in our society experience to a certain extent:

> During her formative years the female dissembles much of her developing functional sexuality in response to societal requirements for a "good girl" facade. Instead of being taught or allowed to value her sexual feelings . . . she must attempt to remove them from their natural context of environmental stimulation under the implication that they are bad, dirty, etc. . . . Yet, woman's conscious denial of biophysical capacity is rarely a completely successful venture, for her physiological capacity for sexual response infinitely surpasses that of man. Indeed, her significantly greater susceptibility to negatively based psychosocial influences may imply the existence of a natural state of psycho-sexual-social balance between the sexes that has been culturally established to neutralize woman's biophysical superiority.

This "biophysical superiority" became apparent as soon as the female patients' negative attitudes toward sex had been reversed by counseling and sensate focus exercises. It was surprisingly easy for supposedly frigid women to become orgasmic (and even multiorgasmic) within a matter of days. Impotent men, on the other hand, were much less responsive to treatment; the 40.6 percent failure rate in cases of primary impotence was Masters and Johnson's "clinical disaster area."

When *Human Sexual Inadequacy* was published, Masters and Johnson predicted that it would become obsolete within a decade, but there has been no great leap forward in therapy techniques or success rates since then. Sexual dysfunction therapy is still available to only a small percentage of those who need it; the few legitimate "sex clinics" are all expensive and have long waiting lists. The book's greatest impact has been on the ordinary sex lives of ordinary people.

Masters and Johnson's sensate focusing techniques were first popularized by encounter and sensitivity groups, which became a national fad that encompassed everything from radical experiments like Esalen and Sandstone in California to groups of Kansas City businessmen lying on the floor with their heads on each other's stomachs. Soon suburban housewives were buying *The Sensuous Woman* and spending their afternoons in bed—with electric vibrators, not delivery boys—doing their "sensuality exercises" and practicing the Butterfly Flick and the Velvet Buzzsaw. "J's" message to sexually unresponsive women was simply a lowbrow version of Masters and Johnson's: "All you have to do is relax, clear your head of those preconceived notions that have been stumbling blocks to sensuality and open yourself up to new signals." *The Sensuous Man,* who came along two years later, was still a goal-oriented "chauvinist," but at least he took time for plenty of "nibbling,

nipping, eating, licking, and sucking" on the way. By the time *The Joy of Sex* appeared in 1972, the best-seller lists were ready for a new price range in sex books ($12.95!) and a more sophisticated approach. Its editor, Dr. Alex Comfort, called it "the first explicitly sexual book for the coffee table"—but my copy tends to fall open at too many embarrassing places for that.

Joy and its sequel, *More Joy,* were written for people whose sexual responses are already "adequate," to use Masters and Johnson's terminology. The basic assumption is that merely adequate sex isn't good enough; the goal should be "high-quality sex" between "adventurous and uninhibited lovers who want to find the limits of their ability to enjoy sex." As Dr. Comfort and his two anonymous coauthors define them, those limits are pretty far out—too far, in the opinion of reviewers who were shocked by the passages on fantasies, fetishes, role-playing and bondage "games." There are dangers in these sorts of things, of course, and the books are full of warnings about them. But the warnings are much less explicit than the descriptions of techniques. Readers who are anxious about whether their sexual appetites are "normal" are told not to worry, that abnormality is an outmoded concept, and that they shouldn't make the mistake of practicing "do-it-yourself psychoanalysis." That seems like pretty unrealistic advice to offer people who have spent the night following instructions like these:

> [Bed] is the place to experience things you can't possibly act out, and to learn your partner's fantasy needs. Their fantasies can be heterosexual, homosexual, incestuous,

tender, wild or bloodthirsty—don't block, and don't be afraid of your partner's fantasy; this is a dream you are in. But be careful about recording such dreams, as they can be disturbing at the daylight level . . .

One imagines the couple at breakfast the next morning, glassy-eyed over their orange juice and poached eggs.

"Sex is the most important sort of adult play," the Joy books keep telling us—but the kind of sex described in these books requires a great deal of practice, time, and effort, which is why the "joy" of sex ends up sounding so much like work. One reason these books are so popular may be that they fit perfectly with the Protestant ethic; there's always another technique to be learned, another position to be tried. The old goal ("Did you come?") has been replaced by an open-ended and ultimately indefinable one ("Was it good for you? *Really* good?"). This is certainly an improvement and a lot more fun, but it can become just as anxiety-producing in the end.

It is unfair to blame Dr. Comfort and his colleagues for this, of course, or for our tendency to go overboard on technique at this point in the sexual (r)evolution. We need only remember the Kinsey reports to see how far we've come—many of the couples who were having two-minute sex with no preliminaries and the woman flat on her back in 1949 are now reading *The Joy of Sex* and discovering slow masturbation, chastity belts, and Chinese penis rings. Dr. Kinsey would be amazed.

NANCY BANKS

Above the Fruited Plain

Gay Life in San Francisco, 1974

11

> *It is an odd thing, but everyone who disappears is said to be seen at San Francisco. It must be a delightful city, and possess all the attractions of the next world.*
> Oscar Wilde, 1891

In 1975, people are still disappearing from straight heterosexual lives and turning up in San Francisco, where there has always been a gay scene, and, since the late 1960s, an active gay liberation movement as well.

In 1948 (the same year that Kinsey reported that 37 percent of white American males had had at least one homosexual encounter), the first major homophile organization—the Mattachine Society—was founded in California. This and subsequent groups—One, Inc., the Society for Individual Rights, and the lesbian organization Daughters of Bilitis—concentrated on establishing the respectability of homosexuals, on winning church support, on individual counseling and assistance—in short, on integrating the homosexual-as-outsider into American society.

In 1969, alongside the militant agitation of other oppressed minorities, Gay Power blossomed. In San Francisco, the Committee for Homosexual Freedom organized a protest against a shipping company which had fired an employee after a photograph of him hugging another man appeared in the *Berkeley Barb*. Demonstrations at the mayor's office and radio and newspaper offices followed soon after similar incidents. In New York, the Stonewall riot—gays fighting back as the police raided the Stonewall Inn, a bar on Christopher Street—and its publicity established gay pride as a force to be reckoned with, a radical political movement which questioned heterosexual values in all spheres of life. The slogan had changed from *Gay is Good* to *Blatant is Beautiful*!

Throughout the country gay liberation groups proliferated; publications multiplied; manifestoes appeared; demonstrators disrupted medical and psychiatric conventions, demanded their rights from universities; gay communes, coffee-houses, consciousness-raising groups (alternatives both to cruising in bars and baths and to heterosexually imitative monogamy) sprang up; gays were coming out of the closet.

In 1970, lesbians who had formed women's caucuses of gay liberation groups, or gay subgroups of women's liberation organizations, left both groups to form their own movement, creating Radicalesbians in New York and other groups around the country. Gay men and lesbians have occasionally united for marches and Gay Pride celebrations since then, but separate ideologies, activities, and objectives—outweighing the common ground of homosexuality—have largely put the gay scene for men and for women in two unconnected worlds.

In 1970, Carl Wittman wrote, in "A Gay Manifesto" in the February 1970, issue of *Liberation* (Vol. 14, #10):

> San Francisco is a refugee camp for homosexuals. We have fled here from every part of the nation, and like refugees elsewhere, we came not because it is so great here, but because it was so bad there. By the tens of thousands, we fled small towns where to be ourselves would endanger our jobs and any hope of a decent life; we have fled from blackmailing cops, from families who disowned or "tolerated" us; we have been drummed out of the armed services, thrown out of schools, fired from jobs, beaten by punks and policemen.
>
> And we have formed a ghetto, out of self-protection. It is a ghetto rather than a free territory because it is still theirs. Straight cops patrol us, straight legislators govern us, straight employers keep us in line, straight money exploits us . . . In the past year there has been an awakening of gay liberation ideas and energy. How it began we don't know; maybe we were inspired by black people and their freedom movement; we learned how to stop pretending from the hip revolution. America in all its ugliness has surfaced with the war and our national leaders. And we are revulsed by the quality of our ghetto life.
>
> Where once there was frustration, alienation, and cynicism, there are new characteristics among us. We are full of love for each other and are showing it; we are full of anger at what has been done to us. And as we recall all the self-censorship and repression for so many years, a reservoir of tears pours out of our eyes. And we are euphoric, high, with the initial flourish of a movement.

Many gays remain in closets, many lead subdued or banal lives. But what is most visible of the gay scene in San Francisco are the public events, many of which are shown here—from the masquerade balls to a softball game against San Francisco's police department, to an ad campaign aimed at gays by Acme Beer Company, supplier to the bars. The photographs in this chapter were taken by Robert Hopkins at gay events in San Francisco spanning a period of slightly more than a year in 1974. No statement is being made concerning any of the persons pictured, except that the camera and the subjects were at the same place at the same time. Some of the photographs have been previously published in the *San Francisco Sentinel*.

Above the Fruited Plain

The annual Gay Pride parade.

Above the Fruited Plain

Above the Fruited Plain

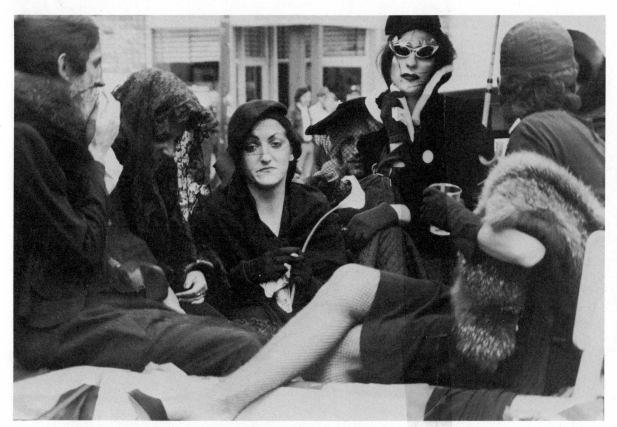

The Gay Pride parade.

Above the Fruited Plain

Competitors for the title of
Miss Gay San Francisco, 1975.
Tammy Lynn, *left,* was the winner.

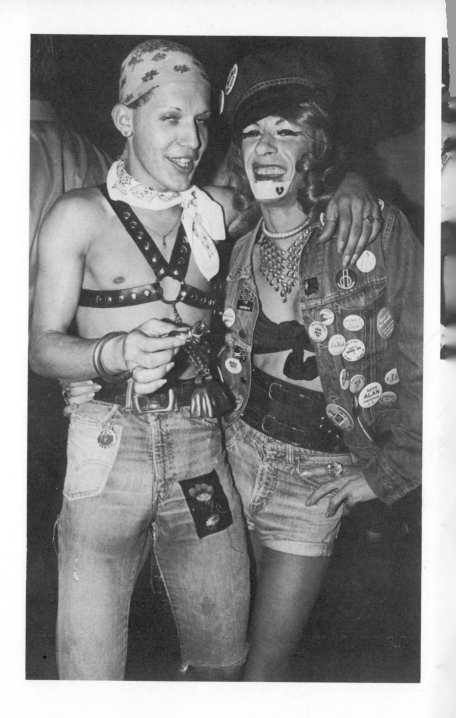

California Motorcycle Club carnival.

Above the Fruited Plain

Above the Fruited Plain

Above the Fruited Plain

Above, judge and contestants on the
Acme Beer Company promotional trip.
Opposite and following pages, a
Halloweeen party.

Above the Fruited Plain

Above the Fruited Plain

Above the Fruited Plain

Slightly Far Out in California

12

It's another Saturday night and Sam Cooke ain't got nobody. He's singing it on the stereo and I'm in the kitchen eating corn chips with dip.

"*I just wish I had someone to talk to,*" he sings, and I can dig it, I can dig it. You should see this party. Halloween in California. Every light in the house is on. As soon as I got out of the car I said it, oh no-o-o. This is one a those *light* parties. I hate light parties. *You can see what people look like.* No, man, I want a serious party, where nobody's talking and everybody's slow dancing and nobody's moving. I want to meet a woman in the *dark* and lose my mind. And you can't go to a party in this town where that's going to happen. There's no commitment here.

You're lucky if you don't get depressed.

At the last party, which was a housewarming (there always has to be an *occasion,* Saturday night isn't good enough), every woman had gone home by eleven and I was left, wonderfully drunk on wine with no one to turn to. I remember singing "Who Can I Turn To?" like Tony Martin. But it wasn't a joke. I had boogied, woogied, fallen in love a few times, and laughed all night, and there I was with three tables of

vegetarian food and *Hey, man, I'm alone. Again,* and I panicked. Suddenly everything I lacked in life had climbed out in front of me and started calling me names. In two minutes, I got right back down with what had never gone away and said, "Here I am again." Six months of getting it together straight down the drain.

Desperation is not cool in California.

It's OK for New Year's Eve or the first day of spring in Philadelphia or any day of the week in Iowa City, but not in Santa Cruz. I've seen whole bars in this town where no one feels bad. Just as I've seen whole parties where no one gets too excited. There's no commitment.

So this party I'm not getting excited, or loaded, I'm grounded tonight, and if the poison oak on my arms flares up I won't scratch, I'll *stand* it. I will *not* pass Go. This is a costume party and my name is Dumbo, with a three foot rubber trunk and a fear of flying, and I am going to sit by these corn chips all night and listen to Sam sing and feed the elephant. Later I may walk the elephant.

Wandering about me, in other rooms, in soft voices, witches, goblins, and gorillas touch and relate to each other, and struggle to maintain eye contact through their masks. They're big on eye contact out here; it's a major industry. I prefer to look somebody in the mouth, I don't know, maybe I'm antisocial but the mouth seems to reveal more, and you don't have to divide your attention between listening and *looking* like you're listening which is what happens when somebody's got me by the eyes. I've got friends in Chicago who talk three feet to the right of each other. I don't know what they do in front of a mirror. How do they shave? Use two mirrors?

I eat a corn chip. Sam is singing directly to me but it doesn't help, I feel lousy. As usual. I've been considering applying to the Guggenheim Foundation for a grant to continue my research into self-pity, using the last three women I've lived with for references. I could name the project "How Low Can You Go? by peter ellis," but they'd probably award the money to some junkie with a good act. (And is there an ex-junkie in the country who doesn't make his living rehabilitating junkies and ex-ex-junkies?) Why am I going on like this, what is this itch to bitch? Come on, *listen to Sam sing.*

OK. Sing, Sam. *Eat.* I eat. I close my eyes.

I was born by the river, in a little tent,
and just like the river, I've been runnin ever since,

Sam sings. I'm right with you, Sam.

And it's been real hard every step of the way . . .

Yeah. I know what you're trying to say, go on . . .

. . . . . my change, my change is gonna come . . .

That's right, that's right. I dip, I eat, *crunch.* Yeah, but what happened, Sam, and I wonder about where the mystery woman who visits his grave was when he needed her. Or was she the one who shot him in his motel room? Or was that Jackie Wilson? Some chick shot him in the neck and he was never the same again. His voice changed.

"Hey Bambi, you remember Jackie Wilson?" I say. Bambi is standing by the end of the table.

"Who?" she says.

"You know, Jackie *Wilson.*"

She's never heard of him. Amazing. Where am I? My dog's heard of Jackie Wilson. "He sang, what is that song. . . . *Lonely Teardrops,* yeah, that's it . . . *mine will nev-er dry up . . .*" She's not listening and has moved over to the liquor table to admire a gorilla, and I keep singing, *lone-ly tear-drops,* just in case anyone thinks I was singing for her benefit. I stop.

The gorilla who is stealing the show is a plain young woman named Lori, who is usually allowed her own space at a party.

"Come on, who *is* that? Who's *in* there?" Bambi says, playing the game. Bambi by the way is dressed as a *duck.*

"It's me. Lori."

"Far *out.* What a neat costume!"

"Yeah, at midnight I turn into a princess."

"Far fucking *out.* Where did you ever *get* that?"

I can tell you where she got it. I was at the Costume Bank before she was and saw the gorilla suit, and *I* wanted to rent it too but not for thirty-six dollars for twenty-four hours. Dumbo was only nine dollars and, well, you know, like *for what*?

Jon comes over to them. He looks like one of

those strong men in the soap operas those worried women look up to. Even when they say "Hello, Bob," it's laden with meaning.

"Hello, Jon," Lori says.

"Hello hairy. Is it hot in there?"

"Oh, don't worry, I use *Dial. Don't you wish everybody did?* Oh Jon, I'd like you to meet Bambi. She was the one in my *train* dream."

"Hey, sure." Jon strains to see if there is an attractive woman under the duck's costume. "I like your name, Bambi."

"I like it, too," she says, and they laugh.

"Jon is a very special friend of mine," Lori says.

Bambi nods and offers her hand. "Hello Jon."

He squeezes it. They look at each other without blinking. Something passes between them. "*Really*," he says, and they laugh again, something is happening, they are relating beyond life as we know it. A moment of peace passes. "How have you *been*, Bambi?" It is a joke and they laugh, still holding hands. She turns serious.

"I've been *good, good.*"

"That's great, that's just *great.*"

Slightly Far Out in California

"It *feels* great."

He nods, and then shakes his head from the breeze of the thought that just went by him. "*Wow.* Bambi, did anyone ever tell you . . ."

"*Yeah.*" She is right with him.

He can't believe it. "Beautiful."

"*No shit,*" she says, and they laugh, fall against each other and hug, I know what he's thinking. They have got it off, but will they get it on? That remains to be seen. It's possible they've totally misunderstood each other.

I dip a corn chip and remind myself to multiply everything these people say by zero. I've seen pinball machines with larger vocabularies. Language in California is on the way out, and for good reason; words cannot convey feelings, and LSD has already shown us the arbitrariness of thought—so why talk, especially when people

want only to agree? Slang out here has been reduced to a few unchanging catch-alls, *really, out of sight, far out,* and *wow,* which provide a certain stroke value and mean simply *I hear you* and *I like you* and *it doesn't matter what you say, I can dig it.* Thirty-year-old men say *groovy* without embarrassment. *I don't think, therefore I am* is satori, and within reach of half the state.

"Hello, Dumbo." Someone pats me on the shoulder.

"Hello, Trisha."

"It's good to see you. I've been thinking about you."

"I've been here all the time."

"I know. Hey, what's the matter? You look like you're in pain, excuse me a minute . . ." She touches my shoulder and is gone. *Gone.* She says you-look-like-you're-in-pain and *leaves.* Where to? To talk to Jon? Hello, Jon. Man, Dumbo's an elephant, not a worm. *Stand back, bitch.* I think I'm going crazy. OK, OK, ease up, relax, you've been looking forward to this party for a month. *I'm in pain. She said it, look . . .* You're not in pain, Dumb-bo, relax, listen to the sounds. I listen. *Eat.* I eat. Aretha is now singing.

I think about her husband walking on stage to borrow money from her, and going backstage to shoot her manager. I think about Johnny Ace shooting himself, and Al Green getting boiling hot grits poured on him by a woman as he got out of the bathtub, and I dip and eat and think about Johnny Mathis who never got into trouble, who has ten million dollars and not one paternity suit, and I eat, hunched over the table now and shoveling the loaded chips directly into my face, in such a way that anyone passing will keep on going.

Slightly Far Out in California

I dip I eat I dip I eat I despise myself when I'm like this. Maybe next group I'll work on getting in touch with the Pig-in-me, or with why I punish myself for despising myself, (and for another thirty dollars, why I despise myself for feeling good about punishing myself for despising myself; no wonder people don't feel anything out here, it's too complicated). I'll just accept where I'm at, assume responsibility— *OK*—I'm despicable. Despicable. Hey great, it works, no *pain*.

The hostess of the party comes by. I load up a chip and bend my head to catch it. She looks away in disgust.

I swing my trunk under her nose.

"My compliments to the chef. This dip's terrific," I say.

She smiles weakly. "Yes, it's got ginger in it." Selecting a single chip, she dips and eats it and walks away. What is called a *success d'estime* I take it.

"Hey, save some for me," I call out, and laugh, and finish laughing, and twenty minutes goes by since I was laughing. "I care for you," I tell the corn chips and begin to slap them into my mouth by the handful. *Crunch*. My trunk flops into the dip. I'm coming apart. I believe the first stage of loathsomeness is at hand. How much further down before the drill strikes shit?

"More chips," I call out, digging into the last bowl. When I'm done with that maybe I'll kill myself—what else can you do after two pounds of chips—but as long as I don't punish myself for killing myself, it's OK. *Yeah*. You know, two days ago my mother calls me on the phone. She says, "What're you doing out there? You're thirty-one years old. Look, if you need some money, we'll be glad . . ." Look, I tell her, I'm

happy. "You're *happy*? Do you expect to spend the rest of your life being *happy*?"

I think maybe I should have a drink, maybe two drinks. I'm not doing myself much good like this. Make it three drinks. Yeah, I'm going to start coasting this party. *Hey, man, what's happenin, man?* That's the only way to do it out here. On the Coast you coast. I mean, this is Santa *Cruise*—all year round. Where people over thirty can retire and rotate in the sun, and if you have a Ph.D. you're entitled to forty-six dollars worth of food stamps a month.

I eat some chips. I don't *want* to cruise. That isn't me. I'm an all-out guy—just like Charlie Parker who, in this book I read, ate more, drank more, fucked more, and played more music than anyone—except that I don't play an instrument and I don't like the *taste* of liquor and I'm, well, in between affairs, OK OK, so maybe I'll get up, *in a minute,* and start circulating, go from room to room in case I'm missing some of the action, right? And then what do I do, start leaning in doorways with a drink in my hand, waiting to be trapped into conversations, "And what have *you* been up to?" And what then, start talking the equivalent of eating corn chips? Anyway I'd probably blow it because this aloofness that I've demonstrated, once pierced, degenerates quickly into a compulsion to confess. And what then, cry? Yeah, and in five seconds mobilize this party into a group therapy session in which I would be pushed from every side to spill my cookies entirely.

Although the last time I got unhappy in public about ten California smiles absorbed everything I was feeling. A woman hugged me and said, "Let me be your emotional ground." And that one bad acid trip I had when this guy kept screaming LET IT BE into my ear, as though down a well, LET IT BE. They had to pull me off him. I was ready to kill him and he still said it, LET IT BE.

Oh, for a good cool draught of the East Coast, where people know how to be miserable and enjoy themselves. Sometimes I wonder why I don't go back. Dudes with daggers, women with sharp teeth, that's why. Being blissed in Santa Cruz may be too weak a sensation, but being hassled, scared, undermined, and horny in Philadelphia is second best to anything. I got out of Philly like Nixon abandoning the rats, and drove 3,000 miles watching my eyes in the rear view mirror.

When I got to Santa Cruz I was ready to get down on my knees before someone. Which is how you should arrive here, like clay. I got myself a used Volkswagen, some used clothes, and went looking for the new me. I lived in three cabins in the woods and two tract houses by the sea before I finally got to sleep with a California blonde with long legs and a *Chiclet* smile. She was hitchhiking and I was causing a traffic jam hitting the brakes. She was out of work and feeling down and her bicycle was in the shop and I said I was holding four aces, and we got it off. I convinced her not to hitchhike anymore; you never know who might pick you up.

Cynthia was lovely in bed but after a while I felt I was impressing her like footprints in sand. There was always another wave. One good night did not seem to imply there should be other good nights. Was this called living for today or did she just not like me? She was kind to everybody, everybody was kind to her, and what was I wringing my hands about? I didn't have four aces. Give me three cards.

I met another woman, and again drew cards. What was wrong? These were nice people. The wildness I was feeling began to build; the paranoid who constantly rode shotgun on my shoulder needed someone to shoot at. But these people offered no resistance. And no real friendship because I could sense no bottom to them. No hot no cold. Extremes of anything were conveniently shut down in order to achieve a more perfect and painless nothing.

The friction and aggression of the East Coast, where I first heard the words *You rat motherfucker,* were absent on the West. Here life was more Yes-oriented, and more feminized, intuitive, passive. The men had abdicated and everyone wanted to be a woman or a child, and get back to the garden and see, smell, hear, touch, and taste, and be open to change and *into* everything—painting, belly dancing, writing, macrame—which meant usually a commitment only to keep moving and trying new things. People demanded space—*give me my space*—to breathe and grow and true commitment threatened limits, and suffocation; it followed of course that commitment to feelings, anger, excitement, passion, even to finding the right words, could be similarly hard and dangerous work.

My reaction to this is to eat corn chips for a living. I wouldn't mind any of it if white people both East and West didn't have such wonderful ways to hide from their sexuality. You want to see some eye contact? Go to a nude beach. Until you turn your back, it's just eyes on eyes. No one looks down. Except on the gay strip of course. There, my beautiful watermelon ass did not go unnoticed. *Hey, white thighs.*

I wish this *party* were gay, a good faggot ball where everybody's ripping each other apart and bitching and seething with sex, and there's none of these gentle compliments about *what a neat costume.* The only bar in this town where people dance with each other and don't just throw out their hands and self-express is the gay bar, Mona's Gorilla Lounge. Most of the lesbians aren't much fun to watch; they dance stiffly, like men, but the gay dudes swing and pop and talk with their hips.

The best dance I had was with a drag queen. It had been a mistake, I thought she was a woman, she had the sweetest tightest ass in the place and a red sensuous mouth. Well, I asked her and fortunately it was a fast dance. Still, she stayed close, licking her full lips, flaring her nostrils, and I began to think, this is too good, a woman wouldn't do this . . . would she? *No, no,* this dude's a femininity and then in time to the music, she went down on her knees and made like a snake. I began to sweat—*let yourself go, enjoy yourself*—her mouth opened, *no, she ain't no woman, let me the fuck out of here, I ain't like that,* she flicked her tongue, *no . . .*

"Give me some of that wine?" I call to Bambi who is standing by the liquor table.

"The Zinfandel?"

"Yeah." I think I'll have to get drunk at this party. I'd like some sweet pink wine and lemon juice so I could get *rotten* drunk, but this'll do. Drop some moth balls in it and I'll never quit. I'm coming, folks; the elephant is ready.

I pour off a glass and drink.

"Trisha, give me a hit of that dope." I suck on the joint. An hour ago I was talking that alcohol and dope are anti-people and make it easy not to relate, but this is California, a state with no memory, and give me back that joint.

"You still thinking about me, Trisha?"

"Are you still in pain, Dumbo?"

I run my trunk up her dress and she grabs it and laughs. I mimic her voice. "Trisha, I took some amyl nitrates last night and thought of you."

"Oh, I see. So you are in pain."

I finish off the wine and refill the glass. It is hard to drink when you're smiling. Trisha is all right. Once in a while we sleep together; I say that casually because it *is* casual. Now there is *no other woman* I'm sleeping with at present, a situation not arrived at by choice, and I refuse to go out every night and hunt for one (of course I go out every night and hunt, in every *bar*), but when I'm with Trisha, it's strictly casual. I don't know how it started, I think we woke up in the same bed together, and now every few weeks or so when I'm tired or slightly drunk I'll stop by her house and pet her cat, whose name I can never remember. It is good to be tired and sort of *I don't know* with Trisha. That's her frequency, and tired and goofy we lay in bed together and she never seems to know if she wants to ball until we're balling, and even balling she seems to require her own space. Afterwards there's that moment, and she says, "Where are you? Hey, are you all right?" Yeah.

Once I said *No, I wasn't* and got angry and told her where I thought all this shit was at and she just looked at me, as though through the bars of a cage, and said "Cool *out.*" The same phrase she later used on a growling dog, Cool *out.*

Anger, of course, is one of the Seven Inconveniences. And one of the nine ways to put your trip on somebody. You can get angry in therapy, or if somebody says something about your therapist. *You say somethin' about my therapist?*

I had a psychiatrist friend who wouldn't get angry, even if you had had the good fortune to sleep with his wife. Now, we had already done it, it was maybe a year later, and we were seated with a group of people in the living room. Alan had just come back from *his* therapist with a videotape of what had been a *breakthrough* session. We were going to witness the tape. Well, in it he comes clean of all the women he'd slept with during his marriage. All of this was news to his wife, and a room full of people were watching her face while she watched the video-

tape of her husband crying that he was sorry because he slept with so many beautiful women. Alan has a way of making himself look good no matter how much it hurts.

His wife's face showed no emotion but I knew I was dead. In the name of honesty and pure vengeance, she was going to spill the beans. What saved me though was, while she had slept with me once (okay, *twice*), she had slept with the guy across the room for a year. In therapy with Alan, he had been agonizing for months about some problem he could not explain.

In the morning, Alan put his arms around me and said *I love you,* and he kissed the guy from across the room. Three days of this and the guy left town; it wasn't until six more months of therapy that my friend got in touch with what a poisonous person I was. He said it between his teeth with a hissing sound. "I find you to be a poisonous person." It was like being sentenced.

I do not eat any chips. I am on my feet and mobile, and drinking entering the living room, with a strong temptation to get down on all fours and invent a new dance. The Elephant, part II. I spin around, drink deeply from the tall glass of red wine, and produce a very wide and contagious smile.

"Hel*lo*," a pretty woman says.

I bow from the waist and for a moment become a headwaiter I used to work for; the wine is working, and it takes a half a minute to straighten up. "Hello." She laughs. This isn't such a bad party. Marvin Gaye is singing "*Don't you love to love somebody, makes you feel so good,*" and walking I stumble but recover by turning it into a dance step which, off balance as I am, carries me three steps backward, two steps to the side, and seven steps into the kitchen. I

Slightly Far Out in California

eat a stalk of anise, a raw floweret of cauliflower, refill my glass, and return to the living room. I turn off a light and no one complains.

"It attracts mosquitoes," I say, and somebody actually laughs. We smile and look into each other's eyes, I like this man who laughs, and lifting off the elephant part of my head, I let him see who I am and say hi.

"What are you?" I ask.

"I'm a ghost," he says, and then it becomes clear. He has a sheet over his head.

I drink. As Hemingway would say, it is a *fine* party. My friend who once loved me is here with his wife. She is bellydancing in the dining room for a room full of people, turning on the women and the men, and my friend is going around hugging everyone. I go into the dining room. Boy, can she dance. You could go crazy watching her dance. She stares at me, her hips swivel and beckon, and the air goes out of me, my face forgets how to look, and those hips keep talking. I drink down half the glass. Yes, Ernest, this is a fine party.

Two women are dancing together, getting it on for fair. Two other women are sitting on a large pillow discussing how hard it is for women to let down and really get to know each other, and while they talk and keep talking, the women dancing keep getting it on. It is good to see. I ask one of the women on the floor if she'll dance, then I ask the other one, then I change rooms. Tell me, can a woman still love a man after she's tried the real thing? Jack, that bitch looked at me like I didn't *count*.

I laugh. Not this time, baby. And then I see her, the one I've got to touch. She is beautiful, no way around it, even in her leather jacket and aviator's cap. Amelia Earhart. My trunk is stick-

ing straight out. I remove it. One can only hope she likes men.

Casually I approach and say a few words of encouragement to this loser I know who's sitting beside her. How are things, that's good, you still working at . . . oh, excuse me, would you like to dance . . . Amelia?

I smile like Burt Lancaster.

"But the record's over," she says.

"But the next one's about to begin." And it's Barry White and it's slow, very slow, sugar.

"OK, excuse me a minute, Frank." She pats Frank on the knee and pops up.

We go into the dining room. Barry White begins the opening rap of an eight minute cut. It is a deep voiced pimp's rap. . . . *sit down, baby, I just want to talk to you. You see I have this problem, this VERY serious problem, I . . . I just get so emotional over you sometimes . . .*

"Can you dance to this? He's just talking," Amelia says. Bless her.

"We can try. I think he starts to sing after a while." I know this record by heart.

I take her in my arms, I take her to my heart. We're hardly moving, hardly at all, I listen with my body to her breathing, she has a wonderful body, soft, with wonderful breasts and wonderful legs, a small back, and and. . . . and and and . . . and and, oh, sing the song Reverend White, yes, we are dancing—just as a doctor goes to school for nine years so he can charge somebody fifty dollars for five minutes, I have practiced dancing all my life, with a thousand women, for this moment—I can feel her body

Slightly Far Out in California

through her clothes, my hands are under her jacket, steering her back, she glides bends like a tree in a breeze, slightly ever so slightly this way, circling, that way, come on, baby, nothing wrong with love, let yourself go, I follow her every move, ride her rhythm until I float weightlessly with her, I'm inside her, I'm outside her, don't go away, baby, please stay, that's right, baby, I've never felt this way before, our legs brush, this way, that way, and slowly I begin to shift her rhythm, follow the circle her body moves in and then take her back along mine, and she is loose now and letting me take her, pull her, holding it, swaying in, moving away so that only my hands on her back, her forehead on my cheek and our knees occasionally brushing are touching, our thighs, it is the rhythm which is making us drunk, and Barry in that slow slow slow space and and and and, oh we are fine, children, all I can feel now is good, she kisses my cheek, I pull back and gently taking her face in my hands, just hold it and close my eyes still holding it, and we are floating, the music ends, I bend to kiss her and it is as it could only be, like butterfat on milk, and she won't quit, *let's get out of here,* I finally say, it is understood, *my place or yours,* I say, let's go to the creperie, she says, *what?* the creperie, we can have some tea and talk, *ain't this a shame, yeah, right, whose car,* it's all logistics now, both cars, *fine, I'll follow you.*

At the creperie she takes off her jacket and she is built like she felt, from the *b* to the *t.* She really wants to talk about us, because she wants to get straight what is going on between us; things like the way we were dancing don't just

happen to her that often and before she lets herself into anything she wants to know a few things.

What things? I don't want to open my mouth. Everytime I get into a conversation with a woman, I'm dead, especially if it's a good conversation—it will never lead to bed, and that's not me talking, that's experience.

"Are you interested in a Primary Enduring Relationship?" she says.

I request clarification, and she begins to clarify, and what has been a gentle passionate tip to toe desire to love her body and soul, becomes as she begins to catalogue the pitfalls and demands of the kind of relationship she is willing to enter, a kind of porno fantasy of how I'd like to nail her. We drink four pots of spearmint tea before she successfully manages to kill the magic that has brought her here. Everything has been fed into her computer and come out words.

Am I married, gay, or living with a woman? Because she wouldn't want to hurt a sister. Am I willing to commit myself to what is actually her *controller,* her need to know what cannot be known in advance. Perversely, I give her the wrong answers. *Look, I just want to suck your pussy.* She laughs, understanding that it is just the child in me talking, as it was the child in her that had danced with me, the parent in her says. *But will you let me suck your pussy?*

She leaves me. A friend of hers is playing Scrabble at another table and she joins him. I order another pot of tea. The tension and wildness have gone out of me and I feel extraordinarily calm. I put my thumbprint on the glass of ice water and straighten the napkin. The world seems so simple when you're not getting any. I sip the tea, and look at the teapot until it becomes real to me, three dimensional, and slowly I accept that it is there and I am here and it can never be my friend, but that I am aware that it is a teapot and I am alone.

PETER ELLIS

Slightly Far Out in California

Index

Abolitionist movement. *See* Anti-slavery movement
Abortion, 44, 45, 46, 102, 129, 138
Ace, Johnny, 216
Acme Beer Company, 198, 208
Adam, 81, 82
Adams, John, 43
Adams, John Quincy, 44
Addams, Jane, 110
Adler, Polly, 112, 119
Adultery, 7, 8, 10, 20, 35, 43, 47, 85, 91, 101, 102
Adventures of Lucky Pierre, The, 146
Aetios, 125
"A Gay Manifesto," (Wittman) 198
All the Loving Couples, 152
Alpert, Hollis, 146
Amana Colony, 85
American Coalition of Patriotic Societies, 131
American Medical Association (AMA), 128–129, 132–133
American Woman Suffrage Association (AWSA), 67, 74, 75
Anarchists, 95–96, 110
Andrews, Stephen Pearl, 69–70
Ann, Mother. *See* Lee, Mother Ann
Anthony, Susan B., 64, 65, 67, 68, 77
Antislavery movement, 61, 63, 64, 65, 68, 72

Arbuckle, Roscoe "Fatty," 54, 55, 56
Aroused, 143–145
Awful Disclosures of the Hotel Dieu Nunnery of Montreal (Monk), 45
Automobiles, 157–177
  and courtship, 159
  custom, 163, 170–173
  marketing, 162–163, 165
  as a place for sex, 157, 159–161. *See also* Car-sex
  production, 159
  as sex objects, 162, 169–174, 176

Babb, Kroger, 139
Baby Bullett, 163
Back-Seat Dodge (Kienholz), 172
Barbary Coast, 106, 107
Barris, George, 172
Bascom, Dickens, 170
Bastardy, 20, 101, 102
Battle Axe, The, 89
Baumeler, Joseph, 83, 84
Beaux Arts Ball, 205–207
Beecher, Catherine, 74
Beecher, Rev. Henry Ward, 46, 47, 48, 49, 54, 56, 74, 75
Bemis, Johnny, 28
Bennett, James Gordon, 44, 46
Bergman, Ingrid, 51, 52, 53, 54, 56

Bestiality, 9, 11, 12, 13, 179
Better Half, The: The Emancipation of the American Woman (Sinclair), 61, 77
Bigg, Bertha, 153
Birth control, 88, 89–91, 121–135, 138
  devices:
    coitus interruptus, 89, 124–125
    condoms, 89, 122, 124, 125, 126, 128, 134, 135
    diaphragms, 122, 130, 132, 134
    douches, 125, 126, 132
    folk medicine, 122
    IUDs, 133, 134
    male continence, 126
    movement cures, 126
    pills, 133, 134, 135
    rhythm, 132–133, 134
    spermicides, 126, 130, 134
    sponges, 122, 125
  effectiveness chart, 132
  and the government, 129, 130, 135
  information, 124–126, 128, 129–130, 135
  legality of, 121, 126, 128
  and the medical profession, 128–129, 132–133, 135
  and passion, 121–122
  and racism, 130–132

  techniques of, 134
  and women, 125, 128, 129
Birth Control Review, 130
Bishop Hill, Ill., 84
Blacks. *See also* Racism, Slavery
  on the frontier, 19
Blackwell, Antoinette Brown, 65, 67
Blackwell, Henry, 65
Blaine, James G., 49
Blood, Colonel, 69, 70, 75
Blood Feast, 149
Blood Trilogy, 149
Bowen, Henry C., 46, 47
Boys on the Bus, The (Crouse), 52
Bradford, William, 10–13, 14
Bradstreet, Anne, 6, 7, 14
Breasts, 190
Brenner, Joseph, 142
Brisbane, Albert, 93, 95, 97
Brook Farm, 95, 96
Brooks, Alden, 15, 17
Browning, Tod, 150
Buffalo Evening Telegraph, 49
Buick Le Sabre, 164
Bulette, Julia, 26–27, 31
Burlesque films, 140, 141
Burr, Aaron, 43
Burton, Richard, 35, 88
Butler, Benjamin, 70
Butterfly Flick, 194

Cadets, 109, 110, 111
California, 213–224
California Motorcycle Club, 202–203
Callender, James Thomson, 43, 44, 51, 54
Call houses, 112
Capitalism, 79, 98
Cars. See Automobiles
Car-sex, 161–169, 172–176
    and police, 161–162, 168–169
Casanova, 124
Catholics, 4, 7, 21, 45, 46, 167
Celibacy, 80–85, 97, 105
    Amana, 85
    Puritan, 4, 7
    Rappite, 82, 83
    Shaker, 81, 82
    Swedish Messiah, 84, 85
    Zoarite, 83–84
Censorship
    film:
        California, 149
        Chicago, 142
        community, 137
        Hays Office, 138
        industry, 137, 138
        Kansas, 150
        Maryland, 142
        Motion Picture Production Code, 138
        National Board of Review, 137
        New York, 141, 149
        and nudity, 141, 142, 149
        Seattle, Wash., 146
        Supreme Court, 141, 142
        and violence, 150, 153
    mail, 68, 126, 127, 128
Cervical caps, 122, 132
Chandless, William, 88
Chastity, 37, 105, 159
Chicago Historical Antique Auto Museum, 163
Child Bride, 139
Chinatown, 106, 170
Church of the Latter Day Saints. See Mormons
Civil War, 30, 37, 105
Claflin, Tennessee, 68, 69, 75, 77

Claflin, Tennie C. See Claflin, Tennessee
Claflin, Victoria. See Woodhull, Victoria
Cleveland, Grover, 49, 50
Cleveland, Oscar Folsom, 49, 50
Clinical Sonnets, 180
Clitoris, 186, 190, 191
Coffin, Tristam, 160, 161, 177
Coitus interruptus, 89, 124–125
Coitus reservatus, 126
Collector, The (Fowles), 150
Color Me Blood Red, 150
Comfort, Dr. Alex, 194–195
Coming, 39, 167–168. See also Ejaculation, Orgasm
Commentary, 189
Committee for Homosexual Freedom, 197–198
Common Law Cabin, 150
Communes. See Communities, utopian
Communism, 69, 79, 83, 98, 183
Communities, utopian, 79–99
    anarchist, 95–96
    and capitalism, 79, 98
    map of, 80
    religious, 80–93, 97
    socialist, 80, 93–95, 97, 98
Comstock, Anthony, 126, 127, 128
Comstock Law, 68
Concubinage, 102
Condoms, 89, 122, 124, 125, 128, 134, 135
Continence, male, 89–91, 92, 126
Contraception, 102. See also Birth control
    technology chart of, 132
Cooke, Sam, 213, 214
Corporate Queen, The, 146–147
Costello, Mme., 44, 45
Cotton, John, 4, 6
Courtship
    and the automobile, 159
    in the nineteenth century, 60
Cox, Ross, 18, 20, 21, 23
COYOTE (Call Off Your Old Tired Ethics), 117

Cragin, George, 91
Cragin, Mary, 91
Crib girls, 106
Cribs, 106, 109
Crouse, Timothy, 52
Curse of the Flesh, The, 153
Custer, General, 18

Daughters of Bilitis, 197
Daughters of Lesbos, 153
Davis, Kingsley, 115
DeCenzie, Peter, 145, 146
Decisive Confirmation of the Awful Disclosures of Maria Monk (Smith), 45
Defilers, The, 150
de Lahontan, Baron, 17
de Leon, Count Maxmillian. See Muller, Bernhard
De Mille, Cecil B., 138
Demos, John, 10, 14, 119
Depression, 112, 159
de Sévigné, Mme., 124
Desmond, Judge Charles, 141
Diaphragms, 122, 130, 132, 133, 134
Diary of Samuel Sewall 1674–1729, The, 8–9, 14
Dichter, Dr. Ernst, 162–163
Dickmobile, 173
Divorce, 4, 8, 32, 65, 67, 86, 91, 93, 98
Dixon, William, 17, 31
Double standard, 183
Douches, 125, 126, 132
Douglas, Mary, 56–57
Douglas, Stephen, 36
Drive-in theaters, 139, 142
Drug addiction, 138, 139
Dyspareunia, 192

Earhart, Amelia, 221
Edison, Thomas, 137
Eisenhower, Dwight D., 129
Ejaculation, 90, 191, 192
    premature, 184, 185, 192
    See also Orgasm, Sperm

Ellis, Havelock, 111–112
Ellis, John B., 79
Ellis Island, 110
Emigrants. See Immigrants
Engels, Friedrich, 98
English Riding Coat, 124
Equal Rights Party, 47
Erotica, 146
Europe in the Raw, 146
Eve, 6, 81, 101
Eve and the Handyman, 146
Everleigh sisters, 110
Everts, Kellie, 142
Excelsior Pictures vs. the Board of Regents, 141

Fallopius, 124
Family
    Amana, 85
    and capitalism, 98
    in Colonial New England, 101
    Harmonist, 83
    Hutterite, 85
    Modern Times, 97
    monogamous, 95
    Mormon, 86–88
    New Harmony, 93
    in nineteenth century communes, 79–80, 98
    Perfectionist, 91–92
    Puritan, 6, 10
    in the South, 101–102
    Victorian, 102, 105
Family Limitation, 130
Farber, Leslie H., 189
Faster, Pussycat! Kill! Kill! Kill! 150
Fatima, 137
Fear of failure syndrome, 191–192
Federalists, 43, 44
Female, The, 150–151
Feminism, 59–77, 117. See also Women's rights
Fiedler, Leslie, 145–146
Film Comment, 149
Films, exploitation, 137–155
    burlesque, 140, 141

nature, 141
nudist, 141–142, 145
and nudity, 138, 141–142, 145, 146, 149
peep-show, 137–138
race, 139
roughies, 149–150, 153
silent, 137–138
stag, 138
violent, 149–150, 153
First Amendment, 141
Flexner, Abraham, 110
Foam, contraceptive, 134
Forbidden Oats, 139
Ford, Edsel, 158, 159
Ford, Henry, 157, 158, 172, 173, 176
Ford,
    Model A, 159
    Model F, 158
    Model T, 159, 160, 172, 173
Fornication, 7, 8, 10, 91, 101
"Forty Thieves," 139
Fourier, Charles, 93, 95, 97, 98
Fourteenth Amendment, 141
Fowles, John, 150
Freaks, 150
Free love, 47, 51, 52, 69, 70, 72, 74, 75, 79, 91
Free Love and Its Votaries; or, American Socialism Unmasked (Ellis), 79
Free Ride, A, 138
French device, 124
French Letters. *See* Condoms
French Peep Show, The, 145
French Secret, 126
Freud, Sigmund, 11, 157, 186
Friedan, Betty, 185
Friedman, David F., 141–142, 146, 149, 150, 153
Frigidity, 191, 193, 194
Frontier, 15–40
    and Indians, 17–24
    and miners, 25–32
    and Saints (Mormons), 32–37, 86–88
Frost, R. Lee, 150
Fruits of Philosophy (Knowlton), 125

Gall wasps, 179
Garden of Eden, 81
Garden of Eden, 141
Garrison, William Lloyd, 61
Gaye, Marvin, 220
Gays. *See* Homosexuality
Genius of Universal Emancipation, 96
Gergler, Dr. Edmund, 186
Gluckman, Max, 41, 57
Goldilocks and the Three Bares, 142
Goldman, Emma, 75, 110–111, 119
Gorer, Geoffrey, 182–183
Graham, Rev. Billy, 179, 185
Grand Trip Across the Plains (Brooks), 15
Greeley, Horace, 95, 105
Green, Al, 216
Griffith, D. W., 138
Grimké, Angelina, 61, 62, 63, 77
Grimké, Sarah, 61, 63, 77
GTO, 169–170
Gurney, Robert, Jr., 146
Gynecology, 123. *See also* Birth control

Halcyon Matrimonial Co., The, 71
Halpin, Maria, 49, 50
Hamilton, Alexander, 42–43, 51
Harmonists. *See* Harmony Society
Harmony Society, 82, 83, 84, 93
Harper's Weekly, 33, 66
Hays Code, 138
Hays Office, 138
Heavenly Bodies, 146
Hefner, Hugh, 157
Heidrich, Bob, 146, 149
Heller, Louis, 183
Hemings, Sally, 43, 44, 54
Henry, Alexander, the Younger, 20–21
Henry, Hank, 149
Her Morning Exercise, 138
Herrick, O. E., 128
Hidden Persuaders, The (Packard), 162–163, 177
Hippocrates, 133

"History of Sex in the Cinema" (Alpert and Knight), 146
Hitchcock, Alfred, 154
Hollywood, 51, 52, 54–56, 138, 139
Hollywood Nudes Report, 141
Holton, Harriet, 89
Homosexuality, 91, 179, 180, 182, 183, 199–211
Honky Tonk Girls, 139
Hoover, J. Edgar, 179, 185
House Committee to Investigate Tax-Exempt Foundations, 183, 185
Hull House, 110
Human Sexual Inadequacy (Masters and Johnson), 192, 194
Human Sexual Response (Masters and Johnson), 75, 187, 189, 190
Hunt, Morton, 8, 14
Hutterites, 85–86, 97

Idaho Historical Society, 30
Immigrants, 15, 28, 29, 30, 31, 110, 111, 122
Immigrant's Protective League, 110
Immigration, 17
Immoral Mr. Teas, The, 145, 146, 154
Impotence, male, 4, 192, 194
Incest, 91
Independent, 47
Independents, 49, 51
Indiana University, 179, 180
Indians, 15, 17–24
    and adultery, 20
    and bastardy, 20
    and blacks, 19
    and children, 20
    and first encounters with white men, 18–20
    and hospitality, 18
    and marriage to whites, 20–23, 31
    and prostitution, 24
    and rape, 31
    and rituals, 21, 23
    and squaw towns, 23
    and venereal disease, 24

and virginity, 17, 20
and white men's lust, 18
Indian tribes,
    Aricara, 18
    Cheyenne, 20
    Cree, 20
    Flathead, 21
    Huron, 17
    Iowa, 21
    Mandan, 20
    Pawnee, 38
    Piute, 31
    Saultern, 21
    Spokan, 20, 21
Intercourse, sexual, 67, 74, 190–192, 193
    and the college-educated, 184–185
    observed, 185
    outside marriage, 180, 182, 183
    premarital, 180, 182, 183
International Convention of Women, 65
Intolerance, 138
Intrauterine devices (IUDs), 133, 134
Invitation to Ruin, 153
Irwin, May, 137
IUDs. *See* Intrauterine devices

"J," 194
Jacobi, Abraham, 128–129
Jamestown, Va., 16, 17
Janson, Eric, 84–85
Jefferson, Thomas, 43–44, 51, 142
Jelly, contraceptive, 130, 133, 134
Jewett, Helen, 44
Johnson, Edwin, 51–52
Johnson, Virginia E., 75, 185, 187–194
Joseph Burstyn, Inc. vs. *Wilson,* 141
Joy of Sex, The (Comfort), 194
Judge, 50

Kansas State Board of Censors, 150
Karezza, 126
Kienholz, Edward, 172

Kimball, Nell, 106, 108–109, 112, 119
Kinsey, Dr. Alfred C., 159, 179–186, 187, 195
Kinsey Institute Collection, 138, 180
Kinsey's Myth of Female Sexuality (Gergler), 186
Knight, Arthur, 146
Knowlton, Dr. Charles, 125
Koedt, Anne, 75, 77
Kurz, Rudolph, 21

Labia, 186, 190
Lamb, John, 142
Lancaster, Burt, 221
Lareux, Napoleon, 44
Lasko, Edward, 145
Lautz, Leo, 132
Lee, Mother Ann, 81, 82
Leeds, Lila, 61
Lehman, Ernest, 145
Leigh, Janet, 154–155
Lerner, Gerda, 63, 77, 119
Lerner, Max, 190
Lesbians, 109
Lewis, Herschell G., 149, 150
Lewis, Meriwether, 18, 19
Life, 73
Life of An American Madam by Herself, The (Kimball), 109, 119
Lippard, George, 46
Lippman, Walter, 159
Little commonwealth, 6, 10, 101
Livingston, Edward, 51, 54
Look, 180
Lorna, 150–153
Love, 6, 7, 15, 17, 66, 179, 182–183
Lynn, Tammy, 204

Madams, 106, 108, 109, 110, 112. *See also* Prostitution
Magnetation Method, 126
Mahon, Barry, 149, 153
Maitland, Lorna, 150
Male continence, 89–91, 92, 126
꯭nn Act, 112
꯭he, Zulma, 44, 46

Marriage, vii, 35, 66, 71
Amana, 85
Brook Farm, 95
celestial, 87
complex, 88–92
group, 89–92
Harmonist, 93
Hutterite, 85–86
Indians and whites, 20–21, 23, 31
Modern Times, 96–97
monogamous, 95
Mormon, 32–37, 86–88
in the nineteenth century, 59, 61, 63, 64–65, 66
Perfectionist, 89–92
phalanx, 95
as prostitution, 47, 111–112
Puritan, 4–8, 10, 14
quartet, 91
reform, 65, 67, 68
as slavery, 61
Married Woman's Private Medical Companion (Mauriceau), 125
Marsh, Julian, 153
Mart, Paul, 146
Martin, Tony, 213
Marx, Karl, 98
Maryland State Board of Censors, 142
Mason, Connie, 149–150
Mast, Gerald, 138
Masters, Dr. William H., 75, 185, 187–194
Masturbation, 91, 165, 175, 180, 183, 185, 186, 192
Mathis, Johnny, 216
Mattachine Society, 197
Mauriceau, A. M., 125–126
Mawra, Joseph A., 153
Mayflower, 10
McCarthy, John, 149
McGovern, George, 52
McLuhan, Marshall, 176
Medical and Surgical Reporter, 128
Mencken, H. L., 3, 46
Mensinga diaphragms, 130, 132
Menstruation, 126, 132
Meyer, Russ, 142, 145, 146, 150, 153, 154

Michel, Pierre, 21
Michigan Medical News, 128
Millain, John, 27
Millenial Church. *See* Shakers
Millenium, 83
Millett, Kate, 113, 119
Milner, Dr. Jean S., 183
Miners, 24, 25–32
Mishkin, William, 142
"Mistress Versus Wife" (Dichter), 162–163
Mitchum, Robert, 139
Modern Times, 96–97
Mom and Dad, 139
Monk, Maria, 45, 46
Monroe, James, 43
Monticello, 43, 44
Moral Physiology (Owen), 9, 124
More Joy (Comfort), 194–195
Morgan, Edmund S., 4, 7, 8, 10, 14, 119
Mormons, 32–37, 86–88
Mother Earth, 111
Motion Picture Production Code, 138
Motor Psycho, 150
Motor Trend, 165, 177
Motown Records, 172–173
Mott, Lucretia, 63, 64
Moulton, Frank, 48
Movement cures, 126
Mrs. Satan. *See* Woodhull, Victoria
Mud Honey, 150
Muhlenberg, Frederick, 43
Muller, Bernhard, 82
Muncy, Raymond, 86–87, 88, 99
Muscle Cars, 169–170
Musitanus, 121–122
Musketeers of Pig Alley, The, 138
My Bare Lady, 141
Myotonia, 190
"Myth of the Vaginal Orgasm, The" (Koedt), 75, 77

Nash Ambassador, 165, 166, 177
Nashoba, Tennessee, 94–96, 98
Nast, Thomas, 70
National Board of Review, 137

National Council of Jewish Women, 110
National Geographic, 141
National Woman Suffrage Association (NWSA), 65, 67, 70, 72, 74, 75
National Young Women's Christian Association, 110
Naughty, Naughty Nudes, 149
Nauvoo, Ill., 32, 33, 86
Nauvoo Expositor, 34
Negroes. *See* Blacks
New Harmony, Ind., 93, 95, 96
New Lanark, Scotland, 93
New Orleans, La., 26
Newspapers, 42, 44, 48, 49, 54
New York Court of Appeals, 141
New York Herald, 44, 45
New York Herald Tribune, 95
New York Magdalen Society, 27
New York Post, 190
New York, Regents of the University of the State of, 141
New York Society for the Suppression of Vice, 128
New York State Education Department, Motion Picture Division, 141
New York Tribune, The, 54
Not Tonight Henry, 146, 149
Noyes, John Humphrey, 88–92, 97, 126
Nuckolls, C. K., 32
Nude and the Prude, The, 141
Nude Las Vegas, 149
Nude Scrapbook, 149
Nudist films, 141–142, 145

Oberholtzer, Dr. Emil, 8, 14
Of Plymouth Plantation (Bradford), 10, 14
Olga's Girls, 153
Olga's Massage Parlor, 153
Onanism, 89
Oneida, N.Y., 88, 90–92, 97, 126
One, Inc., 197
1,000 Shapes of the Female, 141
One Too Many, 139

One Way of Taking a Girl's Picture, 137–138
Oral contraceptives, 133, 134, 135
Orgasm, 182, 186, 189–191
  clitoral, 186
  female, 186, 189, 190, 191, 192
  male, 180, 184–185, 186, 189, 191
  multiple, 186, 191
  premature, 184–185
  vaginal, 75, 77, 186
Orgasmic platform, 190–191
Oui, 173
Ovulation, 132
Owen, Robert, 93, 97, 98
Owen, Robert Dale, 93, 95–96, 124–125

Packard, Vance, 162–163, 177
Paige, Steven Hastings, 173
Pantarchists, Utopian, 69–70
Paramore, Ted, 146, 149
Pardon My Brush, 149
Parker, Charlie, 217
Parking, 163–165, 166–169, 173–176
Parlor girls, 106, 107
  on the Barbary Coast, 106, 107
Parlor houses, 106, 108, 109, 110
Peale, Norman Vincent, 179, 184
Peep shows, 137–138
Penis, 90, 190, 191
  artificial, 187, 191
Perfectionism, 88–89
Perfectionists, 88–93
Perkins, Anthony, 154–155
Phalanx, 95
Pilgrims, 10. *See also* Puritans
Pill, birth control, 133, 134, 135
Pimps, 109, 110, 117
Pincus, Dr. Gregory, 133
Piute War of 1860, 31
Planned Parenthood Federation, 133
Playboy, 146, 149–150
Pleasuring, 193
Plymouth Church of Brooklyn, 46, 47
Plymouth colony, 10, 11
Polygamy. *See* Polygyny

Polygyny, 80, 86–88. *See also* Mormons
Pomeroy, Wardell B., 183
Pornography, 3, 36
Port of Missing Women, 138
Portnoy's Complaint (Roth), 145
Pregnancy, 10, 102
Presley, Elvis, 157
Press. *See* Newspapers
Procurers. *See* Pimps, Cadets
Progressivism, 137
Prostitute's Protective Society, 153, 154
Prostitution, 27, 44, 91, 101–119, 138
  on the Barbary Coast, 113
  Chicago's guidebook to, 108
  on the frontier, 26–32
  of Indian women, 24, 31
  legalization of, 105, 108, 115, 117
  and marriage, 111–112
  in Mormon towns, 36
  and slavery, 106, 109–111
Prostitution Papers, The (Millett), 113, 119
Protestants, 4, 21, 45, 46
Protestant ethic, 195
Prude and the Parisienne, The, 146
Psycho, 154–155
Punchinello, 72
Puritans, 3–14
  and bastardy, 20
  and bestiality, 9, 11, 12, 13
  and celibacy, 4, 7
  and divorce, 4, 8
  and the family, 6, 10
  as farmers, 4
  and God, 4, 6, 7, 10, 11, 12, 13
  and love, 6, 7
  and pregnancy, 10
  as Protestants, 4
  as prudes, 3, 8, 13–14
  and punishment, 7, 10, 11, 12, 13, 101
  and religious utopia, 9, 10
  and sex in marriage, 4–7, 8
  and sex outside marriage, 5, 7–8, 10, 14
  and sin, 7, 8, 10–13
  and Victorians, 3–5, 7, 8, 9–10

Puritans and Sex, The (Morgan) 4, 14
Putney, Vermont, 89, 91

Quakers, 81

Racism, 130–132
Radicalesbians, 198
Raleigh, Sir Walter, 15
Rape, 31, 102, 105
  statutory, 162, 168
Rapp, George, 82, 83
Rappe, Virginia, 54
Rappites, 82, 83, 93
Raw Ones, The, 142
Reader's Digest, 179, 182, 186
Reece, B. Carroll, 183
Refractory period, 191
Republicans, 36, 44, 49
Research, sex, 179–194
Restell, Mme., 46
Revier, Harry, 139
Revolution, The, 65–67
Reynolds, James, 42–43
Reynolds, Maria, 42–43
Rhythm, 132–133, 134
Rhythm of Sterility and Fertility in Women, The (Lautz), 132
Rice, John, 137
Richter, Kurt, 153
Richter, Dr. Richard, 133
Riva, Ann, 153
RKO films, 51, 52
Roanoke, Va., 15
Robinson, John, 6
Robinson, Richard, 44
Rockefeller Foundation, 180, 183
Rockefeller White Slavery Commission, 138
Rolling Stone, 172–173
Ronnie and the Daytonas, 169–170
Roosevelt, Theodore, 130
Rossellini, Roberto, 51, 52, 53
Roth, Philip, 145
Rubbers. *See* Condoms
Ruined Bruin, The, 149
Rumble seat, 161
Russell, Bertrand, 142

Sachs, Sadie, 129
Sadistic Lover, The, 153
Safes. *See* Condoms
St. James, Margo, 116, 117
Salt Lake City, Utah, 35, 37. *See also* Mormons
Salvation Army, 179, 184
Sanger, Margaret, 75, 129–131, 133, 135
Sanger, Dr. William, 105, 110, 117, 119
Saunders, W. B., 180
Scandal, 41–57
  and the anonymous, 46
  and gossip, 41, 54
  nature of, 41–42, 51, 54, 56, 57
  and the press, 42, 51, 52
  and the prominent, 46
  and women, 56
Schickel, Richard, 150–153
Scrotum, 190
Seabury, Judge, 112
Searle, G. D., Company, 133, 135
Seattle, Wash., 146
Seduction legislation, 46
Seneca Falls Convention, 64
Sensate focusing, 193, 194
Sensuous Man, The, 194
Sensuous Woman, The (J), 194
Separatists. *See* Zoarites
Serpent of the Slums, The, 138
Sewall, Samuel, 8–9, 14
Sex and Marriage in Utopian Communities (Muncy), 86–87, 99
Sex flush, 190, 191
Sexism, 67
Sex Kick, The (Coffin), 160, 161, 177
Sex-sell, 162–163
Sexual Behavior in the Human Female (Kinsey), 183
Sexual Behavior in the Human Male (Kinsey), 180, 182, 183, 184–185
Shainess, Dr. Natalie, 192
Shakers, 81–82, 83, 89
Shaking Quakers. *See* Shakers
She Did It His Way, 142
She Freak, 150
Show, 145–146
Silent films, 137–138

Sinatra, Frank, 149
Sinclair, Andrew, 61, 77
Sinderella and the Golden Bra, 146
Six Companies of China, 28
Slaver, The, 139
Slavery, 96, 101–102
  and women, 153
Sleeve job, 115
Smith, Joseph, 32–34, 86
Smith, Mrs. Joseph (Emma), 32, 86
Smith, S. B., 45
Socialism, 79, 80, 93–95, 97, 98
Society for Individual Rights, The, 197
Society of the True Inspirationists.
  See Amana colony
Sodomy, 10
Solange, 118
Sonney, Daniel, 142
Soranos, 122, 125
Soule, J., 126
South, 101, 102
Sparking, 82
Sperm, 38–39, 43, 112, 125, 126
Spermicides, 126, 130, 134
Spiritualism, 69, 70, 71, 74, 75
Sponges, 122, 125, 126
Sporting house, 109. *See* Parlor
  houses
Squaw town, 23
Stag films, 138
Stanton, Elizabeth Cady, 48, 63–64,
  65, 67, 68, 70, 74, 77
Stanton, Henry, 63, 64
Stems, 132
Stirpiculture, 92
Stone, Abraham, 186
Stone, Lucy, 65, 67
Stonewall riot, 198
Storm, Tempest, 141, 145
Storyville, New Orleans, 106, 108–
  109, 112
Stowe, Harriet Beecher, 74
Strip Tease Girls, 141
Stromboli, 51

Suffrage, women's, 32, 46, 59, 64,
  65, 67, 70, 74–77
Swedish Messiah, 84
Swiving, 82
Syphilis, 124

Teas, Bill, 145–146, 154
Television, 139
Testes, 190
Thalberg, Irving, 138
Tilton, Elizabeth, 47, 48, 49, 74
Tilton, Theodore, 47, 48, 49, 74, 75
Time Store, 96
"To My Dear and Loving Husband"
  (Bradstreet), 7
Touch of Her Flesh, The, 153, 154
Toy, Ah, 106
Traffic in Souls, 138
"Traffic in Women, The"
  (Goldman), 111
Tricks of the Trade (Wells), 115
True Womanhood, cult of, 102, 105,
  119
Truteau, Jean Baptiste, 17, 20
Turan, Kenneth, 141
Turner, Daniel, 124
Twain, Mark, 25, 35
Two Thousand Maniacs!, 148, 149,
  150

United Order of Enoch, 86
United Society of Believers. *See*
  Shakers
U.S. Supreme Court, 141, 142
Universal Pictures, 138
Utah territory, 32, 37. *See also* Mor-
  mons
Utopia. *See* Communities, utopian

Vagina, 90, 186, 190, 191

Vaginismus, 192
Vanderbilt, Cornelius, 69
Vans, 172
Variety, 149
Vascocongestion, 190
V-8, 170
Velvet Buzzsaw, 194
Venable, Abraham, 43
Venereal disease, 24, 91, 105, 117,
  123–124, 138
Vespucci, Amerigo, 18
Victorians,
  and the family, 102, 105
  and morality, 139, 157
  and pornography, 3
  and prostitution, 3
  and Puritans, 3–4, 7, 8, 9–10
  as source of American prurience,
    3–4, 8
  and women's sexuality, 59, 69, 72
Virginia City, Nev., 26, 27, 31, 32,
  36
Virginity, 17, 20, 35
Viva, 173
Von Stroheim, Erich, 138

Wages of Sin, 139
Walker, Betsy, 44
Walker, John, 44
Wallingford, Conn., 88
Warren, Josiah, 93, 96, 98
Warrick, Ruth, 139
Washington University, 187
Weiss, George, 153
Weld, Angelina Grimké. *See*
  Grimké, Angelina
Weld, Theodore, 61, 62–63, 77
White, Barry, 222, 223
White slavery, 28, 30, 31, 106, 109–
  111, 138, 139
White Slaves of Chinatown, 153
White, Theodore, 52
Whitman, Walt, 67

Wild Weed, 139
Williams, William Appleman, 97
Wilson, Jackie, 214
Wimbish, Dr. John W., 183
Winthrop, John, 7
Winthrop, Margaret, 7
Wishbones, 132
Wittman, Carl, 198
Women's liberation movement, 31.
  See also Women's rights
Women's rights, 59–77
  and the antislavery movement,
    61, 63, 64, 65, 68, 72
  and divorce, 65, 67
  and marriage, 17, 59, 61–63, 64–
    65, 67–68
  and sex, 59, 67–68, 70, 75, 193.
    See also Prostitution, Suffrage
Women's Rights Convention. *See*
  Seneca Falls Convention
Woodhull, Canning, 69
Woodhull & Claflin's Weekly, 68, 70,
  74, 77
Woodhull, Victoria, 47, 49, 51, 68,
  69, 70–72, 74, 75, 77
Worcester Foundation of Experi-
  mental Biology, 133
World Antislavery Convention, 63,
  64
World War I, 112
World War II, 162
Wright, Frances, 93, 94, 95, 98
Wyoming territory, 32

Young, Brigham, 33, 34, 35, 36, 37,
  86, 87

Zito, Stephen, 141
Zoar, Ohio, 83
Zoarites, 83–84, 85